'Too often we race through the we[ek] packed with countless errands [and] Before we know it, we've lost si[ght] happy. In *The Weekend Effect*, Katrina Onstad offers a powerful argument, and practical advice, on the importance of reclaiming your leisure time to live a happier and more fulfilling life'

Gretchen Rubin, *New York Times* bestselling author of *Better than Before* and *The Happiness Project*

'In our frenetic era of total work devotion and breathless busyness, the idea of making time for leisure has become almost a sacrilege. But Katrina Onstad makes a compelling case in her terrific new book, *The Weekend Effect*, that true leisure – time for reflection, connection, play and joy – knits together the social fabric of community, soothes the weary soul and, at heart, is what makes life worth living. A welcome romp of a read'

Brigid Schulte, award-winning journalist and author of the *New York Times* bestselling *Overwhelmed* and director of The Better Life Lab at New America

'Modern life means we are more plugged in, but less connected to each other than ever before. Too often work and technology erode our ability to connect meaningfully face-to-face, intruding into the critical time we need to recharge ourselves. In Katrina Onstad's insightful and compelling book, *The Weekend Effect*, she offers an urgent call to arms on the essential need to take back our weekends'

Dallas Hartwig, *New York Times* bestselling co-author of *It Starts With Food* and *The Whole30*

'Masterfully researched and beautifully written, *The Weekend Effect* urgently makes the case that our hard won free time is essential to our survival, and needs to be reclaimed. Pick up this book, and get ready to rekindle your love of the weekend! Your emails can wait until Monday'

David Sax, author of *The Revenge of Analog*

'*The Weekend Effect* is a call to action – or even better – a call to inaction. It proves its case that by staking a claim to your weekend, your work and home life (and your health and wellbeing) benefit every day of the year. Take the time to read it like I did, over a weekend. It's a great way to start'

Kirstine Stewart, media and technology executive and author, *Our Turn*

THE WEEKEND EFFECT

The Life-Changing Benefits of Taking Two Days Off

KATRINA ONSTAD

piatkus

PIATKUS

First published in Canada in 2017 by HarperCollins Publishers Ltd
First published in Great Britain in 2017 by Piatkus

13 5 7 9 10 8 6 4 2

A CIP catalogue record for this book
is available from the British Library.

ISBN 978-0-349-41118-7

Printed and bound in Great Britain by
Clays Ltd, St Ives plc

Papers used by Piatkus are from well-managed forests
and other responsible sources.

Piatkus
An imprint of
Little, Brown Book Group
Carmelite House
50 Victoria Embankment
London EC4Y 0DZ

An Hachette UK Company
www.hachette.co.uk

www.improvementzone.co.uk

To my parents

Living is the least important activity of the preoccupied man;
yet there is nothing which is harder to learn.

—SENECA

CONTENTS

THE WEEKEND EFFECT

SUNDAY NIGHT LETDOWN

Q UILT CHIN HIGH on a Sunday night, by the light of his bedside lamp, my young son asks, "Was that the weekend?" "Yes, it was," I reply.

"But it didn't *feel* like a weekend," he says, employing his "rip-off" voice, the one reserved for bad trades in baseball and empty cereal boxes.

At twelve, he poses this question many Sundays—it's a macabre family tradition—thereby prompting a review of my own weekend, which frequently looks something like this: hockey; work email; groceries; an ensuing onslaught of emails about the first email; homework help; hockey; dog wrangling; family dinner; cleanup; laundry; work reading. To keep Sunday distinguishable from Saturday, I might top off the above with some light toilet cleaning. We do change it up in summer, however: the kids play soccer instead of hockey.

I

For many of today's (gratefully) employed, the workweek has no clear beginning or end. The digital age imagined by science fiction is upon us, yet we're lacking robot butlers and the three-day workweek that economist John Maynard Keynes predicted in 1928. Working more than we did a decade ago is the norm for most employees, and those devices designed to liberate our time merely snatch it back. The weekend has become an extension of the workweek, which means, by definition, it's not a weekend at all. Many Americans work longer hours today than a generation ago, and most work hundreds of hours more per year than their counterparts in European Union countries of similar economic status. A 2014 paper from the U.S. National Bureau of Economic Research reports that 29 percent of Americans log hours on the weekend, compared to less than 10 percent of Spanish workers. If the Spanish are too life-loving to bring home the hurt in that statistic, here's another one: even fewer of the diligent Germans work on the weekend, at 22 percent. U.K. workers are the exception among Europeans, racking up almost as many hours on weekends as Americans. They call this, unflatteringly, "the American disease."

I recognize this disease. Years ago, for a brief, not-so-fun time, I was an au pair. Mostly, I was shuffling through the post-college years, hiding in a small village on a windswept shore of northern France for a few months. Every Sunday, as far as I could tell, France shut down. There was no work. There was—and this shocked my North American mall rat self—no shopping. Instead, there was The Visit and The Activity. Three kids in tow, my single-mom boss and I visited grandparents, or brought flowers to a family friend in a nursing home. Some weekends, neighbors came to the house unannounced, and food and conversation would stretch into the night. There was always an outing: a hike along the beach shore; a bike ride; a stroll through the streets of a nearby village, peering in the windows of closed shops. We could look, but not buy. These weekend days felt like ritual, embedded in the culture; something sacred. Time seemed to slow itself. These were weekends of the imagination, rich with experience, a clean break from what came before and what would come next, on Monday.

Now, with my own kids and a job as a writer that leaks across the days, my Saturday often feels hardly different from a Wednesday. Sometimes, in fact, Saturday feels busier. On weekends, I'm always responding to the e-needs of clients and sources, even when technically off duty. But who's off duty, ever? I've attended soccer games where parents are on iPads between perfunctory cheers. "TGIM," jokes a friend at Monday morning drop-off, gratefully exchanging the children's myriad playdates and activities for the relative calm of an office.

This borderless work life is no longer just a freelancer's reality, or the domain of high-billing lawyers and Silicon Valley creative-class innovators. Post-recession, work means a patchwork of part-time gigs for many people, with no set pattern to the week. Millennials tend their brands around the edges of precarious work. My husband is a teacher, and he spends his nights and weekends managing emails from anxious parents and students, then scrambling back to his analog duties like marking and lesson planning. "It's like we're all doctors now, forever on call," I tell him, leaning in the doorway late at night, taking in the familiar sight of his back turned to me as he punches away at the computer. "Really low-stakes doctors."

Too many weekends, The Activity is deferred. The Visit is deferred. Pleasure and contemplation are deferred. "Sunday night is the new Monday morning," a headline in *The Boston Globe* trumpets, noting that many workers are getting a jump on Monday morning emails by spending Sunday night in the Inbox. The executive recruiter and the venture capitalist interviewed for the article sheepishly give what amounts to the same reason for ceding their Sunday night: *Since everyone else is doing it, I'd better do it, too.* No one wants to be left behind, and so we are running, scurrying, our days streaming past.

For this blatant neglect of leisure, Aristotle would be mad at us. In Aristotle, leisure isn't just the time beyond paid work. It's not mindless diversion or chores—a binge-watch weekend or a closet overhaul. Leisure is a necessity of a civilized existence. Leisure is a time of reflection, contemplation, and thought, away from servile obligations. But today, leisure smells lazy, a word connoting uselessness and privilege. Somewhere along the line, the joyless Protestant ethos became a reality, if not a mantra: "Live to work," not "Work to live." To understand how sullied the idea of leisure has become, look no farther than the "leisure suit"—a louche fashion-crime, hopelessly out of date.

I offer feeble comfort to my son. But I feel it, too: something missing; a profound absence altering body and soul. I remember my own child self anticipating the weekend on Friday morning, the great expanse of possibility before me. My parents' friends, and my friends, would fill the house. Bad TV was waiting to be consumed in the early-morning shadows. Mostly, I remember being bored, and in that boredom picking up a pen and paper, and discovering that writing felt better than any sport I'd tried or picture I'd drawn. Time wasn't tight, but roomy, a space to explore.

These moments of vivid weekend experience are fewer now, and not only because I'm older, and farther from wonder. My time is bleeding out, and my days and nights are consumed by work and an endless chain of domestic pursuits that leave me snappish and unfamiliar to myself. In a 2013 survey, 81 percent of American respondents said they get the Sunday night blues. Surely this melancholy isn't just about anticipating the workweek ahead, but about grieving the missed opportunity behind—another lost weekend.

After too many Sunday nights turning off the light in my kids' rooms with an apology for the lameness of the previous two days, thereafter collapsing in exhaustion, I decided to dig deep into the weekend problem: how we lost it, and what it means to live without it. When I started investigating, two things became clear: I'm not alone with my Sunday night letdown, and smarter people than I are fighting to preserve the weekend—and winning. I talked to people who fiercely protect their weekends for the things they love. There are CEOs who are reinventing the workweek to spend time with their families, and successful corporations that are beginning to offer four-day workweeks, and companies that now ask their employees to drop their phones off on Friday night and pick them up on

Monday. Shonda Rhimes, the ridiculously prolific and successful writer-producer-showrunner behind hit shows like *Grey's Anatomy* and *Scandal*, no longer responds to emails at night or on weekends—and she's a single mom with three kids as well as being busier than the average head of state. Everyone needs to do what she says.

I've tried, on occasion, to follow the lead of these people who have committed to a new relationship to time, one in which leisure is as precious as any material good, any professional accolade. An interesting thing happens when you reclaim your weekend: you reclaim your childlike abandon and sense of possibility. You unearth the self that's been buried beneath the work. You discover that a well-lived weekend is the gateway to a well-lived life.

This is a book about how we won the weekend, and how we lost it. Mostly, it's a book about how to take it back.

CHAPTER I

WHAT IS A WEEKEND?

W HAT IS A WEEKEND?" sniffs the Dowager Countess, that cranky truth-teller in the series *Downton Abbey*. It's been voted the most beloved quote in the show's history, delivered by Maggie Smith while the Crawley family sits sparkling around the dining table in beaded dresses and dinner jackets as the (overworked) footman ladles the gravy.

Set in the first blush of the twentieth century, the PBS series shows one English family's slow tumble through the decades as society shifted from aristocratic rule to the more egalitarian modern age. The Dowager Countess's line gets the laugh because, for the British nobility, the idea of a week divided into days of work and non-work is incomprehensible—an abstraction. It simply does not apply. In the corridors of abundance where the Crawleys dwell, every day really is like Sunday— to steal a line from Morrissey—filled with tea, gossip, and directives like "Mrs. Hughes, do see to the marble bust of the Earl of Carnarvon today. Gleam is lacking."

The Dowager Countess's line resonates with today's audiences because we, too, ask the question "What is a weekend?"—but for very different reasons. A century ago, workers were striking and marching and shedding blood to win the weekend. Today, many people can't remember the last time they had two full days off in a row, even when they have a legal right to take them.

The fading of the weekend goes hand in hand with new ways of working. Gone are the days of long-term employment in one organization, with decades of mutual loyalty and a gold watch at retirement; job security is a relic of the past, like a butter churn, or a Slanket. For many, work is painfully insecure, a patchwork of short-term contracts or a series of small jobs that add up to one fragile living. With a swipe, our phones can conjure up workers: if you need a doorknob replaced or a microwave hauled, call Task Rabbit, an odd-job service; if you have a wedding to attend, call Glam Squad, on-the-go makeup and hair stylists. One person's leisure becomes another person's labor. It's worth remembering that there are people on the other end of those swipes, living on high alert, 24/7, their workweek ever-changing. For some, that fluidity is liberating; for others, it's the end of the weekend.

With the decline of manufacturing and the rise of so-called knowledge work, ideas, not widgets, are the white-collar stock-in-trade. But ideas, by nature, are hard to quantify; an idea doesn't really have a beginning or an end. Just like work. The economist C. Northcote Parkinson is credited with "Parkinson's law of efficiency," which holds that "work expands so as to fill the time available for its completion." The phrase came from a 1955 humor essay in *The Economist*, but it's only funny because it's true: Work is like a goldfish that grows to fit the bowl. Work will always take up all the space. And when we're digitally connected to the office at any moment, day or night, work is virtually—pun intended—limitless. We're bowl-free, and the goldfish is growing to monstrous, horror movie proportions. *Attack of the Work Goldfish*—a movie no one wants to see.

But the prospect of taking two days off sounds like lunacy in a flatlined economy where there's fierce competition for jobs—even mediocre ones. Job insecurity is a strong predictor of poor health, and increases risk for depression. It nestles into the body like illness, this feeling of being constantly in competition with our hypothetical replacements (possibly "foreign"; probably robotic) as well as with the guy at the desk one over, who never seems to leave early for a doctor's appointment or take off before 8:00 p.m. on a Friday.

For the luckiest workers, the relationship to leisure is complicated by the fact that we like our work. We've all had those periods of being lost in the myriad satisfactions of the job; we know the thrill of completion and flow. Another ripple effect of the global economy is that much of the drudgery of white-collar work has been eliminated by smart technology, and—if troublingly—farmed out to offshore workers. A certain kind of privileged knowledge worker might argue that we work more because work just isn't as bad as it used to be. If one is lucky enough to have a job that requires thinking and creating, then working long hours straight through the weekend might not feel like a loss; it might not even feel like work at all. One might even take a certain pride in not having leisure or weekends. And letting everybody in the office know about those long hours and work-inflected weekends is a strategy—even a subconscious one—to manage anxiety about not having a job at all, an insurance policy against redundancy in downsized times.

But what if all that work is distorting your view of the world, clouding your perception of what matters, acting a little like . . . brainwashing? Welcome to the "cult of overwork," which is a no-fun cult, free of sex and drugs. In this particular cult, workers have accepted fifty-, sixty-, eighty-hour workweeks without weekends as status quo, or worse, as a credential of success. But in fact, working *less* makes you *more* productive. Overworked and under-rested people are bad employees. They make mistakes. They burn out. You don't want them operating on your kid, and you probably don't want to hang out with them because they're boring. And, most urgently, members of the cult of overwork are missing out on their lives.

A weekend is the break that reminds you that you are more than a worker. That was the original promise of the Sabbath: God prescribing a day away from the monotony of labor. Exodus is filled with passages in which the bad boss Pharaoh admonishes the slaves about the bricks they're being forced to carry back and forth to his endlessly expanding empty warehouse space: "You are lazy, lazy! . . . Go now, and work! . . . You shall not lessen your daily number of bricks!" But God has other ideas, and as He frees His people, He mandates a day of rest, like the one He took on the seventh day, tired from all that creating. He stuck the Sabbath into the commandments as a reminder that life isn't defined solely by production, or its little friend, consumption. He built humanity into the week.

A brick is a pretty obvious burden, but so much of today's labor doesn't leave marks on our bodies; it breaks our spirits, which is an invisible kind of wearing down. The result is tangible: overwork leads to exhaustion, or even depression and suicide. Maybe we continue on in a kind of Stockholm syndrome state because accepting work's bottomless infringement is a survival technique, a delusion to get through another leisure-free month, or year. But if your occupation is your preoccupation all the time—every weekend—the risk is the possibility of missing your life; of only doing, and rarely being. Even if you love your work, what's going on? What is a week too full to allow for forty-eight hours of restoration? What is a life without reprieve?

IN ANSWER TO my son's pleas for better weekends, I sat down with my laptop and did a quick, informal audit of my good and bad weekends. Three columns: Friday, Saturday, Sunday. Then the activities, as best I could remember. There they were, laid bare in their monotony and occasional doses of pleasure. There was kid stuff (*hockey, playdates*); domestic stuff (*cleaning, groceries, laundry . . . so much laundry*); work stuff (*emails, article polishing, invoicing*); some pleasure (*dinner out, K. visited from Calgary, run by the water*); and then back to the domestic stuff (*basement overhaul, buying the kid running shoes again because running shoes are now made out of tissue paper*). Reviewing a few months of weekends (ignoring those occasional special getaways and big events), it was easy to see that the least-satisfying ones were all the same: chores; shopping; work; screens. Repeat.

But the best weekends always included a few key elements, in various iterations: connection; pleasure; hobbies; nature; creativity. I can't imagine a weekend where I feed all those needs, unless I can, as is my dream, transition to a one-day workweek so my weekends are six days long (please call me if you know how to make this happen). But I came to discover that, with some diligence, at least a few of those ingredients for a good weekend are available to anyone.

When I started writing this book, I wanted to understand what makes a good weekend by talking to people who take them. I thought I'd turn a cool, journalistic eye on the situation, notebook at the ready. But pretty quickly I realized that I needed to start copycatting these good weekenders. In the year it took me to write this book, I went from casual observer of good weekends, to occasional participant, to something of a convert (albeit a work in progress, who spent a chunk of last Saturday answering emails and then watched three *Lord of the Rings* movies . . . okay, rewatched). It turns out that there are all kinds of unique ways to build a good weekend, but the contours are the same: real leisure isn't just diversion, it's making meaning. A good weekend is alert to beauty. A good weekend embraces purposelessness. A good weekend wanders a million different paths, but always involves slowing down and stepping out of the rushing stream of modern life. This moment we live in is defined by what David Levy, professor in the Information School at the University of Washington, calls the "more-faster-better philosophy of life." The Industrial Revolution established the mind-set that we must always be "maximizing speed, output, and efficiency."Now, technology and a global economy that never sleeps have accelerated what was already grueling. Getting more, and getting it faster and better, takes time. We can be rich in stuff, yet starving for time. Which is why the weekend is more imperative than ever: it's the corner of the week ordained to slow time.

Protecting forty-eight hours in a row in this day and age is a superhero move. It takes courage. But if you can put up your hand and hold off the rush, just for two days, you create space for all kinds of experiences that aren't about success and acquisition, but about that humanity the Sabbath was put in place to safeguard.

On hearing the Dowager Countess's question, the footman should have stopped ladling the gravy and answered for all of us: The weekend is when we put down the brick and remember what matters.

CHAPTER 2

THE RISE AND FALL
OF THE WEEKEND

W E MADE UP the weekend the same way we made up the week. The earth actually does rotate around the sun once a year, taking about 365.25 days. The sun truly rises and sets over twenty-four hours. But the week is man-made, arbitrary, a substance not found in nature. That seven-day cycle in which we mark our meetings, mind birthdays, and overstuff our iCals—buffered on both ends by those promise-filled forty-eight hours of freedom—only holds us in place because we invented it.

The weekend begins, then, with an enduring love of seven. The clean, sleek digit is our preferred dose of dwarves, sins, and brides for brothers. As a baby name, Seven has been on the rise for both boys and girls since the 1980s (hardly anyone is named Four). Ancient civilizations loved seven: the Babylonians saw seven celestial bodies, and imbued the number with mystical significance, using it in incantations and exorcisms. Seven is special: the only number between one and ten that cannot be multiplied or divided within the group.

This very ancient idea that seven signifies totality and uniqueness carried over into ever so slightly less ancient Jewish liturgy (perhaps because the Jews were exiled in Babylon, absorbing Mesopotamia's astrological leanings). In the Old Testament, when God dictated rest on the seventh day, He was not kidding around: "Whosoever doeth any work in the Sabbath day, he shall surely be put to death."

Surely it wasn't only death threats that prompted most religions to protect one day out of seven, though. Humans possess a deep, unassailable need for repose. Hindus, Buddhists, and Taoists all exhort a day of rest. Roman emperor Constantine shifted the calendar to emphasize Sunday as the Sabbath day, a move befitting a Christian convert looking for a way to distinguish the new Church from Judaism. The prophet Mohammed decreed that Muslims required one special day in seven for prayer and congregation, and Friday got the nod; some scholars maintain this is because Saturday and Sunday were taken and there was a little three-way competition to attract that coveted undecided pagan audience. Jumu'ah, as Friday public worship is called, isn't strictly a Sabbath, as work halts for a short time only, long enough for an hour of prayer and a sermon. But for that hour, businesses shutter and a community comes together, even if most congregants return to their daily lives right after. So all three monotheistic religions have anointed one day per week as spiritually significant and set apart from work, and all three of those bump up against one another: Friday, Saturday, Sunday. The outline of the weekend is etched in the sacred.

By 1725, most American colonies had passed Sabbatarian legislation banning Sunday work, but the other six days often started and ended in darkness for the laboring class. Newspapers frequently ran anonymous editorials by workers fuming about their epic hours and lousy pay, including one in *The Philadelphia Independent Gazetteer* by "An Old Mechanic" who complained, in 1784, that his lot "have barely sufficient time to acquaint themselves with the true interests of our country." The mechanic was too spent after a fourteen-hour workday to down a glass of ale let alone participate in bettering the republic. Framing this plea in nation-building terms may have been an easier sell to eighteenth-century powers-that-be than the more contemporary, first-person strategy many of us shout in our fantasies: "Please, boss, let me go home before eight so I can eat with my family." But the old mechanic was sincere: the citizens of the fledgling country knew that the success of the great New World experiment required—and revered—a hearty Protestant work ethic. Yet as Benjamin Kline Hunnicutt, historian and professor at University of Iowa, points out in his book *Free Time: The Forgotten American Dream*, work wasn't virtuous in and of itself, but as a means to a higher end. For the religious majority, that end was God's kingdom on earth. For Walt Whitman, writing in the century after the mechanic's lament, the true work of the citizenry must be oriented toward "higher progress." America was already realizing its dream of political freedom and material abundance, meeting the physical needs of its citizens—but then what? Whitman's "higher progress"—the goal of the new American—called for the pursuit of the arts, the spirit, and the body in nature. He pleaded for attention to "the interior life."

But when, during these long, hard days, was the average worker permitted to tend his humanity? As Hunnicutt told me, "In the nineteenth century, as industry is becoming more and more efficient, Walt Whitman is writing this beautiful poetry, these democratic vistas, as if he were on a hill looking forward into the future and he sees this coming era when people would be able to meet their material needs with less and less effort." (Whitman didn't anticipate email.) "It's not that work is a bad thing at all; work is absolutely essential for the human creature. But after a certain point, after you get enough, acquire enough, it's time to move on to those things that are more important, things that constitute the best of the possibility of our humanity."

HOW THE WEEKEND WAS WON

We abuse time, make it our enemy. We try to contain and control it, or, at the very least, outrun it. Your new-model, even faster phone; your finger on the "Close" button in the elevator; your same-day delivery. We shave minutes down to nanoseconds, mechanizing and digitizing our hours and days, paring them toward efficiency, that buzzword of corporate America.

But time wasn't always so rigid. Ancient cultures like those of the Mayans and the pagans saw time as a wheel, their lives repeating in stages, ever turning. The Judeo-Christians decided that time was actually linear, beginning at creation and moving toward end times. This idea stuck, and it's way more boring than a wheel. Straight time means that we are rushing toward an invisible finish line, one without ribbons or high-fives. Our sprint through time, if you really think about it, is because we're trying to outrun the inevitable: death. Isn't that ultimately what's behind the need for speed? Becoming efficient is a way of saying *I'm going to conquer time before it conquers me*. To slow down, to stop fighting time, to actually feel it—this is an act of giving in, which is weakness. Bragging "I never take a weekend" is a gesture of strength: *I corralled time, I beat it down*. Actually, taking a weekend means ceasing the fight with time, and letting it be neutral, unoccupied. Why isn't this a good thing?

Not long ago, free time was a defining political issue. The first instance of American workers rising up in unity wasn't about child labor, or working conditions, or salaries—it was about shrinking long work hours. Those who came before us fought—and died—for time.

For about a hundred years, through the eighteenth and nineteenth centuries, one of the central campaigns of the organized labor movement was getting time off for workers. But before the two days of a weekend could even become imaginable, they had to tame that rangy workday, and the first U.S. strike over hours occurred in May 1791. A group of Philadelphia carpenters walked off the job, asking for a day's work that would start at six in the morning and end at six at night, with two hours for meals. Their strike had no immediate impact, but it did articulate the end game of what came to be known as the "10 Hour Movement." Hundreds of organized protests and strike meetings (perhaps announced by a town crier) took place throughout the late nineteenth century, in big cities like Boston and Detroit and smaller manufacturing towns like Lowell, Massachusetts, and Rochester, New York.

In 1835, in the wake of one such strike, labor leaders released a fiery document called the *Ten-Hour Circular*: "We have too long been subjected to the odious, cruel and unjust and tyrannical system which compels the operative Mechanic to exhaust his physical and mental powers by excessive toil, until he has no desire but to eat and sleep, and in many cases he has no power to do either from extreme debility." The authors disdainfully noted that many bosses plied their workers with "a half pint of ardent spirits" on the job, essentially drugging them to work longer and harder. (Remember this next time you imbibe at your office's "Beer Friday" hang.)

The short, articulate circular catalyzed the movement: the first general strike in U.S. history was about hours worked. Over several days in June of 1835, the Philadelphia Trades Union organized a mass strike across the trades where coal heavers, housepainters, leather dressers, cigar makers were all fighting together under the banner "From 6 to 6." They won. Within months, Philadelphia had legislated the ten-hour day for municipal workers, with no reduction in pay. Even as other states followed suit, however, a shorter workday was still mostly theoretical, rarely enforced, and often evaded by industry. In the weeks leading up to the implementation of ten-hour-day laws in New Hampshire, corporation agents set out to corner workers to sign "special contracts" that would circumvent the new rules. Those who didn't sign were often fired or blacklisted.

As the Industrial Revolution changed the very nature of work, things got worse. The new machines required uninterrupted tending to avoid the costs of starting and stopping. Dickensian misery abounded. Windowless factories locked in darkness. Rats scurrying. The deformities of child laborers with soft, bendable bones and knees pointed inward from standing in the cotton mills. The "mill girls" who populated the factories of Lowell complained of working the looms in the dark at both ends of the day, their eyes strained by the candles that provided their only light.

All of this was happening on the clock; the clock became the ubiquitous new boss. Previously, workers tended to complete their work organically, in accordance with natural laws: the fisherman's tasks beholden to the tides; the farmer's to the seasons. But with industrialization, clocks now determined the task, and the measure of productivity was how much labor could be wrung out of a worker over a period of time. As historian E. P. Thompson wrote, it was the moment when work went from "task time" to "clock time." Time had a dollar value, and became a commodity, not to be wasted. "Time is now currency: it is not passed but spent," wrote Thompson. Clocks in factories would often mysteriously turn forwards and backwards. Bosses were stealing unpaid hours from workers, who feared to carry their own watches for, as one factory worker wrote in his memoirs in 1850, "it was no uncommon event to dismiss any one who presumed to know too much about the science of horology."

EIGHT HOURS FOR WHAT WE WILL...

A ten-hour day was still grueling, and eventually workers set their sights on shaving off two more hours. The eight-hour day we know came a little closer with the birth, in 1771, of Robert Owen in Montgomeryshire, Wales. Owen was a middle-class, bookish kid, a fan of rationalist thought and the utopian ideals of Thomas Paine. He loved a big idea—various biographies describe him as a "dreamer," and in portraits he has a curious face with raised eyebrows like two footbridges. Later in his life his big ideas got a little nutty, and he lost most of his fortune trying to start a utopian society in New Harmony, Indiana. But as a younger man, in the early nineteenth century, he was running new-model cotton mills in New Lanark and Clyde, Scotland, that were widely admired as living examples of social reform. His ideas for improving the lot of his workers were simple. He set up a company store so employees could buy goods cheaply rather than getting fleeced by unscrupulous shopkeepers. He banned alcohol. He established a school for workers (the syllabus included geography, math, and dancing in kilts). Owen's factories proved profitable because—as every good boss knows—happy workers are better workers. So for his next big initiative, Owen seized upon working hours, noting that shorter workdays made laborers both more efficient and more cheerful. He's credited with coining the phrase that defined the ideal working day: "Eight hours' labor, Eight hours' recreation, Eight hours' rest."

Owen's maxim showed up, revamped, in a poem written by American activist J. G. Blanchard and set to music by the Reverend Jesse Jones, published in 1878. Their popular version allotted the workers a little more autonomy: "Eight Hours for Work, Eight Hours for Rest, Eight Hours for What We Will!" The catchy phrase fit tidily onto a banner and was held high at protests, which were frequent. From 1881 to 1885 in the United States there were at least 142 strikes around the issue of work hours.

Advocates presented the eight-hour workday as a two-sided coin, a boon to both labor and industry. Shorter workdays would lead to the creation of jobs for those without them and leisure for those already employed. A higher standard of living for all workers would mean more consumption. Consumption would stimulate the economy, and stave off overproduction, and the dreaded boom-and-bust economic cycle would be halted

Around the world, the movement for a manageable workday was rumbling in economically developed countries. Melbourne stonemasons held a strike in 1856 for an eight-hour day, arguing that the extreme Australian heat necessitated shorter hours. In England in the late 1880s, the Eight Hour League successfully pressured the Trades Union Congress, which represented (and still does) the majority of unions in Britain, to adopt the eight-hour day as one of its major goals in bargaining. On April 15, 1872, in Toronto, a group of two thousand printers paralyzed the publishing industry by striking for a shorter workday. Starting downtown, the small group snaked through the city's core, gathering bodies as it moved. By the time it reached the legislative buildings at Queen's Park, the group had swelled to ten thousand people—one tenth of the city's population.

But it's Chicago's Haymarket Affair that remains the best-known Eight Hours demonstration, darkly famous for its blood-soaked, tragic climax. On May 1, 1886, in booming, industrial Chicago, at least thirty thousand workers walked off the job. In his book *Death in the Haymarket*, labor historian James Green describes the strangeness of the day, when the thick gray smudge from the smokestacks that usually coated the city was absent, the sky over Lake Michigan clear. The "great refusal" picked up thousands more as it headed toward Haymarket Square, closing businesses as it moved through the factories on the South Side. Side by side in the square, the demonstrators were now eighty thousand strong. The ranks of the unions and the workers, thick with European immigrants, celebrated day's end in Swedish beer gardens and Irish pubs. German anarchists gathered in large halls, toasting one another.

One of the strike leaders was August Spies, editor of the German socialist paper *Arbeiter-Zeitung* and an ally of the robust anarchist movement. On May 3, Spies delivered a speech about the eight-hour day to a small group of German and Czech lumber shovers. When the bell rang for the end of the day at McCormick Reaper Works, the scab-riddled factory nearby, a few hundred men from the crowd marched toward the gates, some with stones in their hands. The stones begat police bullets, and a striker was killed by gunfire. Several others were injured.

Despite the combustible atmosphere, the crowd that gathered the next night in Haymarket Square remained calm. By 10:00 p.m., as the sky darkened and rain began, only about five hundred people were listening to the speaker when a wall of policemen suddenly appeared, calling for the group to disperse. As people were doing so, a red light arced through the air, and in seconds a bomb exploded. In the ensuing chaos, police began firing. Six police officers would die of wounds in days to come. At least three protesters, too, lost their lives.

Anarchists were rounded up and held accountable for the attack on the "hero cops," as the press anointed them. There was no evidence proving who had thrown the bomb, and the trial was considered a farce, a pre–Court TV spectacle played out in the papers, pitting patriotic Americans against the immigrant agitators. In the end, all eight men were convicted of murder, and seven of those eight were sentenced to death. One killed himself in jail by setting off a cigar-shaped bomb in his mouth. Four were hanged in public, August Spies among them.

Because of Haymarket, and the chaos and violence that came in its wake, workers' rights were no longer an abstraction; sacrifices had been made for the cause of time, and the issue would not be abandoned. In tribute to the affair, May 1 is still known as May Day, a holiday to honor worker solidarity, and protest, celebrated around the world.

BEFORE THE WEEKEND became official, many workers took it anyway. Between the late eighteenth and mid-nineteenth centuries in England, vast numbers of employees didn't bother to show up on Monday, playing the religious holiday card by saying they were "keeping Saint Monday" (there is no Saint Monday, it turns out). Benjamin Franklin rather prissily bragged that as a young man he got promoted simply by showing up on Mondays for his job in a London printing house: "My constant attendance (I never making a St. Monday) recommended me to the master."

Binge work leads to binge play, and many workers were hungover on Mondays, recovering from bar games at alehouses, outdoor dogfights, and boxing matches. They were paid on Saturday, and stuck in church on Sunday, so they stole that Monday to burn through their paychecks and have some fun. By the 1840s, popular pastimes included day trips out of town on the new railways, or perhaps a cricket match—recreation that's the stuff of our own modern weekends. An 1867 memoir from "A Journeyman Engineer" named Thomas Wright describes, in slightly condescending terms—behold the casual use of the term "great unwashed"—how the average worker filled his day off: "On Monday everything is in favour of the great unwashed holding holiday. They are refreshed by the rest of the previous day; the money received on the Saturday is not all spent; and those among them who consign their best suits to the custody of the pawnbroker during the greater part of each week are still in possession of the suits which they have redeemed from limbo on Saturday night." Nothing says weekend like getting the suit out of hock! (The idea of the weekend as the time to blow the paycheck holds today: Americans spend the most money on Friday and Saturday nights, and the least on Mondays and Tuesdays.)

Monday absenteeism was a chronic problem for the bosses. In 1855, a London-based group called the Metropolitan Early Closing Association began advocating for a "half-Saturday"—a 1:00 p.m. closing. In *Waiting for the Weekend*, Witold Rybczynski writes that while the group was genuinely concerned about the eighteen-hour workdays endured by many shopkeepers, it was also a Christian organization, and angling for a higher turn-out at Sunday services. By locking the doors at 1:00 p.m. on Saturday, they hoped workers would wring out their baccha-nalian inclinations on Saturday night and then head straight to the pews on Sunday.

Low-paid workers—the aforementioned "great unwashed" —were actually willing to lose out on a much-needed day's sal-ary in exchange for a day of freedom, so deeply felt was the need for two days' reprieve. It's a trade-off most of us make all the time: time versus money. Do I pay the parking ticket or challenge it and lose an afternoon to the process? The financial hit of that lost Monday was real, so when the paid half-Saturday was offered, most workers were glad to accept the comprom-ise. Saint Monday faded from tradition, and the half-Saturday holiday became the standard in Britain in the 1870s. The full day off wouldn't take hold until sixty years later, but the first recorded use of the word "week-end" that seems to fit our cur-rent definition appeared in 1870 in *Food Journal*, according to the *Oxford English Dictionary*: "'Week-end,' that is from Saturday until Monday,—it may be a later day in the week if the money and credit hold out,—is the season of dissipation"—with "dissi-pation" in this context meaning "movement" or "activity." An affluent British family in the Victorian era was likely to spend the weekend socializing at a country house, enjoying eight-course meals between shooting, embroidering, and matchmaking. The first weekends were about escape and movement—and the best ones still are.

One of the key agents in normalizing the weekend for the rest of American workers was actually a staunch anti-unionist, auto tycoon Henry Ford (he was also a well-known anti-Semite, which makes his championing of the Sabbath a little delicious). In 1914, Ford raised the daily wage in his factories from $2.34 per day to $5.00. It was a radical move, and a PR sensation. Thousands showed up hoping for work, causing a near riot that was damped down when the police department turned fire-hoses on men in bitter winter. But the raise wasn't exactly the Owen-style socialism it superficially resembled; Ford was convinced to go along with an increased wage only when his vice president, James Couzens, pointed out that not only would the move be great publicity, but more money would give the workers an incentive to spend—perhaps on cars. In 1926, Ford echoed this argument when he introduced the five-day workweek. "People who have more leisure must have more clothes," he argued. "They eat a greater variety of food. They require more transportation in vehicles."

Ford, probably by accident, articulated a contradiction that sits at the heart of the weekend as we have come to know it: it's both a time of rest and a time of consumption. A Marxist might point out that the weekend is an act of corporate trickery, a dangling carrot that keeps workers tethered to their jobs.

As the economist John Kenneth Galbraith put it, the mission of production—and business—is to "create the wants it seeks to satisfy"—and the weekend is the time of satisfying wants.

All of which is probably true, but it's just as true to say that the yearning for a weekend doesn't arise solely from a desire to shop. With work quelled, space opens up in which to be with others, or in solitude with the self—or both. The clock that propels us all those other days is silenced (or quieted, at least), and time opens up, awakening our own desires, our thoughts and impulses. In *The Sabbath World*, Judith Shulevitz likens the Sabbath to a psychoanalytic session, tough but profound, as it "takes you out of mundane time and forces you into what might be called sacred time—the timeless time of the unconscious, with its yawning infantile unboundedness, its shattered sequentiality."

It was less poetry than pragmatism, however, that finally cemented the two-day weekend. During the Depression of 1929, many industries began cutting back to a five-day schedule. In a tumultuous, underemployed economy, fewer hours for some would mean more work for others (an idea that still reverberates in some European countries: in Germany, the response to the 2008 economic crisis was to implement a nationwide work-sharing program called Kurzarbeit, meaning "short work"). Americans experienced what it was to work less, and—shocker—they liked it. Politicians noticed. Guided along by organized labor, with President Roosevelt signing off, the Fair Labor Standards Act of 1938 enshrined the modern weekend: Americans were now promised the eight-hour day, and the forty-hour workweek.

The weekend was inching closer to realization. But it's worth noting that what looks like progress was, in a way, a return to what came before. The long, work-tethered week was really a two-hundred-year (approximately) blip in history, a product of the rise of industrial capitalism and the shift away from feudal life. In other words: you, right now, with all your gadgets and time-saving devices, probably work longer hours than a medieval peasant. In medieval times, work and play were less distinct categories. Serfs were beholden to their lords, but they were in "task time," living where they worked, taking sustenance from the land where they lived, and finding leisure there, too. Unlike the archetypal work martyr who refuses to take a vacation, these people were not afraid of holidays: before the Reformation, a European church calendar might note as many as 156 holidays, a clever way of keeping parishioners loyal. One estimate is that the average English medieval peasant spent about one-third of his year on leisure and holiday time. In fourteenth-century England, during a period of high wages, there were lots of good reasons not to work: weddings, births, and deaths; a juggler passing by; Sunday. The work itself was drudgery, and physically draining, but there was unoccupied time to buffer it. (Of course, most of us would not choose to go back to lives of hand-plowing and famine, no matter how excellent the perks.) "The tempo of life was slow, even leisurely; the pace of work relaxed," writes Juliet Schor, professor of sociology at Boston College, and author of *The Overworked American*. "Our ancestors may not have been rich, but they had an abundance of leisure."

Working five days a week is a relatively new concept, and we still haven't got it right.

The weekend skipped across the globe over the next several decades. By 1955 the two-day weekend was standard in Britain, Canada, and the United States, and short Saturdays were common across Europe. By the 1970s, no European country exceeded a forty-hour workweek—many worked less—and all observed the weekend.

In the Middle East, Friday-Saturday weekends became the norm over the last half of the twentieth century, while some Gulf and North African countries booked off Thursday and Friday. But as economies have reoriented from local to global, the financial boon to a country that keeps hours in line with the West has altered the shape of the weekend. Oman switched from a Thursday-Friday weekend to a Friday-Saturday weekend in 2013. The same year, Saudi Arabia followed suit with a royal decree that looked a lot like an open-for-business sign.

The state of the weekend is an ongoing battle in Israel, where the official weekend is the day and a half that constitutes the Sabbath, from Friday evening through Saturday. I remember walking the streets of Jerusalem on a Friday at dusk, where in a matter of minutes a flurry of activity transformed the thick crowds and bustling market stalls to shuttered businesses and empty, tumbleweed-ready streets. It's quiet and otherworldly (but buying a sandwich is nearly impossible).

Israel's weekend is changing, too—tensely. Some Orthodox Jews, appalled at Sabbath-breakers, have reportedly thrown stones at Israelis taking the bus on Saturdays. Yet Saturday is also a big shopping day in Israel. Many malls are open because the day-and-a-half-long weekend is so short. When exactly are working people supposed to get stuff done? ask the shoppers. With Arabs and Christians to please, there have been calls for a full, two-day Friday-Saturday weekend to accommodate holy days for all groups. In 2016, a bill for six three-day weekends per year was before the Knesset, with much grumbling on all sides of the debate.

Israel's conundrum is a tidy illustration of the confusion so many of us face about the weekend: the need to tend the domestic front collides with the need for a sacred, protected pocket of time in which we do nothing. Our urge to protect time is in constant conflict with the need to spend it. Whether it's motivated by the push of business or the pull of the soul (or some combination of the two), two days off is what feels normal and human. After hundreds of years of debate, bloodshed, and dogma, a weekend should be an enshrined right—yet that isn't exactly what happened. It took a century to win the weekend. It's taken only a few decades to undo it.

THE FALL OF THE WEEKEND

Recently, on an airplane, I sat next to a young man who appeared to be masquerading as an adult. His face was teen-smooth yet he wore a suit, like a kid playing the dad in a middle-school play. He initiated the awkward, kiss-close chitchat of the airplane companion with a line I hadn't heard before: "So—what keeps you busy?" It was, he explained, his favored icebreaker, a Millennial alternative to the uncool, old-fashioned "What do you do?"

He was an executive from the car-sharing service Uber and one of the oldest guys in his office. "I just turned thirty," he told me cheerfully. As he described his workplace, with pride and affection, a picture emerged: open concept, filled with twenty-somethings who worked deep into the night, every night. I mentally embellished with Ping-Pong tables and wandering Labradoodles and clear-glass refrigerators stuffed with Red Bull. "So—what do you do on the weekend?" I asked, trying out my own new line. He informed me, puffing with pride, that in his life, there were no weekends. Work kept him busy.

There's an historic cord linking Haymarket Square to my neighbor on the plane, or rather, a severing thereof. Those forty-eight hours, so hard-earned, have been slowly whittled away, and with little to no marching from a post-organized-labor work-force. This was not supposed to happen. In 1930, British econo-mist John Maynard Keynes, rose-colored glasses perched firmly on nose, published his famous essay "Economic Possibilities for Our Grandchildren." For decades, he'd seen a decrease in work-ers' hours as technology accelerated the pace of production. This would surely continue, he predicted, and leisure would replace labor as the driving force in people's lives. The world was becoming global; an age of abundance was at hand (the market crash of 1929 was just a blip, he assured his audience). By 2030, Keynes imagined that his grandchildren would work a fifteen-hour workweek. Here was capitalism at its best, liberat-ing citizens from the "love of money as a possession" and instead allowing them to see money "as a means to the enjoyments and realities of life." This future swell of leisure would upend avarice; the central desire would be the "good life": "We shall honour those who can teach us how to pluck the hour and the day virtuously and well, the delightful people who are capable of taking direct enjoyment in things, the lilies of the field who toil not, neither do they spin." Keynes was far from the stuffed-shirt stereotype of the economist, living among the artists and intellectuals of Cambridge's Bloomsbury group, commiserating with his friend the writer Lytton Strachey over their various affairs. From that vantage point, he saw the upcoming leisure surplus as a creative possibility, time to appreciate "the art of life itself."

But he also expressed concern. What if all this free time led to a "generalized nervous breakdown"? Leisure anxiety sprouted up right alongside leisure promise. Boredom—the province of aristocrats—would trickle down to all Americans, becoming a curse. "We spring from a long line of compulsive go-getters," read a panicked article in *Life* magazine that ran in 1964. "And the joys of contemplation are not a part of our tradition." Theorists and economists wrung their hands over the upcoming onslaught of leisure, a result of American ingenuity that no one was prepared for. Some predicted a utopia where man would finally realize his full potential, emotional and artistic; others fretted over an undereducated (unwashed?) class that would fritter away its free time doing nothing, a slacker nation in waiting.

Of course, it didn't play out that way. It's true that workers in almost every advanced economy in the world are putting in fewer hours on average than a half century ago, including in the United States, so Keynes's starry-eyed soothsaying wasn't entirely wrong. But, as Derek Thompson points out in *The Atlantic*, this statistic is an average: overall, hours haven't declined significantly in thirty years, and looking more closely it turns out that, in North America, educated, high-wage earners are working longer hours than fifty years ago, while less-educated, lower-wage workers are working less (i.e., are underemployed and unemployed, stuck with only part-time work). Economists call this phenomenon of the rich having less leisure than the poor "the leisure gap," and it's relatively new. In 1965, college-educated men had more leisure than men with a high school degree; by 2005, the college grads had eight hours less leisure than the high school grads. The rich are no longer the leisure class.

One explanation is the "substitution effect": people earning high wages are less inclined to take time off because it means giving up more money. Since the 1980s, the salaries of those at the top—the 1 percent—have risen exponentially, while the salaries of those below have stagnated, or declined. The inequality gulf actually encourages the rich to work more and the poor to work less. But the group working the most hours with the least leisure are single mothers, who feel the most time-crunched. So even if workers have more free time on average, for those at either end of the income scale it feels like much less.

The United States ranks high for a worker's average annual hours at 1,790—that's 200 more hours than France, the Netherlands, and Denmark. It works out to about 35 hours a week. But a separate poll, conducted by Gallup, found that, when self-reporting, workers admit to a much higher average—somewhere between 41 and 47 hours weekly for those in full-time employment. Most alarmingly, nearly 40 percent of employees report working 50 or more hours per week. They don't stop on Friday, either. According to time-use surveys in the U.S. and abroad, 29 percent of Americans said they perform paid work on weekends, more than three times the rate among Spanish workers. Then there's all the un-noted work time added on to the week when we check our phones or speed-type an email while in line at the grocery store. Britain comes in a close second with four in ten managers saying they put in more than 60 hours a week—that "American disease."

Emma is a young lawyer in private practice in Toronto who recently made partner, and when she talks about how work bleeds into her weekends, she invokes illness as a metaphor. "I don't have a healthy relationship with work. I worry it's an addiction," she tells me. "But I brought it on myself." Her hours are empirically brutal: Monday to Friday, she's at work before the sun comes up, around 7:00 a.m. If she's lucky, she gets home between 8:00 p.m. and 9:00 p.m., but many days she's not home until 10:00, and occasionally midnight. On either Saturday or Sunday, she's right back at her desk (albeit a little later, like 9:00 a.m.). For a while, she worked both Saturdays and Sundays, but she's been trying to keep it to one of the two. If she is at home on the weekend, sometimes, while doing a useless task, like watching TV, Emma will think to herself: "In that hour, I could have been billing." She's not proud of this instinct of measuring time in dollars. She feels guilty when she's not working, as if she's letting down her clients and her boss. But then she feels guilty about being the kind of person who works all the time. Her nights and weekends are also time to drum up more clients with coffee, drinks, lunches, breakfasts—meetings that resemble fun, and may actually be a little fun, but are still work. When Emma is at home on weekends, her phone is never off and her laptop moves around the house with her. She answers all pings within minutes.

This is the new normal: smartphone-carrying professionals report interacting with work 13.5 hours every workday. We can barely get through three waking hours without working. The average smartphone user checks his or her device about 150 times per day, with younger people checking most often. Even if many of those swipes are just to check the social feed, we are in constant, perpetual proximity to work. We carry our jobs in our purses and packs, on our bodies. There's no physical separation; we can always be reached, and work can always reach us.

Some research suggests that well-off families are disproportionately likely to complain about time crunch. Professor Daniel S. Hamermesh of Royal Holloway, University of London, analyzing international time-stress data in a paper with Jungmin Lee, came up with his own name for the fact that the highest-paid members of society are also the most anxious about their lack of time: "yuppie kvetching." I get it: it feels indulgent to pine for leisure when unemployment has left so many burdened with too much time, and millions of working poor are holding down two and three minimum-wage jobs but still living below the poverty line. Where's the urgency in a conversation about restoring the weekend?

I'd argue that our new digital reality is a great class equalizer: the lack of control over time is something shift workers, whose schedules change week to week and day to day, have always contended with. New technologies mean that blue-collar workers on the frontlines of the patchwork economy are easier than ever to reach, pulled in for extra hours with a text "request" that feels compulsory. The loosening of Sunday shopping laws around the world affects lower-paid service and retail workers most of all. A "weekend"—if one is lucky enough to get it at all—is often two days somewhere in the week, and not necessarily back to back.

But a culture of overwork among the educated doesn't deserve to be trivialized as "yuppie kvetching," as if suffering can be quantified, or there's not enough empathy to go around. Lacking the time to tend our lives—our families, our souls— is serious, with social implications, and personal ones, all of which are cross-class concerns. Research suggests that 80 percent of working parents feel rushed, and both men and women report that finding work-life balance is very difficult. Brigid Schulte, journalist and director of The Better Life Lab at New America, described how the deluge of work and personal demands effectively grate time into ever-tinier fragments that she calls "time confetti."

In Toronto, where I live, half of all jobs are deemed "insecure" or "precarious," meaning no benefits and no job security. The engine of the "gig economy" is Schulte's time confetti, where workers' time is divvied out among obligations. A solid block of time away from work is a luxury many contract workers rarely experience. On one hand, this is an amazing moment to be a worker: the Internet has freed creative people from corporate constraints, and small businesses don't require the bricks-and-mortar outlay that can cripple entrepreneurs. But there's an anxiety-inducing aloneness in precarious work, too: no paid vacations, no benefits, no retirement plans. Research has shown that the stress of job insecurity may actually be worse for your health than being unemployed.

Rebecka, twenty-two, is a Millennial hyphenate. In one week, she works as a restaurant hostess, a tour bus guide, a free-lance journalist, and a volunteer at a media organization. She spends hours outside her jobs every day nurturing the career she wants—digital media—by contributing to websites (often for little to no pay), and she almost never gets Friday or Saturday off because she's hostessing. She doesn't care if she gets a conventional Judeo-Christian weekend; she would, however, like two days off in a row, something that has happened only a couple of times since she graduated from university. "I love it when I get two days off back to back because that's when you really know you're off. The first day off is just coming down from the week, but the second day, you can actually relax." Of course, wage workers don't usually get paid for days off, no matter where those days fall in the week.

In the province of Ontario, a group called the Urban Worker Project is trying to unify this growing population, lobbying for more protections and benefits for freelancers. They're asking for reforms that prevent employers from forcibly classifying full-time workers as "independent contractors," a common strategy to circumvent providing sick days and parental leave. Equally unstable, a generation of aspiring academics at universities and colleges in Canada and the U.S. are stuck working as adjunct (or sessional) professors as tenure track positions vanish. The halls of higher learning are filled with gloomy, debt-burdened PhDs earning low wages with no guarantee of a course to teach next semester. I met a young drama professor named Michelle who's an adjunct at three universities in the Toronto area. She has no office or library carrel, and moves from campus to campus throughout the week like a traveling band. On weekends, she preps and marks. "Every day feels like a Friday and every day feels like a Monday," she says.

It's not just young people who are working in insecure conditions. A middle-aged friend who's a very successful journalist and novelist (he's at the point in his career that Rebecka perhaps hopes to hit in twenty years) describes being on high alert at all times, waiting for a story to break, to see if he'll be called in for a hit of radio or TV punditry. He admits that he almost never says no to work when it's offered, so panicked is he that he might never be wanted again. During a hard-earned holiday in Belize recently with his son, he had to return to the hotel to accept a surprise assignment. Nurturing his brand—even a high-profile one—doesn't stop on Fridays. "The gig economy killed the weekend," he says.

At what point do we declare this way of living a public health issue? Here's a short list of the very real effects of being perpetually "on." Our bodies literally release stress hormones when the Inbox pings. Too much time on our devices means we lose the ability to focus. Working long hours brings weight gain and increases anxiety levels. The risk of stroke among employees who work fifty-five or more hours per week is 33 percent higher than those with a thirty-five- to forty-hour week.

Losing free time usually means losing sleep. The kind of deep, almost spiritual sleep that restores (let's call it "weekend sleep") is becoming rare. Most of us are sleeping less, and more poorly, than a decade ago. Forty percent of American adults are considered sleep-deprived, getting less than six hours of sleep per night. The lack of sleep is linked to obesity, lost cognition, even Alzheimer's and cancer. President Donald Trump brags that he sleeps between ninety minutes and four hours a night, as if this is a sign of virility or a corporate success strategy. But diminished sleep is actually an alarming predictor of erratic behavior.

Lack of sleep breeds a more intimate loss, too. Matt Walker of the Sleep and Neuroimaging Laboratory at Berkeley has written about the negative effects of losing "slow-wave sleep." During this stage of sleep, slow-moving electrical waves travel between regions of the brain. Information moves far and wide during this process, forging associations and building "big tapestry frameworks of understanding," said Walker in a podcast called Inquiring Minds. "It's the difference between knowledge, which is learning individual facts, and wisdom, which is extracting overarching understanding." This feels intuitively right: when we're too exhausted to sleep, when our rest time is depleted, there's a diminishing of a fundamental intellectual part of one's self, the part that matters most—our wisdom, which requires respite to flourish.

WORTH DYING FOR?

In Japan, the word *karoshi* means "death from overwork." Statistically, Japanese workers log slightly fewer hours per year than Americans, but the prevalence of unpaid overtime makes the number spurious. One estimate holds that one in three Japanese men aged thirty to forty works over sixty hours a week. Literally dying from all that work—sometimes just dropping at the desk—is a phenomenon real enough that 813 families were compensated by insurance companies for "*karoshi* deaths" in 2012. For a legally designated "*karoshi* death," the government may pay surviving family members around $20,000 a year. A company may have to offer compensation up to $1 million in damages. Recently, China—in a sad display of its developed-world bona fides—seems to be mirroring Japan, as *China Youth Daily* reports an epidemic of overwork among white-collar workers. In 2014, banking regulator Li Jianhua reportedly died after staying up all night to finish a report before the sun came up. The Chinese press noted that the country has borrowed the Japanese word for its own epidemic of death by overwork—*karoshi* becomes the new Chinese word *guolaosi*.

And if we need tragedy from outside Asia to encapsulate the seriousness of the cult of overwork, let's look at twenty-one-year-old Moritz Erhardt, found dead in the bathroom of his East London flat, lying beneath the shower, which was still running.

Erhardt's too-brief life is so high-achieving that in describing
it, one pictures him as a hurdler, arms pumping and legs flying,
clearing one obstacle after another. According to a lengthy article in *Der Spiegel*, he was a star student in high school in Staufen
im Breisgau, a town in southwestern Germany at the foot of
the Black Forest. Next, he triumphed at a high-powered business
school called WHU – Otto Beisheim School of Management,
near Dusseldorf. The elite character of the institution coheres
perfectly with the graduation gift each student receives: a large,
red book that holds the contact information for alumni, a kind of
Willie Wonka Golden Ticket to the corridors of power. Erhardt
then completed a semester abroad in Ann Arbor, Michigan,
where he sailed through his studies at the Stephen M. Ross
School of Business, described in *Der Spiegel* thusly: "There are
60 hours in a normal workweek at Ross. Overloading students is
part of the concept. Moritz learned to be efficient, goal-oriented
and fast. He had no opportunity to slow down." In Erhardt's narrative, there is no moment of slowing down, no rest. His twenty-
one years were all in fast motion. He cleared the Ross hurdle,
too, and took a summer internship at Bank of America Merrill
Lynch in London, in the investment banking division.

The finance industry, at its most extreme, relies on a way
of working that dumbfounds those on the outside, a combination of sleep-deprivation experiment and hazing ritual. Newbies
hold all-nighters and "roundabouts," where teams of young
interns drive together to each other's flats, and wait while one
runs in and changes clothes, only to return to the cab and get
back to work. Adderall and cocaine help some young bankers

stay awake. Abdurahman Moallim, twenty-one, a former intern at a major multinational bank, told *The Guardian* that the profession thrives on one-upmanship. "All-nighters are often worn as a badge of honour—it's common for interns to brag in the morning about the long hours they've worked the night before. Everybody wants to show they have what it takes to succeed in an industry which demands stamina." On Wall Street, interns joke that they work nine to five—9:00 a.m. to 5:00 a.m.

Erhardt's parents said they regularly received emails from him at 5:00 a.m., presumably from the office. Before collapsing in the shower, evidence suggests that he stayed awake, on a work stint, for a staggering seventy-two hours. An autopsy found that he had suffered an epileptic seizure, and had been taking medicine to manage the condition. The coroner reported that while findings were inconclusive, exhaustion could have played a part.

Either way, the young banker's death became a rallying cry—What madness is *this*? What kind of life was *that*? Media fixated on a photo of the handsome young man dressed as Gordon Gekko, the fictional 1980s tyrant and tycoon portrayed by Michael Douglas in the film *Wall Street*. Gekko was the greasy, pinstriped physical manifestation of his motto: "Greed is good. Greed works." Erhardt's parents decried the interpretation; their son was just a kid playing dress-up at a costume party during his student days in Germany. Their son, like all kids, contained multitudes.

Of course this is true, but the theatricality in that photo resonated darkly. He was a guy playing the part of a successful worker; he was *passing*, and so many of us have felt like that at work. We play the part of a person who doesn't need a weekend, a person who denies the need for any experiences that don't service the career's progress. The young man's Gordon Gekko picture seemed emblematic, a performance of the epic hours demanded in finance that's recognizable to workers in other fields, too. Long hours and missed weekends look good. Even those of us who don't work like bankers felt a twinge at Erhardt's story, seeing a variation of ourselves in the insanity, and wondering if that kind of machismo had trickled down to us, in our less glamorous occupations in which we face another Saturday night at the laptop, another Sunday visit to the office.

Months after Erhardt's death, Goldman Sachs announced reforms to its internship program. Now it caps interns' hours at seventeen per day, and encourages them to come in no earlier than 7:00 a.m. and leave by midnight. Sorry, but seventeen-hour days still sound totally insane. More impressive than that dubious gesture were the words of chief executive Lloyd Blankfein, who admonished his interns that they shouldn't give over their whole lives to the firm. "You have to be interesting, you have to have interests away from the narrow thing of what you do," he said, which is another good argument for why the weekend matters: it's the time to dig down into your non-work self, and discover what makes you who you are. That might make you a better employee, but it will absolutely make you a better person. All of this work, no matter how fascinating the content, makes us boring. As Blankfein said: "You have to be somebody who somebody else wants to talk to."

◇◇◇◇

THERE IS NO compelling reason for anyone to work like this. Since the first research on productivity was published in the 1900s, experts have found, over and over, that workers are most productive when working eight hours a day, up to forty hours per week. As social futurist Sara Robinson wrote in an article on AlterNet: "On average, you get no more widgets out of a ten-hour day than you do out of an eight-hour day. Likewise, the overall output for the work week will be exactly the same at the end of six days as it would be after five days." There may be some gains in a short-term increase in hours—a couple of weeks of overtime on a big project at sixty to seventy hours per week—but after the second week of working long and late, productivity drops off rapidly.

A system that's overloaded wears down and doesn't function efficiently. A paper by John Pencavel at Stanford University showed that reducing work hours actually improved productivity. Pencavel examined a study from World War I, when the British government asked researchers at the Health of Munition Workers Committee (HMWC) to crunch data gleaned from munition workers to explore ways to maximize productivity. Their conclusion, a half century ago, was that workers needed to work less to produce more. In 2014, Pencavel rechecked the research. Output was relatively easy to measure, as workers were paid by the piece. What Pencavel found was a non-linear relationship between working hours and output. After a fifty-hour workweek, employee output—the number of weapons produced—fell. After fifty-five hours, it crashed. Putting in seventy hours produced no more munitions than fifty-five; those fifteen hours were the definition of wasted time. Researchers from 1917 noted that Sunday labor, in particular, caused a decrease in productivity, and increased sickness rates, writing that "the effect of long hours, much overtime, and especially Sunday labor, upon health is undoubtedly most deleterious."But the theater of long hours and missed weekends endures. Sadly, it may reward those who participate, too. Erin Reid, a professor at Boston University's Questrom School of Business, interviewed over one hundred people working at a high-powered global strategy consulting firm. Theirs is a culture of sixty- to eighty-hour workweeks, with the expectation of being on call all weekend, and ready to hop on a plane at the drop of a hat. As one consultant described it, in Reid's paper: "You don't really have the latitude of saying 'I can't really be there.' And if you can't be there, it's probably because you've got another client meeting at the same time. You know it's tough to say I can't be there because my—my son had a Cub Scout meeting."

But, of course, real life does occasionally interfere with work: a funeral, a dental appointment. Reid found that in the event of these kinds of personal events, women were more likely to request formal accommodations—an afternoon off or a flexible schedule—while men were inclined to simply take the time on the down-low, without making arrangements with their superiors. To maintain work-life balance, male consultants were more likely to use "under the radar" strategies, like booking clients closer to the office or working from home, stealth techniques that would allow them to turn up at the recital without their absence being noticed by the boss.

For voicing their needs and working transparently, female consultants were often marginalized, poorly reviewed, and overlooked for promotions. On the contrary, men who worked just as little but didn't talk about it and passed as workaholics were usually rewarded as ideal employees. Those men who acted more like women—i.e., behaved transparently with official requests for work-life balance—were punished just like their female counterparts. One male consultant requested a three-month leave when his daughter was born, but ended up getting only six weeks of unpaid vacation, and subsequently, a terrible performance review in which he was chastised for "the donut" of those missing six weeks.

So Reid's research uncovered one more reason that women may struggle to ascend at work, and affirmed the bleak but unsurprising news that many businesses are still rigidly resistant to the kind of institutional change that would acknowledge the real-world realities of their employees' lives. Sociologists use the term "greedy institution" to describe workplaces that require total commitment and availability of their employees, creating a kind of hermetically sealed, all-in universe. What's greedier than a workplace that infantilizes its workers and measures success not in output but in minutes clocked behind a desk?

But what's most notable about Reid's study is that managers really couldn't tell the difference between employees who actually worked an eighty-hour week and those who faked it. Researchers found no evidence that those employees who logged the longest hours accomplished more, or that those who occasionally stepped out of the work stream and into real life accomplished less. But the theater of busy-ness, the optics of exhaustion, dominate office life. When I worked as a broadcast executive, competitive busy-ness was the norm. On Friday around 5:00 p.m., one particular colleague always seemed to hover near the exit to let it be known that he wouldn't be using it. "Have a good weekend," I'd say, readying to go. "Weekend? What weekend?" he'd gloat, all giddy in his sacrifice, one-upping me in a game that no one wins.

But the joke's on him: it turns out there's no correlation between long hours and economic success. In fact, the OECD's annual measure of productivity backs up the conclusion that short hours win. In the countries ranked highest for productivity—output per working hour—people work shorter hours. These are seven of the ten countries with the highest GDP: Luxembourg, Norway, Switzerland, Netherlands, Germany, Denmark, and Sweden. The same seven make the Top Ten list of countries with the shortest working hours. And countries with long hours prove less competitive. Koreans and Mexicans work the longest of economically developed countries, and both nations rank extremely low in productivity.

The country with a productivity ranking similar to that of the United States is France, and France is also just moderately productive. But consider this when slumped at your desk next Sunday: workers in France also have thirty days of annual paid vacation, excellent scarf-wearing abilities, and subsidized child care. Alone among advanced economies—shamefully—the United States has no paid vacation policy.

In some cases, long hours can lead to far-reaching tragedies. Investigations into the *Challenger* explosion and the *Exxon
Valdez* disaster found exhausted, burned-out workers in the line
of decision makers who may have contributed to those terrible
outcomes. The medical profession is blighted by long, almost
abusive hours that can lead to bad medicine, even patient death.
The weekend—a forty-eight-hour break from occupied time
—matters. Whether we have it or not is truly a matter of life
and death.

THE WORKPLAY FAKE-OUT

How did our relationship to work—and, by extension, our relationship to leisure and the weekend—get so messed up? The
young Uber lawyer I met on the plane, bragging about his
holiday- and weekend-deficit, embodied a particular high-tech
hipster attitude that may provide a clue.

The original team of Macintosh designers wore T-shirts
that read: "Working 90 hours a week and loving it!" It's a
nerd brag of the first order, yet productivity experts estimate
the first Mac might have been completed about a year earlier
if they'd worked half as many hours per week instead. But
"Working 45 Hours a Week and Loving It!" makes for a meh
T-shirt slogan.

The T-shirt comes from Silicon Valley in the mid-1980s,
and that may be the petri dish that bred some of our present-
day misguided attitudes toward work. As many advanced economies have shifted from manufacturing and industrial work to

knowledge-based commerce, the way we work has changed, too. Long, rangy days and nights where ideas flow freely across the aforementioned Ping-Pong table is the idealized image of modern work—a snapshot of urban studies theorist Richard Florida's definition of the much-vaunted "creative class." It's a big, baggy category of white-collar work that, says Florida, includes workers "in science and engineering, architecture and design, education, arts, music and entertainment whose economic function is to create new ideas, new technology, and new creative content." In this kind of work, output is much less easily measured than in a munitions factory; work is inherently shapeless, with no beginning, middle, or end. Project-driven deadlines aside, if the things being made are ideas, then when do you make enough of them to shut off the lights and go home? And why would you, when it's Red Bull and office parties at work anyway? Writing online in *Al Jazeera America*, Sarah Leonard puts it succinctly: "What Silicon Valley has so masterfully done is disguise labor as a lifestyle choice. . . . It's hard to feel exploited while wearing flipflops, balancing gently on an exercise ball."

Let's call this professional mode of melding work and fun "workplay." Workplay is even manifest in office design, with the rise of communal work spaces in bright candy colors that resemble those at kindergarten carpet time. At the San Francisco company Livefyre there are alcoves lined with blue felt, big enough for workers to sit together cross-legged. At Evernote, rather than a receptionist, clients might be greeted by a barista with donuts. This may be par for the course in digital, but at a media complex housing a children's publisher in Toronto, I was surprised to see a slide in the lobby. No one will say donuts and slides aren't awesome, and a welcome alternative to the sterile veal-fattening cubicles of the 1980s and '90s. But the endgame of these aesthetics isn't as cute as the design: it's to make you forget you're at work, so you won't mind staying late, or coming in on Saturday. These super-cool offices are designed to keep you in them.

Katherine Losse was one of the first women hired at Facebook, joining the neophyte company when it was just a group of hungry Harvard dudes in Palo Alto, California. In her memoir *The Boy Kings*, she writes about spending her first day in customer service scanning the office for Mark Zuckerberg. He was nowhere to be seen. She quickly learned that Zuckerberg worked at night "when he had a home-court advantage over VCs and other businesspeople used to keeping regular daytime hours." Boy genius Zuckerberg is always at the top of *Vanity Fair's* Power Lists, and was worth an estimated $56 billion at the time of writing. His is the start-up success story of the century; he's the father of a product that has changed wholly how we live and relate to one another. The Facebook success is mythic, yet the work itself looks informal, as Silicon Valley always has in contrast to the buttoned-up, high-finance wage-slave work of yesteryear. As economic power shifts westward from the reputation-scarred corridors of eastern seaboard finance to the sparkly digital world on the Pacific coast, so shifts our way of working toward flip-flops and bouncy balls.

Losse describes a Facebook culture of late nights and weekends at a beach house rented by Zuckerberg, where engineers and less-techie (and lower-paid) staff like her ate, partied, and slept. In those early start-up days, Facebook staff, for the most part, were young and childfree. Our twenties are when many of us don't mind turning our office-mates into proxy families; a job is still a shiny new object that we don't want to put down. "When there was nothing else to do, we could always run around the empty office after midnight tinkering with the toys and games the boys had accrued and lolling around on the body-sized bean bags that are Silicon Valley's furniture of choice," writes Losse. "In many ways, the atmosphere of our lives that year was like an oversized preschool." These companies are excellent at offering the perks that make work feel less like work and more like a self-contained world that one would never want to leave. Out is the word "headquarters," with its Cold War–era connotations; in is the chummy "campus." Tech campuses may contain gyms, concierge services, dry cleaners, and masseuses. One retired programmer remembers being moved into a condo on the campus of a large gaming company, where he was told the residence was for "artists"—an ego-boosting label that's flattering enough to get most of us to work a little harder.

We're a few decades into the rise of superficially anti-hierarchical, highly social offices. In his 1985 book *Brave New Workplace*, Robert Howard called these "enchanted workplaces": jobs that cast a spell over workers. Howard noted that these open, super-fun offices are vulnerable to abuses of power and intrusion into workers' lives. Thirty years later, digital devices—which bring us so much pleasure—have thickened this sauce of work and play, and the result is work-filled weekends.

If Silicon Valley brought the illusion of nonstop fun to work, it's also a place known for epic, cruel hours. In 2004, a gamer calling herself "ea_spouse" posted on *Live Journal* about the insanity of her husband's job as a programmer at Electronic Arts. He was working six days a week, putting in twelve hours a day, on the game *Lord of the Rings: The Battle for Middle-Earth*. Those were "pre-crunch" hours; in actual "crunch mode"—the time before the product must be brought to completion—he worked seven days a week, 9:00 a.m. to 10:00 p.m., averaging 87.5 hours per week, with no overtime pay. Occasionally, employees would get a Saturday evening off, starting at 6:30 p.m.

"The stress is taking its toll," she wrote. "After a certain number of hours spent working the eyes start to lose focus; after a certain number of weeks with only one day off, fatigue starts to accrue and accumulate exponentially. There is a reason why there are two days in a weekend—bad things happen to one's physical, emotional and mental health if these days are cut short. The team is rapidly beginning to introduce as many flaws as they are removing."

Her article created a maelstrom online and in the mainstream press, and a class action lawsuit ensued. EA settled with claimants for a reported $15.6 million to compensate for unpaid overtime.

A decade on, work-life balance in gaming is a bit better, according to Kate Edwards, the executive director of the International Game Developers Association (IGDA), which lobbies for better working conditions in the industry. But one recent survey by IGDA found that while 62 percent of developers experience crunch time, only 37 percent are financially compensated for it. "There's a certain glorification that happens, tied to this notion of being a band of brothers in a battle—it's a male dominated industry—and that battle happens to be crunch time. I've had developers tell me: 'Hey, remember that crunch of 2012? We were under our desks for 2 weeks—we didn't take a shower—that was awesome,'" she says. "And I'm like: 'No, it wasn't.'"

So how are a bunch of gamers working on their wizards in dark rooms in California relevant to the rest of us? It's an extreme version of creative-class overwork, the kind that sucks up our weekends. Here is the machismo of "work hard, play hard" on full display in the enchanted workplace—what's more enchanting than wizards, people? And that enchantment leaves the door open to long hours. "When we ask people who build games why they do it, the responses are consistent with artists—songwriter, author, painter. They tell us they love it, and they will never stop," Kate Edwards tells me. "You are dealing with artists that are so passionate about the work. My job is to point out that it's actually different: we are both an art form and an industry."

Most of us prefer to feel more like artists than workers—and maybe some of us really are—but that mind-set paves a path to exploitation. And if we believe that work isn't actually work, we lose the sense that leisure is an altogether different category of existence. Work time—with its dollar value, and transactional nature—*is not* play time, which is free, in all senses of the word.

The workplaces that are regarded today as the most innovative, admired, and successful are, paradoxically, often described as terrible places to work. They also trade in the conquering of time: Facebook, Huffington Post, Amazon—they never close. As Sheryl Sandberg, the Facebook CFO and "lean in" guru, wrote, "Facebook is available 24/7 and for the most part, so am I. The days when I think of unplugging for a weekend or vacation are long gone."

The products of these companies are also available twenty-four hours a day, seven days a week, delivering—sometimes within the hour, possibly by drone—our posts, our books, our news. If they succeed at their mandate, then we forget that it takes time, and human labor, to manufacture these services; every late-night click of a button summons a person up a ladder in a warehouse. They sell us immediacy. They refuse the pause. Why would the workers along the supply chain at these companies be inured to this acceleration, or allowed to rest, or tarry?

With its outsize cultural significance, the Silicon Valley workplay mode seems to have shifted from digital into other spheres, too. The website franchise Huffington Post runs editions across the world, gathering every crumb of news and celebrity flotsam that drifts across the Internet, an inherently panic-inducing proposition that's reflected in reports of what it's like to work there. The writers, editors, video producers who churn out the content reportedly turn over fast. Emails fly at all hours, even from Arianna Huffington, the founder and face of the company. Some workers claim she only stops hitting send between 1:00 and 5:00 a.m., which, if true, is ironic given that Huffington is also a self-styled better living guru, promoting lots of sleep and "digital detox" and offering meditation and yoga rooms to staff. These initiatives were introduced when she herself collapsed in her office from exhaustion, waking in a pool of blood and with a broken cheekbone after logging eighteen-hour days working, and sleeping four to five hours a night.

Amazon has been chastened in the media for inhumane conditions in factories, from severe heat in its warehouses (ambulances sat on retainer outside one Pennsylvania warehouse to handle overheated workers) to mechanized, Orwellian employee surveillance. That's the blue-collar piece, but in the most commented-upon article to run in *The New York Times* in 2015, Jodi Kantor and David Streitfeld reported on the white-collar downside of the behemoth company. They spoke to employees who allege that it's not unusual to receive emails after midnight, and then text messages querying about the unanswered emails. Weekends and evenings can be sucked up by conference calls; availability is often expected on Easter and Thanksgiving. The website Gawker ran a story by an employee who alleged being berated for turning off his phone while at a movie on a Saturday.

For every miserable worker, there's another employee who thrives under the kill-or-be-killed conditions, and worships the samurai warrior methodology of the company's founder, Jeff Bezos.

But what about the rest of us? Hours logged are easy to measure, the same way the speed of an email response is quantifiable. The quality of that response, and the quality of that work, requires a more carefully calibrated measure.

Making empirical data the measure of success is passed off as cutting-edge, trumpeted by companies lauded for innovation, but it's actually painfully old-fashioned. Their expecting crippling hours from digital employees is no different from the Victorian foreman waving his pocket watch at the sooty factory workers. The quality of the output is the only measure that should matter. "You can work long, hard or smart, but at Amazon.com you can't choose two out of three," Mr. Bezos wrote in a 1997 letter to shareholders. But actually, you should choose: the last two. The first one is bullshit.

TWO DECADES LATER, the long-hours ethos is being called out by different power brokers—even in the most upper echelons of Silicon Valley.

A couple of years ago, Dustin Moskovitz was delivering a speech to a group of high school students, and a key message was not landing. These were bright, driven kids in a highly selective summer program for young math and science students, many gearing up for careers in tech. Moskovitz must have appeared to them like a bodily manifestation of the digital get-rich dream, the burning bush speaking to a bunch of baby Moses-es.

At Harvard, Moskovitz shared a dorm room with Mark Zuckerberg, and they ended up founding Facebook with three others. Moskovitz is now worth an estimated $10 billion, according to *Forbes*. He left Facebook, and in 2011 he launched Asana, a web and mobile application that helps teams track their work. He's also signed the Giving Pledge created by Bill Gates and

Warren Buffett, promising to donate most of his money to charity before he dies.

Still, the kids were unimpressed with the idea that Moskovitz most wanted to impart. "They kept asking me a bunch of questions that were getting at the same thing: 'What can we do to optimize our chance of success while we're in college? What kind of activities should we be doing? What were you doing at our age?'" he recalls. "And I just kept coming back to these answers that were like, 'Oh, I wasn't enough of a whole human, you guys should focus on that.' And they weren't having it. They were like 'No, no, but what kind of work, what kind of skills can I learn?'"

The event spurred Moskovitz to write a post for Medium calling for a new way of working. He wrote: "2006 was one of the best years for Facebook, and one of the worst years for me as a human."

A few months later, I meet him in the glass boardroom at the Asana offices in San Francisco (yes, bicycles parked in the center of the wood-floored, open concept space; yes, a salad bar; yes, wandering twentysomethings hunched over their phones, thumbs flying, narrowly avoiding banging into one another). He still looks like a freshman, except for the steady, wary gaze that reminds you how strange his trajectory has been. On his belt loop most days he wears a Spire, a device that measures his breathing and will alert him if he's been tense for too many minutes, sending a reminder to take a deep inhale-exhale.

When he worked at Facebook in his twenties, Moskovitz wasn't much of a breather. He suffered panic attacks, scarfing back soda and energy drinks and working late and through the weekend. A sneeze could throw out his back, which he now believes was a function of stress and lack of exercise. But would Facebook have succeeded without that extremity? asked the high school students.

"Actually, I believe I would have been *more* effective: a better leader and a more focused employee," he wrote.

So when Moskovitz and cofounder Justin Rosenstein created Asana, he wanted to actively shape a very different kind of work culture. In the quest for that elusive "work-life balance," Asana offers a menu of "Live Well" policies to its employees: sabbaticals, meditation sessions, limited crunch time, an in-house culinary program with a ping-able on-site nutritionist. Management tries not to babysit employees, trusting them with untracked paid time off. Moskovitz expects people will be available electronically at both ends of the day, but he prefers them physically in the office between 11:00 a.m. and 4:30 p.m. While he runs through this laundry list of happy-making work practices, he mentions a study that found that people have three hours of really solid, productive work in them per day.

"I don't think we should move to three-hour days, but there's some wisdom in that; if you're just sitting at your desk trying to do something focused, you're going to get diminishing returns over time. A lot of the people who are working twelve-, fourteen-hour days are just working very, very slowly. The first half of the day is good and the second half of the day is very, very distracted," he says.

Moskovitz's current world view is far from the kind of

mythic culture of overwork that Facebook helped define for the industry. Perhaps this is why, when he interviews people to work at Asana, they sometimes seem a little confused about what they're doing. Prospective employees have asked: "'Oh we're not working seventy-hour weeks so does that mean that there's no urgency to what we're doing?' And my response is, 'No, this is what we think is fastest.'" He'll often point out that marginal returns from additional work decrease rapidly and quickly become negative. "But it's really hard for people to internalize that. Like, 'Well, my friends at this other company are working harder and are they doing it wrong?' And I tell them: 'Yes, they're doing it wrong.' It's just weird to be different, weird and scary, and so we have to be really convicted about it and talk about it a lot."

Moskovitz tries to lead by example. He does his best to protect his weekends by turning off notifications on his phone when he can, and closing tabs if he's on his computer. This isn't always easy; he's teaching himself to turn off. Last year, he went to Burning Man and unplugged for a full week, emerging rejuvenated.

I ask Moskovitz what he wants to do this weekend. "Hike. Putter around the house with my wife. Yoga. My dream is to do nothing."

SAVE THE WEEKEND

In one day, the TV writer-producer-showrunner Shonda Rhimes might get 2,500 emails. At the end of her emails, she has a permanent signature that tells people she won't read or respond after 7:00 p.m. on weeknights, or on weekends. In an interview on NPR, she said: "Work will happen twenty-four hours a day, 365 days a year if you let it. It suddenly occurred to me that unless I just say, 'That's not going to happen,' it was always going to happen. Since turning off my phone at 7:00 p.m., there's never been a thing so urgent that I regret having my phone off."

I'm always trawling media looking for Rhimes-like news hits that flip a finger to Jeff Bezos and his workaholic ilk. In doing so, I've become hopeful that there is a sea change ahead, a collective will to break out of the all-work-no-play illness and take back the weekend. Shifts are happening at all levels: government, industry, and individual.

To wit: In 2015, Scott Walker, the governor of Wisconsin, inserted a provision into the state budget that was essentially an act of weekend theft. The provision would "permit an employee to state in writing that he or she voluntarily chooses to work without one day of rest in seven." This did not go over well. Headlines screamed a variation of Gawker's: "Wisconsin Is Trying to Take Away the Right to a Weekend." An op-ed in the Milwaukee *Journal Sentinel* pointed out that in its 1961 *McGowan v. Maryland* decision the Supreme Court determined that rest laws promoted the values of "health, safety, recreation, and general well-being." One day out of seven is an old and venerable right, protected by law. While Walker successfully dismantled many worker protections in his state, that particular amendment did not pass. Don't mess with the weekend.

Here's another one. In the run-up to the 2016 election, Republican wannabe-nominee Jeb Bush delivered a speech with this line: "We have to be a lot more productive, workforce participation has to rise from its all-time modern lows. It means that people need to work longer hours and, through their productivity, gain more income for their families. That's the only way we're going to get out of this rut that we're in." He quickly backpedaled, saying he was only talking about people who held part-time jobs but wanted full-time ones. Too late. He was pilloried, with *Time* magazine quick to point out his $29 million in earnings filed in tax returns between 2007 and 2013, shorthand for out of touch with the working life. Hillary Clinton tweeted: "Anyone who believes Americans aren't working hard enough hasn't met enough American workers." There are many reasons Jeb Bush did not become the Republican candidate; proposing that Americans need to work longer and harder is my personal favorite.

In contrast to some American politicians' efforts to sabotage leisure, other governments around the world are scrambling to protect it. In 2013, Germany's Labor Ministry banned managers from calling or emailing staff on weekends. On New Year's Day, 2017, an employment law came into effect in France that protects workers' time off by giving them the "right to disconnect" on evenings and weekends. "Good conduct" charters are now required by companies of over fifty people, explicitly laying out the hours on weekends and evenings when staff can back away from the email. Bruno Mettling, director general of mobile giant Orange, who proposed the idea in a research report, said, "Professionals who find the right balance between private and work life perform far better in their job than those who arrive shattered."In the private sector, too, there are signs of a correction. In Dublin, Google tested a program called Dublin Goes Dark, asking employees to turn in their devices before leaving work each day. In 2011, Volkswagen announced that servers would stop sending emails between 6:15 p.m. and 7:00 a.m., affecting four thousand employees across Germany. Deutsche Telekom, EON, and BMW have all taken up their own email management policies.

These companies aren't motivated by altruism; they know they'll get more out of rested workers who are engaged in life beyond work. When the pace isn't sustainable, workers drop out, which is precisely the juicy appeal of a raft of "I'm outta here!" business stories. These anecdotes light up the business pages the way zoo animal escape stories light up Twitter. There was Max Schireson, CEO of a billion-dollar start-up called MongoDB, Inc., who wrote a blog post: "Why I'm Leaving the Best Job I Ever Had." His high-flying job (literally: he was flying 300,000 miles a year) meant that he was absent for his son's emergency surgery; nor could he be there for his family when their puppy was hit by a car. He quit because he didn't want to miss his life. His post sounded a lot like Patrick Pichette, Google CFO, who listed his reasons for walking away from thirty years of nonstop work: "It has also been a frenetic pace for about 1,500 weeks now. Always on—even when I was not supposed to be. Especially when I was not supposed to be." He retired early, and now overstuffs the Internet with pictures of hiking Kilimanjaro with his wife.

My favorite of these missives comes from Brent Callinicos, who walked away from his position as CFO at Uber at age forty-eight. His goodbye note borrows liberally from Simon and Garfunkel's "Hazy Shade of Winter":

Time has a way of passing quickly, easily leaving your heart's desire to "maybe happen later." For me, there is no later. It is now. It is time to do what I have desired for a very long time; time to keep a promise to my wife of not missing another school play, swim meet, or academic achievement of our daughter's childhood. Time; time; time, to encapsulate what matters most to me; time, to admit that every day I work, I lose time with my family; time, to help my daughter understand how important time is before time becomes a blur to her too. It is simply time.

That's a lot of "time"s; thirteen, to be exact.

These stories feel like confessions and warnings, Jacob Marley rattling his chains (though they always contain the requisite "I love my job but . . ." line, ensuring the door remains open at least a crack). They have the ring of a lottery winner cashing out, inviting us to entertain our own "What if . . ." scenarios, imagining what mountains we'd climb were we able to abandon the work ship. Of course, most people will never walk away from billion-dollar companies and the attendant salaries. But millionaires and Deutsche Telekom employees and you all experience time in the same way. We are its victim, and its most privileged guest. We all want to rein in time, and savor it. We all fear that it's leaving too soon.

These little anecdotes from business stars show that even the most privileged—the 1 percent of the 1 percent—struggle with time, and know, deep down, that this way of working isn't just or sustainable. It's hard to begrudge anyone Kilimanjaro, but what if those people stayed and built workplaces that respected their workers' time—and the weekend? These innovators do exist, and they may be the future of the weekend.

A FEW YEARS AGO, my daughter had to design her ideal school. She and her friend came up with a treehouse playground, pool slide entrances to classrooms, and a quiet-time window nook for each student. If adults could design the dream workplace, it might look something like the tech company Basecamp. Some perks include free organic fruit and vegetables delivered to employees' homes, and subsidized hobbies. One employee wanted to learn how to blacksmith, and Basecamp helped pay for it (in return, he gave the office a nail he made). Both meetings and managers are considered wastes of time and are therefore banned.

But Basecamp's most compelling policy is about the weekend. From May to October, employees at Basecamp work a four-day week. This really means summer, with a rub against the shoulder months. Is shortening the week during this particular time period a business decision? "Uhhh . . . I just kind of like seasons," says CEO and cofounder Jason Fried. He has the chill demeanor of the most confident guy in the band at a bad gig, the one who assures his tense bandmates that it's all going to work out just fine.

The reduced workweek at Basecamp doesn't mean longer hours over fewer days either, but fewer hours over fewer days, with the same pay. Basecamp produces web-based project management software (Asana is a competitor), and because its clients use the products all week, the off day is staggered among employees to make sure someone is always available to meet the clients' needs. That means that not everyone gets three days off in a row each week. This incontrovertible reality bugs Fried, and he tries to make it so that most employees do experience the three consecutive days off at least some of the time. "I get it—the pitch is the three-day weekend," he says. "The weekend is the promise."

Basecamp has nice offices in downtown Chicago, with ten-foot-high windows letting in natural light, and cork and felt floors to keep the acoustics relaxing. But most of the employees don't actually have desks there, because the company encourages remote work. One Basecamp customer service rep traveled the United States in an Airstream for many months, logging her nine-to-five hours in front of her laptop while on the road with her two kids and husband.

Life-friendly work policies like remote work and flexible hours are really a matter of faith. Babysitting practices like policing employees, enforced clock-punching, inhumanly long hours—all are the cynical opposite. In his 1952 treatise on work and leisure, *Leisure: The Basis of Culture*, German philosopher Josef Pieper warned against the dangers of "total work": "The world of work is becoming our entire world; it threatens to engulf us completely, and the demands of the world of work become greater and greater, till at last they make a 'total' claim upon the whole of human nature." Managers who do allow employees control over their work environments are saying: *I trust you won't screw me. I don't require every piece of you.* For their faith, they're rewarded with more creative, engaged staff. A large study of a Chinese IT company found that employees who feel more empowered at work display increased rates of "intrinsic motivation"—the desire to do work for its own sake, rather than for external rewards, like a salary or a bonus. Giving up total claim on an employee's time is an optimistic act. Progressive workplace policies acknowledge that humans don't choose "life" or "work" at various points in their weeks, but are, in fact, always living. Good workplaces actively encourage workers to lean toward their humanity.

WHAT WE'RE TALKING ABOUT as cutting-edge policy is actually the offspring of a venerable tradition: Summer Fridays. Its genesis is unclear, but the enduring story is that Summer Fridays date back to the *Mad Men* era of the 1950s, when New York executives locked their office doors after lunch on Fridays to dash off to the Hamptons, beating traffic and heat. The tradition still exists in some fields, particularly publishing and media; according to one survey, 30 percent of workers have access to some kind of Summer Friday. Even though the practice has dropped off somewhat—many publishing houses have been abandoning the idea in the last decade—there still seems to be a slowing down on summer weekends: power consumption actually drops in New York on Friday afternoons in the summer.

Summer Fridays are not exclusively a New York phenomenon, but it's thrilling—subversive, even—that its origins lie in the city that never stops working. If New Yorkers can pack it in sometimes, then why don't we all? We do everything else New York does. New York is why I recently went to a bar in Toronto where the bartender twirled his handlebar mustache and said, "We don't have menus. Just tell me how you're feeling and I'll mix you a drink that matches your emotional state." That's definitely New York's fault. Or at least Brooklyn's.

Either way, let's take New York's lead on the Summer Fridays thing. The concept of Summer Fridays is a flashback to a kinder time, an imitation of an agrarian schedule, where the weather shapes the work. It feels like a civilized, collective act: all of us in this office together agree that summer is fleeting, and we need to take full advantage of our brief time in the sunlight. Summer Fridays expose the concept of total work as fraudulent, and shout the truth that people have lives outside their jobs, and those lives need to be nurtured by sun, and friends. Bonfires and heavy drinking not required, but recommended.

There's been a slight increase in the number of American companies that allow employees to compress their time into a shorter workweek: 43 percent in 2014 versus 38 percent in 2008 (researchers speculate that the 2008 recession accounts for the small size of the increase and some contraction in flexibility arrangements, which had been rising in the decade prior). Smaller businesses tend to be more open to shorter workweek arrangements. They're smarter that way: shorter workweeks make more productive, happier workplaces. *Fast Company* reports that after the tax services firm Ryan introduced shorter workweeks in 2008, the turnover rate dropped from 30 to 11 percent; revenue and profits almost doubled; and clients reported the highest satisfaction scores in the history of the company.

One of the surprise new entries in the field of companies rethinking work is Amazon. Perhaps feeling the fallout of the *Times'* biting reporting on its toxic work culture, Amazon announced in 2016 the launch of a pilot project offering a thirty-hour workweek to some technical teams within the human resources department. Those working thirty hours would receive a 75 percent salary, with full benefits. Amazon framed it as a diversity initiative, suggesting an interest in bringing more women to the company.

Soon after the announcement, former *Redbook* editor Lesley Jane Seymour posted a much-shared, very skeptical LinkedIn article about the move. She pointed out that HR is traditionally a female zone of the corporate world, making Amazon's claims of integration dubious. Furthermore, if men aren't also required to participate in the shorter workweek, reduced-hours female employees may become (further) ghettoized, while full-time men are rewarded just for being around.

Okay—yes. Life-friendly policies can lock women low on the ladder: the words "reduced" and "less" aren't exactly big-winner phrases that smack of advancement. But Amazon is at least gesturing in the right direction, and as society moves toward equity at home, men will be forced to take advantage of these policies at work, too, in order to share the load. A perfectly healthy workweek is a long way off, but it's exciting to see a reckoning with long hours from a company whose boss codified the all-work-no-life philosophy. If it's being rethought at Amazon, of all places, the cult of overwork may find its ranks gradually diminished.

But Jason Fried, who has always had this kind of faith in his employees, isn't convinced that evolved workplace philosophies are going to be the new corporate standard. Basecamp is a small company that's been around since 1999, which is ancient in the digital world. Part of the reason the company can be so innovative is because it's willing to stay small and autonomous, avoiding the pipe dream of most digital companies: the mammoth buyout.

"Our industry is driven by unattainable goals: billion dollar businesses and huge exits," says Fried. "Only a handful will ever make it, but you've got thousands trying, and they're not taking Fridays off. In order to be a billion-dollar company, you have to work Fridays. If that's the goal, then taking Fridays off will be seen as weak and soft and unambitious. A few of the really big companies that employ thousands of people would have to start making those changes, and I'm cynical about that level of change industry-wide. Luckily, I don't care about industry-wide. If one hundred small businesses decide to make a better environment for their employees, that's awesome. It's a great competitive advantage for small businesses."

Basecamp has added a new feature to the most recent generation of its software that embodies the company's work-life balance ethos. It's called Work Can Wait, and it allows workers to send a message to colleagues and clients letting them know the hours when they're available and when they're not, then disables texts and notifications during the off-hours. This is software that actually reinforces the idea that leisure matters. Within a week of announcing Work Can Wait, one thousand Basecamp clients were using it. On the website, it's pitched simply as: "Give work the weekend off . . . Your time is your time."

THE ECONOMICS OF LESS WORK

The wobbly economy is now a decades-old fact. At one end: high unemployment, slow economic growth, stagnant wages. At the other: abundant wealth and a little leisure. And in the middle: time crunch and exhaustion. Not enough work for many, and too much work for some.

The gap feels unbridgeable, but economists with a British think tank called the New Economics Foundation (NEF) see a solution in longer weekends and shorter workweeks. At forty-eight hours, the U.K.'s workweek is the longest of any developed European economy. NEF believes that if all Brits worked fewer hours, more jobs would be created, shrinking the pool of the unemployed and creating more tax-paying citizens, which would benefit the whole. With reduced hours, the environment wins, too, as countries with shorter average hours tend to use less energy. A paper put forward by the Center for Economic and Policy Research posits that shorter work hours are associated with lower greenhouse gas emissions and may, therefore, mean less global climate change. They haven't unpacked the causality, but they hypothesize that reduced work hours translates to less consumption.

But the proposal seems to benefit salaried workers, not hourly ones. If so many people already have an inadequate amount of work, won't the standard of living for low-income people drop even more if they actually work less? "If you make lower workers work a shorter week, you have to increase their hourly rate of pay. You can't have one without the other," says Anna Coote, head of social policy at NEF. But this initial financial hit to businesses should be softened by evidence that those who work less tend to be more productive, hour for hour, than workers who log a forty-plus-hours week.

NEF proposes a gradual transition to a less-work economy. New workers could be offered a four-day week, and older workers could, around age fifty-five, reduce their working week by an hour each year until retirement. These kinds of initiatives would create a critical mass of employees working a shorter workweek. Employees could choose between incremental pay raises or incremental time off. People in the Netherlands, Germany, and Belgium all work fewer hours than people in the U.K. and the U.S., says Coote, and the economies of these countries are robust. In Gothenburg, Sweden, a publicly funded nursing home is in the middle of a much-watched two-year experiment to determine if paying eighty nurses a full-time wage at reduced hours will create enough benefits to justify the costs of hiring extra staff. Early reports suggest absenteeism has dropped by half and quality of care has increased, though the costs of the program have generated controversy. In the same city, Toyota is showing them how it's done: the company switched to six-hour days thirteen years ago, generating a 25 percent increase in profits.

These kinds of shorter-hours experiments aren't just theoretical; they may be the new reality if we run out of work. Futurists have long predicted that automation would hoover up jobs, leaving mass unemployment. To an extent, that future is now; the jobless rate has remained stubbornly high for almost a decade. We've seen robots supplanting humans in manufacturing around the world, and, more visibly, new technologies disrupting industries that once seemed inviolable, like taxis and hotels. Researchers at Oxford University estimate that within two decades 47 percent of American jobs will be automated.

How will people endure the shock of life in a post-work society? One idea is that all citizens should receive a guaranteed annual income from the government, a livable wage that closes the inequality gap and offers a basic standard of living to all. Another potent way to address the robot problem is shorter workweeks, meaning more work to go around.

A long time ago, American industry went down this very road. It's one of those weird jogs in history that our workweeks—and therefore our lives—were once poised to take a very different shape.

In December 1930, at the whim of W. K. Kellogg, the Kellogg cereal plant in Battle Creek, Michigan, switched from three eight-hour shifts per day to four six-hour shifts. During the Great Depression, at a time of mass unemployment, the small town suddenly had four hundred new jobs to offer. The energized employees quickly proved as productive at thirty hours as they had been at forty, inducing pay raises.

The Kellogg experiment was a huge success, and the thirty-hour week seemed like a possible way forward for industry. In 1932, Senator Hugo L. Black of Alabama introduced a pivotal shorter-hours bill that would fix the official American workweek at five days and thirty hours, with severe penalties for overtime work. "Hunger in the midst of plenty is the great problem," he told the nation over the radio, promising the bill would immediately employ 6.5 million out-of-work Americans. In 1933, the "30 Hour Work-Week Bill" passed easily in the Senate. But lobbyists got to work, and it was loudly opposed by the National Association of Manufacturers. President Roosevelt backed off his support. The bill fell in the House of Representatives, and instead, in 1938, Roosevelt's New Deal enshrined the forty-hour workweek.

So the longer workweek became the norm, and that other possibility faded from memory. But the Kellogg factory retained thirty-hour weeks in an ever shrinking number of departments straight through until 1985. When the last shift ended, workers staged a mock funeral at a local bar, replete with a cardboard coffin in which to bury the thirty-hour week.

In a series of 1992 interviews with historian Benjamin Hunnicutt and John de Graaf, filmmaker and founder of an advocacy group called Take Back Your Time, some of the last workers remembered what that shorter schedule did to their lives. Writes de Graaf on AlterNet:

One couple, Chuck and Joy Blanchard, who had both worked
at the plant, claimed that the six-hour day made Chuck a
"feminist" long before the women's movement. He and his
wife shared the housework and he was a "room parent" at his
children's school. . . . The Blanchards spoke to us about how
crime had gone up and volunteering down in Battle Creek
after the six-hour day ended, as people had less time to look
out for their neighborhoods. The Blanchards said they had
little materially, but their lives, blessed with abundant lei-
sure, were happier than those of young families today, who
seem to have so much more stuff, but never enough time.

Their reminiscences embody Keynes's sunny vision for
his grandchildren's future: shorter hours bred a citizenry with
preoccupations beyond the material, and time to devote to
strengthening bonds of family and society. The joy of less work
isn't just an individual experience; it fans out to a greater good.

Even now, these kinds of experiments with leisure are
occasionally taken up by business and government. In Utah in
2008, while the U.S. economy was in free-fall, some public sector workers agreed to change their schedules from five eight-
hour days to four ten-hour days, Monday through Thursday.
The cost-saving initiative meant that though their hours stayed
the same, they got the three-day weekend, and it was a hit.
Evaluations after the program ended had more than half of
the 18,000 state employees who participated reporting that
they were productive on the days they worked, and more than
80 percent said they preferred the four-day week to the five and

wanted to stick to the new schedule once the year was over. Reducing energy at a time of sky-high prices was a goal of the experiment, and it worked: carbon emissions were reduced by an estimated 4,546 metric tons annually, other greenhouse gas emissions by 8,000 tons.

But maybe the benefits of less work don't have to be measured in dollars. A shorter workweek is humane, the kind of gesture that uplifts those intangibles like mood and loyalty. Felicitas Betzl is the managing director at Serps Invaders, a boutique digital marketing agency based in Edinburgh, Scotland, with clients around the world. To keep her company competitive with the bigger ones courting the same in-demand workers, she decided to give her staff (five people, plus twenty or so consultants and freelancers) what she calls "a gift" of the four-day workweek. Digital marketing requires a technical skill set, and consequently there are more jobs than there are talented people to fill them. Serps employees work hard over four days: 9.5 hours per day, picking their own start times. This sounds grueling, and it adds up to 37.5 hours in a week, nearly a full forty. But on Friday, they shut down, leaving one person on call. Clients, to Betzl's surprise, have been very supportive. "They ask me how they can do it in their own offices," she says. In the three years that the agency has been closed on Fridays, Betzl's team has been called in on Friday to deal with an issue only three times.

To make sure everyone can get the work done, Betzl has implemented "productivity hacks" like project management tools and scheduling regular catch-up times. Using time at work efficiently is key to protecting the weekend. So much office time is wasted, and not just with Facebook checks and bathroom sink chat. The overmanaged structure of many workplaces is designed to kill our best work. Most people work optimally in ninety-minute chunks, with breaks on either end; when the day is randomly broken by meetings, that's the end of concentrated engagement. Jason Fried told me that Basecamp banned meetings because the company discovered they suck up the day, leaving people to do their actual work at night and on weekends. But if workers have calm, undistracting environments (turn off your notifications!) that allow them to work, they may get some of their weekend back.

Since the four-day week was implemented at Serps Invaders, overtime has decreased, says Betzl. Employees are more engaged during the week because they can book personal appointments at the doctor's and at the bank for Fridays without the usual skulking required. The downside, some reported, can be late nights (offices close at 7:30 p.m.) and late dinners. But still, no employee has turned down the four-day-week option—it's not mandatory—and reverted to five days.

"When I saw everyone on Monday for coffee after we started the short week, I noticed that they just looked different," Betzl says. "Relaxed. Ready to go." She asked what they did with those three days. Many employees went on trips. One woman had begun running marathons. They saw their kids. Those irritating chores that clogged the weekend could be done on Friday, leaving two days of true respite.

Maybe leisure is a kind of social contagion: if we see others taking the time for good weekends, we feel the pull to do the same. Certainly, Betzl finds herself inspired by her staff to take downtime. Her own hours, once seventy to eighty per week, have dropped by at least a third. "My staff get really angry with me when I don't take time off from work, which is very sweet of them. I know I can, as I fully trust them and their abilities."

I ask Fried at Basecamp for the kind of metrics that will show other businesses that a longer weekend is a viable, profitable strategy. Fried says he finds valuations dubious, and doesn't even know how much the company is worth (enough that Jeff Bezos from Amazon made an investment in 2006). He won't put a dollars-and-cents value on the shorter week, and instead takes the conversation to a more spiritual place. "Are we losing some productive hours? Maybe. Probably at some level. In business everyone is trying to measure this, measure that, but I don't know if I can measure this. I think what we get in return is more valuable. You end up squeezing a lot of waste out of the week. We just have a calmer, more relaxed place. People get to spend weekends doing more interesting things and that in turn creates more interesting people," he says. "It's hard to quantify—but it just feels right. Like, how do you measure the value of saying thank you? How do you measure the value of a smile? You can't measure those things, you just know it's the right thing to do. It doesn't affect our company in terms of being unable to get stuff done or being late on things—so if it doesn't affect that, then why not do it? Why wouldn't you want everyone to have better work-life balance, or more time with the family, or for whatever they need? The four-day week just feels like a right thing to do."

It's a dramatic mental shift to imagine a week where free time matters as much as work, one that upends our deeply held, work-first values. I have to admit that I find it hard to picture myself working only twenty-one hours a week. Like so many of the luckiest white-collar workers, I love my work, and I fear that a sudden onslaught of leisure would deliver me into a slacker state, frittering away those extra hours watching *Friends* reruns and napping. Clearly I've internalized a New World mentality that holds fast to the cinematic idea that all it takes to get ahead is hard work. This is a very nice maxim (I tell it to my kids when they seem lazy; they ignore me and go forth in cheerful laziness), but of course it's a lie. Hard work matters, yes, but a multitude of social advantages and disadvantages lock people in place on the social ladder, often before they've even entered the workforce: economic standing, access to education, race. And yet we trumpet work, work, work as the singular path to happiness and prosperity, not just because the idea of *not* working feels somehow immoral to Puritan sensibilities, but because free time seems so damned scary.

The disorder "chronophobia" appears in some psychiatric manuals: a neurotic fear of time. When a prisoner first arrives at jail, he might feel indifferent, or even relaxed, hopeful that a change in status might be around the corner: a new trial, a reversed decision. But at the moment when he realizes that the verdict is not going to be overturned, and all that's ahead of him is limitless, uncontained time, chronophobia sets in. He may become stressed, overtaken by restlessness and insomnia, and suffer bouts of hypochondria. And then, eventually, the chronophobia subsides, and he is numb to the passing of time, accepting his fate. He waits it out, blankly.

For prisoners, time itself might become a kind of prison, inescapable and fixed. But the rest of us can feel the crawl of chronophobia, too. In boundless time, those unopened, sealed internal places can no longer go unexplored. Our sadness and losses might rear themselves. Our unsettled pasts and unanswered questions about the lives we've lived might surge forward, like a late-night insomnia session loosed in daylight. Unoccupied time means a confrontation with the self, and it's scary in there. Many of us don't want to peek inside the box. We would rather work right past those parts of ourselves that are the most unknown, and possibly the richest.

I mention this possibility of fearing free time to Anna Coote at the New Economics Foundation and she shames me a bit: "It's a sad day when we can't imagine our own freedom. We talk to a lot of people about this, and they are bothered by their relationship to time, and they know they don't have the balance right. But things do evolve. That relationship does change. We used to send children up chimneys. We used to work twelve-hour days."

It's true: we fear free time because we can't really picture it; a short-hours society is unimaginable to us, just as the Victorians couldn't yet see that kids would one day spend their hours in school rather than as human chimney brushes.

Above all, it may be an act of imagining that's required to resuscitate the weekend.

◇◇◇◇

OVER THE PAST FEW YEARS, the will to envision a new kind of relationship to time has led to the micro-trend of unplugging completely on the weekend. There are online challenges and apps that cut you off completely from social media for periods of time. Every March, the Internet alights with testimonials from those participating in a National Day of Unplugging. The manifesto for "digital detox" (the phrase is actually trademarked) at the website DigitalSabbath.com states: "By disconnecting from our devices we reconnect with: ourselves, each other, our communities, and the world around us . . . becoming more present, authentic, compassionate and understanding." This kind of Sabbath is not dictated by scripture; there are no minute observances that will ignite God's wrath if ignored. The goal is both simple and broad: to get people to turn off their devices for an extended period of time—twenty-four hours or more—and prioritize human connection and experience.

One of the first groups to promote the digital Sabbath was Rebooters, a largely Jewish, New York–based nonprofit, which proposed the National Day of Unplugging in 2010. In 2016, it had unplugging participants in 50 states and 206 countries. Dina Mann, one of the organizers, remembers her own Sabbath as a kid. "The minute the candles were lit, it felt like a separate space," she says. "If you're ever in a home right before Shabbat, people are frantic to get things done, and then you light the candles and it's all of a sudden calm. There's a distinct relaxing of time. Unplugging is similar, a way to give gratitude, a way for you to interact with the people you care about."

But unplugging is not actually easy. I tried it on a Sunday, and the first part of the morning was fine. I took my son to hockey and went for a run without my phone, feeling liberated and virtuous. But when I got back to the rink, I had to wait for him, and I grew cold and grumpy. Then I had to stand there watching the Zamboni clean the ice while my son changed, which took several hours, it seemed. Here's a little piece of information about hockey rinks: unless a game is going on, there is nothing to do in them, nothing. I defy you to find a less stimulating environment. They should use hockey arenas as sensory-deprivation chambers in torture sessions. Without a phone or an interest in rereading "PEEWEE CHAMPS 2001" banners for the hundredth time, one is left to watch the water pool on the ice. A person who is fully committed to a Sabbath state might try to find something calming and meaningful in that pooling water—a little "mindfulness" practice, perhaps—but someone who is mentally flabby and freezing cold might start to panic a little and begin checking her pockets for something, anything, to look at (did you know that Extra gum contains hydrogenated starch hydrolysate?).

Later in the day, my tech-naked state was underscored as my traitorous family scattered through the house on their various iPod Touches and computers, wishing me well. So I went for a walk with the dog, and then—it took a while—I kind of got it. Without my phone buzzing in my pocket, we walked farther, and I did feel a kind of unclenching of my brain, like a fist opening. There was no pull of notifications, and when I followed the terrible biological reflex of putting my hand in my pocket (who knew I did this three times an hour?), there was nothing there. The burden of the phone in my pocket lifted, and it was almost physical; I felt lighter. My mind was allowed to wander, and it did. I took in the city, and ran through my thoughts. In that kind of mental space, epiphanies can occur. I didn't have one, but I did feel unusually awake, and I was not deprived of anything. That night, I read in bed for a long time, and I swear I came across this sentence in the book I was reading, which was *Gilead*, by Marilynne Robinson: "Sometimes I have loved the peacefulness of an ordinary Sunday. It is like standing in a newly planted garden after a warm rain. You can feel the silent and invisible life."

When I logged on to my computer Monday morning, the world was intact. I had let no one down. Time, it turned out, was a neutral space. I had been infusing it with stress, and digital panic, but it was actually indifferent to me. For twenty-four hours, I had bent it to my will.

CHAPTER 3

THE NEED TO CONNECT

M Y MOTHER EXCELS at people. She listens closely, eyes locked, leaning in. "Why do you feel that way?" she asks. "Tell me more." She sends thank-you and congratulations cards, remembers birthdays, and volunteers to host any event in need of a home. Throughout my childhood, the industry required to tend these many relationships would take place on weekends. Fridays I would check in about the upcoming social roster: "Who's coming over?" "Leona wrote a book of poems, so I'm making crepes," she'd say. Or, "We're having a slideshow of our trip to Italy." Slideshows and crepes were often enjoyed from a seat on the purple corduroy couch. Yes—the 1970s.

Somehow, she did this while raising two kids and working a full-time job as an adult literacy instructor, not to mention being married to my dad, more of an introvert. Over fifty years he became a very good wingman, and together, they live a day-to-day existence that spokes outward, into the world.

My mom is nearing eighty and has lost her parents and guided too many friends through illness to death. She's hosted a few funeral-related events, the sadness mitigated just a bit by her trademark strong, black coffee. Her two children live far away, and she has her own health and emotional struggles. But she is, I hope, a little insulated from the suffering of age by a life that brims with people who know and love her, whom she loves and knows, on almost every continent. Friends from her time in the 1960s in London, England, and her childhood in Toronto. Relatives. Former colleagues. Neighbors. A new family moves in and my mother drops off a welcome card. She would roll her eyes if I called this a "network." To her, it's life.

The word "connection" has been co-opted by technology—a word for switches, cables, and the speed of zooming bytes. But real connection is born of flesh and time. Here's a blunt "duh" truth: we need each other. We are, in fact, wired to be social. According to Matthew D. Lieberman, a professor and Social Cognitive Neuroscience Lab director at the University of California, Los Angeles, when our brains are "off"—resting between tasks—they slip into a default mode that is identical to our brains when we are being social. Our natural reflex is to connect to others, he writes, with a brain that prompts us "to think about other people's minds—their thoughts, feelings and goals. . . . It promotes understanding and empathy, cooperation and consideration." Lieberman is an evolutionary scientist, so he sees this social reflex as a survival mechanism.

Social intelligence helps the species survive: the cave dweller knew it was better to find a friend to help him through the cold winter than freeze alone.

So deep is our need for social connection that our bodies can literally ache without it. In his book *Social: Why Our Brains Are Wired to Connect*, Lieberman describes an experiment called "Cyberball." A participant is hooked up to a computer where she sees two digital figures on a screen—humans, she is told, wired to remote computers. The three are given a digital "cyberball" to toss back and forth over the Internet. At first, they all play together, but then the other two begin to play with each other, excluding the participant. She believes that they are real people reenacting some form of seventh-grade gym-class trauma, though in reality they're just neutral pre-programmed avatars. Her response to this social ostracizing is physical. A brain scan reveals that the region lighting up is the same one that glows during the experience of body pain. A scientist scrutinizing two scans, one an analysis of physical pain and one an analysis of social pain, would have trouble telling them apart. "A broken heart can feel like a broken leg," writes Lieberman.

My mother's social acuity was exercised most on weekends. No doubt, this is a child's perspective. She was surely nurturing relationships at work and on weeknights, but it's the weekends that I remember, defined by afternoon walks with friends in the nearby woods, and unplanned "drop-ins" at a neighbor's house. There was a particularly languid, shapeless quality to those social events and weekend connections. Even the most formal weekend visits—the elaborate multi-course dinners with the

Julia Child recipes—often segued into something endless and maybe a bit sloppy, involving a piano and political arguments (no doubt an excess of drink helped—did I mention it was the 1970s?). I would crouch, hidden at the top of the staircase, and listen to the rowdy conversation, amazed that the night could stretch so late (2:00 a.m.!).

Now that I might be permitted to join in, I find such evenings rare in my own adult life. It's not just that I've inherited my father's introverted nature rather than my mother's extroverted one, or that I'm not the genius cook she is, because my husband wears that mantle enviably. It's that we are frequently too tired and too busy to socialize on weekends in anything but brief, fleeting get-togethers. On Saturday afternoon, I'm already anticipating the Sunday 8:00 a.m. hockey game, the laundry, and the looming loose ends at work. On Friday I'll announce, "I need a couple of hours tomorrow." Gauntlet thrown. "Me too," says my husband, and we play a marital game of rock-paper-scissors until we figure out who gets to slink off to work while the other meets the kids' myriad needs.

In North America, social isolation has been on the rise for decades. Research suggests that the size of our discussion networks has shrunk in quantity and quality. Neighborhoods have become more stratified, as the economic gap between rich and poor has shrunk that middle-class zone where diversity flourishes—not just of race, but also of experience and perspective. The result is a kind of "social sorting" where we're less likely to socialize with different kinds of people. When we moved into our downtown Toronto neighborhood over a decade ago, we were the white arty couple infiltrating an older Portuguese and Italian working-class community; gentrifiers in the midst. But there weren't that many of us, and we got to know the older people who had built this most recent incarnation of the neighborhood. They were the ones who had stayed behind, resisting the move to the suburbs with their grown kids. Some were our age, second-generation neighborhood natives who had inherited their houses. Our little pocket on the edge of a sprawling park felt diverse in an urban storybook way, with tradespeople next to freelance illustrators and Mandarin and Italian as prevalent as English—the urban theorist Jane Jacobs's dream of a diverse city in action.

Then housing prices in Toronto went mad. Our neighborhood is now domed by a foreboding real estate bubble, which we helped create. Many of our Portuguese and Italian neighbors have cashed out, or passed on. We're surrounded now by a lot of affluence, which isn't always white, but feels uniform: it's a neighborhood of people working long and hard, and while friendly, we're not exactly playing bridge together. Most of our exchanges occur curbside, on our way to work or home from work, with kids hanging off our limbs and coffees in hand. "I'm so tired," we say by way of greeting. "How tired are you?"

Americans socialize much less with their neighbors now than in the 1970s. One third of Americans report no interaction with neighbors at all. In his 2000 book *Bowling Alone*, Robert Putnam posited that as work dominates daily life, the bonds of civic association weaken. We have less time for community groups and volunteering, getting together with friends and family. We no longer bowl in leagues; we bowl alone. One result is an increase in loneliness. A 2010 AARP survey found that 35 percent of adults older than forty-five are chronically lonely, as opposed to 20 percent of a similar group only a decade earlier. Loneliness is worse for your health than obesity and cigarette smoking. Lonely people are at a greater risk for death than alcoholics. It seems strange to admit to loneliness when we are so busy. But if our interactions are manic and rushed, they feel superficial and low-value, lacking the depth of connection we yearn for.

More and more, we seek connection online. Compared to a generation ago, college students today are interacting less with each other IRL (in real life), and more via social networks, according to a UCLA annual national survey of incoming college freshmen. When the survey began in 1987, nearly four in ten students said they spent sixteen hours or more each week socializing (in person) with their friends. By 2015, the number had dropped significantly: fewer than two in ten kids spend that much time with their friends. Now, nearly four out of ten students socialize five or fewer hours a week—a record low. Simultaneously, the time they spend on digital connections keeps rising, with nearly a third of students reporting they spend six hours a week or more on social networks. So if social is social, then adding up the real and the digital socializing could equal eleven hours a week. Nothing to worry about, right?

In some ways, maybe not. Certainly the use of social networks can widen and diversify the scope of one's interactions. Everyone feels something *like* connection on Facebook, or we wouldn't do it. If you go there enough, Facebook starts to feel like a place: a destination where people bump into each other and dead relationships are reanimated, and the world is filtered, curiously, through the eyes (or the feed) of people you know. All of this is social. But being social with a screen in between is not the same as presence. It's a simulacrum of the interaction we're wired to crave; it's one step away. The difference can be read in how e-socializing makes us feel, which, it turns out, is not great. Multitasking different digital media at the same time—checking email while texting and playing a game—can breed depression and social anxiety in people of all ages. Perhaps the most alarming factoid of the UCLA study is that when asked to rate their emotional health in relation to other students', along with incidences of depression, students reported the lowest levels of perceived mental health in the survey's history.

In her book *Reclaiming Conversation*, sociologist and media researcher Sherry Turkle tells a story about the "empathy gap." Teachers at a prestigious private school approached her, asking for help with a peculiar problem: on the playground, twelve-year-olds were behaving like eight-year-olds. Kids seemed strangely oblivious to one another's feelings, casually dealing the kinds of slights and cruelties that kids of twelve should be long past, demonstrating little recognition of the pain they were causing. At the same time, the dining hall had become a sea of kids hunched over their devices—texting, not talking. Without talk, Turkle argues, there is no way to read one's effect on other people, firing up the empathy impulse. These kids were missing out on the give-and-take of conversation, where you sometimes don't even know what you've said until the true weight of it is reflected back at you in the face of your companion. They weren't learning how to read each other. Digital relationships require less emotional risk than human ones: the carefully curated self gently floats past all the other carefully curated selves swimming in the e-water—*blub blub*. There may be the occasional Facebook blowout that mirrors dangerous human confrontation, but those end easily, when one party logs off, or another clicks "Unfriend." Without face-to-face interaction, there's a withering of that essentially human part of the self that rises only when confronted by a fellow being, flesh and blood.

On Twitter, the alienation is of a different cast because the "community" is often composed of strangers. On Facebook, you usually know your "friends," even if you haven't actually exchanged a word since that time in the lunchroom way back when. But the currency of Twitter isn't "friends," it's "followers." And when broadcasting a thought/anecdote/article, the expectation of how it will be received is different than it might be among a community of friends: there's no assumption of goodwill (though, after a time, the most successful tweeters build it). The cultish connotation of "follower" is appropriate: Twitter can make you feel Jim Jones powerful, rousing the crowd to action with a single tweet. We all know the glow of cyber-validation, that rush of adrenaline when the digital throng picks up your tweet and it moves across the Internet like a crowd-surfing body.

But on the flip side, if the tweet, once catapulted out there, generates no replies or likes or retweets, it can feel like a social misstep, a rejection from a wide, unknown group—i.e., the whole world. Lack of response spurs a kind of loneliness that's unique to public, invite-free social media sites like Twitter and Instagram. I've tweeted a goofy joke (probably animal-related; never do animal-related) and an hour later, when the silence became deafening, sheepishly deleted it. I know that's not really rejection, but it stings anyway; erasing is like time-traveling to a pre-rejection moment. Humans are social animals, and the lack of response can feel like shunning from the tribe.

Of course, much worse than Twitter silence is Twitter vitriol. For women particularly, Twitter can be a dangerous place. In 2014, Amanda Hess, an American culture writer who, at the time, frequently covered sex and the Internet, wrote an essay in *Pacific Standard* magazine detailing the hellish experience of being harassed to the point of threats of sexual violence and death. Hess called police, who shrugged and head-scratched, asking, "What's Twitter?"

Twitter, the corporation, has been shamefully lax about policing harassment, and the law is scrambling to keep up with a Wild West it barely comprehends. In the end, Hess had little legal recourse beyond a restraining order. Meanwhile, the 2014 (and on) "Gamergate" scandal saw many prominent women, primarily from the video gaming community, fielding systematic online abuse—hateful, violent attacks from threatened male gamers spitting down from their treehouse. The same charmers—with newly reinforced ranks—went after African American actress Leslie Jones on Twitter, plugging her feed with racist, sexist bile, including images of Harambe the gorilla.

What Hess, Jones, and so many others experience online is good ol' fashioned misogyny and racism, via a fancy new delivery system. But there's also a phrase that helps explain more specifically how social media—supposedly all about connection—can be divisive: "online disinhibition effect." Rider University psychology professor John Suler came up with the term to describe how people online will behave in ways they wouldn't dare in person; the knee-jerk, base behaviors that must be inhibited to make it through the day in the civilized world are set free in the digital one. Sometimes disinhibition is a good thing, allowing us to reinvent, or feel liberated, and open ourselves up to intimacy, realizing all the potential of social media. But Gamergate-type ranting would fall under the category Suler calls "toxic disinhibition," and it occurs because of several factors, including "dissociative anonymity" (feeling no responsibility for one's actions because anonymity erases accountability) and "dissociative imagination" (online is a kind of dream world; we're characters, not ourselves, and the people in it aren't real either).

We disinhibit because we can't see each other. Being together online is not actually the same as being together. And if our weekends are spent online, when do we get that one-on-one time? Reading each other's signals—the curve of the mouth, the stiffening of the body—is connection. If we don't have time together, we aren't practicing our humanity.

For seventy-five years, the Grant Study followed 268 Harvard sophomores from the classes of 1939 through 1944, in one of the most ambitious longitudinal studies of human development of all time. Psychiatrist Dr. George Vaillant took over the research in 1966, tracking the trajectories of his male, privileged subjects (one of whom was John F. Kennedy) in several books that grow richer and more revealing as the men grow older. Some take-aways, gleaned from interviews with the men every two years: alcohol is the single most destructive force in marriage; liberals have more sex than conservatives later in life; men whose youthful relationships with their mothers were warm earned higher salaries than men whose mothers were distant. But when Vaillant was asked "What have you learned from the Grant Study men?" his response was simpler: "That the only thing that really matters in life are your relationships to other people."

Vaillant gave the anonymous subjects colorful, Dickensian names, and their stories read like fables. Behold Charles Boatwright, who initially struck researchers as an unlikely prospect for a "good outcome." If one measures a successful life by money and recognition, then Boatwright is no Harvard poster child. His life is marked by its ordinariness. Boatwright had a happy childhood in an academic New England family. After Harvard, he didn't land the gold-plated career of so many of his peers but jumped jobs often, working in Vermont at a lumber cooperative, as a milk deliverer, and as an artificial inseminator of cattle. Yet, over the years, researchers always found him to be professionally stable and content. "Career consolidation" is one of Vaillant's markers of the maturation process, but Boatwright achieved that only when he bought a boatyard in his fifties, fulfilling a lifelong dream. His second marriage was much happier than the first, and late in life he became a stepfather. He relished the role, conquering the "generative" phase of maturity when one's focus shifts externally, from the self to others and relationships. At eighty-nine, he was still exercising two hours a day and volunteering three hours a week, visiting his grandchildren and shut-in and dying friends. He donated a lot of money to charity, eschewing material gains for spiritual ones, and was always, as he put it, a "cog in the community." He said, of the years between forty and fifty, "I feel a marked change has come over me. I have learned to be more kind, and have more empathy." In his eighties, he said, "I don't give a damn if I'm remembered for anything. I've enjoyed my life and had a hell of a good time. I'm more proud of those times I've helped others."

I include Charles Boatwright here because he strikes me as the embodiment of what we know about the power of social connection. It wasn't just his professional identity or the Harvard pedigree that determined the evolution of his character and happiness, but what he did with his free time: he used it to forge relationships. The body benefits, too: strong social connections can increase longevity and actually strengthen the immune system, speeding recovery from illness.

When I first became interested in weekends and did a quick audit of my family's best and worst ones, the biggest shock was the lack of social connection. We did *okay*. We aren't religious, so church isn't part of our weekends, which immediately eliminates one path to regular community gatherings. Our social group has narrowed as we've waded through the years of parenting; friends are work-related or old standbys. We live in a city far from where we grew up, so family is scattered, and visits are the houseguest kind, concentrated and intense. We love our friends, and yet our interactions can feel fleeting, infrequent, and low-value. We host the occasional dinner or brunch, packing as many people as possible around the table, often determined by a checklist of people to whom we owe a meal. We attend the occasional party or event. But these nights are often loud and furious, bookended by the exhausting labor of finding child care and then watching the clock to get home to avoid a hefty babysitting bill. No wonder the one common refrain at the end of the night is: "Great to see you. Feels like we just scratched the surface."

More alarmingly, I realize how little time I spend with my husband, outside of the trips to Ikea and kid-shepherding. The relationship, too, can take on the shape of a job: delegating and managing, assigning tasks and exchanging information. Those rare times when we are together and the conversation isn't about maintenance work for the life we are building feel shocking to me. I can forget the rest of him, the things I fell in love with. Once, at a dinner party, a little hazy from wine and dark lighting, I heard a man talking at the other end of the table, and thought, "That guy seems cool. I like his take on Nick Cave." Only when I turned did I realize—"Oh yeah, I married him." But other times, I am reminded, painfully, of the line in the Richard Linklater movie *Before Sunset*: "I feel like I'm running a small nursery with someone I used to date."

By deferring our free time, we're deferring our relationships. Lose the weekend, and you lose the time to deepen your relationship to anything but your work. I wanted to find people who were using the weekend to forge connections and build community. I wanted to know who was doing it better.

WHERE YOU BELONG

Just as we approach the doors to the "ecstatic dance party," Nina warns me, "There may be some hugging." I always wondered if I gave off a "no-hug" vibe, and now it's confirmed.

"I thought touching wasn't allowed," I say.

"Consensual hugging," says Nina.

It's clear, once inside the double doors, that staring is also inappropriate, but I can't help notice a guy in rainbow-striped diaper pants leaping like a frog, and a white-haired dancer in her sixties making *va-va-voom* gestures with her hands and then spinning off to the other side of the room. They are fabulous, and worthy of applause, which I'm intuiting, again, is so not done. Some dancers wear workout clothes and move with serious calorie-burning intentions. A couple of kids have hula hoops. Absolutely no one is talking. I'm less worried about unsolicited hugs than the wobbling guy on stilts, who looks as if he might tumble and take out several dancers, like a chainsawed tree in a forest crushing Snow White's animal friends. The room is dark, and the music is good, a Bhangra-thump delivered by a DJ hidden in the shadows.

The ecstatic dance group meets every Sunday, starting at 8:30 a.m., at the Women's Center in the Mission district of San Francisco.

Ecstatic dance has been described as "led conscious dance meets DJ culture," says Tyler Blank, the acro-yoga (yes, acrobatics and yoga, together) instructor who runs the event and is lightly dancing through the crowd. After becoming hooked on ecstatic dance in Hawaii, Blank started the San Francisco group with his then wife, renting an old ballroom in Oakland. Within a few months, between three hundred and four hundred people were gathering on Sunday mornings and Wednesday nights to dance. "Some people treat it as therapy. Some people treat it as spiritual connection, or their social connection," says Blank.

Before the dance starts, there's a kind of sharing circle where people talk about local events and trade news with one another: the feeling in a church before the sermon. The Oakland group is older, and has become a real community: dancers gather when they're not dancing, too, hosting potlucks and fundraisers for various causes, including raising money for a DJ with cancer who couldn't pay his medical bills. Blank sees the group not just in terms of self-expression, but as an experience beyond the self, as a way to break the social isolation that can occur in a city. "It's a safe way to experience intimacy and sensuality without engaging in sex," he says. "It's definitely edgy. You're very vulnerable."

Humans have always gathered to dance, but the "ecstatic" label came out of group dance parties held in Kalani, Hawaii, in the aughts. Blank delivers a complicated origin story that includes a guru-ish guy named Max Fathom, Burning Man, and a meditative dance practice called "Five Rhythms." Pictures of the early ecstatic dances show a cresting, tie-dyed horde grinning happily, hands in the air. Over the past decade and a half, the concept has spread around the world, and now, in cities throughout North America, Australia, and Europe, thousands of people gather at various locations on Sunday morning and pay a door fee (for me, $10) for a dance party. "Party" feels like the wrong word, though; there's no debauchery on the floor, and the rules are rigid: no touching, no talking, no drinking or drugging. I can't confirm that no one is high—I'm looking at you, leaper—but it's certainly not a prerequisite. Also, it feels pretty early for that.

Sociologist Emile Durkheim wrote that ritual creates "belief" and "belonging." He viewed ritual in religious and specific terms—a group gathering around a sacred object—but while ecstatic dance is secular, it shares a ritualistic shape, and perhaps the object in question is the dance itself. The dance is a repeated action at a consistent time—Sunday morning, no less—when people come together, shaping a kind of collective identity. The rules create structure, and the room is a silent, welcoming space, all of which sounds pretty churchy. Durkheim believed that religion wasn't necessarily a theological or a philosophical position, but a social one, a site of experience.

It's a good time to mention that, to an outsider, ecstatic dance looks kind of goofy at first. I have explained to Nina that it's been a long time since I danced, and I was never much of a dancer anyway, with noodle limbs and the misfortune to have come of age when Molly Ringwald's *Breakfast Club* side-shuffle was the height of bodily expression. Yet it only takes about ten minutes for the self-consciousness to drop away. The dim lighting helps, and I am comforted by the rules, which seem to stave off judgment and/or snickering (I hope). The fifty or so of us (the numbers fluctuate throughout the morning) are together, but separate. I'm reminded of *A Charlie Brown Christmas*, where all the cartoon kids have their little spot of floor and do their happy dances alone but in a group; bodies untouching, joy unfettered. The corollary for the feeling of experiencing something intensely personal in a collective space is, of course, prayer, which may explain the peacefulness in the room, even when the music gets louder and faster, and people really start to move.

I heard about ecstatic dance from an old high school friend, Greg, who is married to Nina. They bought their tall Victorian house a few blocks away in an early wave of gentrification, before the San Francisco housing market went crazy, back when the neighborhood was rougher and it wasn't unprecedented to find human feces on the lawn. Now they get to sit by the lemon trees in the backyard with their seven-year-old son as the house increases in value with every breeze. They are very California, in that Californians report the highest sense of well-being in the United States. Their life is a lesson in how to make the most of this short time on the planet: they travel often, and are into their third decade attending Burning Man (I don't think I met anyone in San Francisco who doesn't have a relationship to Burning Man). Even their work is both cool and meaningful: they wrote a book together about the cultural history of coffee, then Nina began working at a gourmet chocolate company that emphasized fair trade. Now, as the pot boom booms, they're setting up a business importing cannabidiol (CBD), a component of cannabis that relieves pain and anxiety without the psychoactive experience.

So these are people who don't defer pleasure, but rather embed it into their lives. In fact, they have figured out how to make careers out of coffee, chocolate, and pot—I tip my fedora to them for that—but mostly, I'm just impressed by how much they *do* with their time. Greg shows me pictures of a holiday he and his son took last summer to Camp Tipsy, a weekend where campers gather to build rotten boats out of junk and found objects. Their son is flying off the end of one of these crazy, Seussian structures, straight into a reservoir, with a "Wheee!" face.

On some Sunday mornings, Nina takes her leave of the family and hits the ecstatic dance party. "I always loved to dance," Nina says. "It was a huge part of my life before having a family, and I'm always trying to find ways to reconnect with who I was before I had a kid. I feel like if I don't take that time, I'm not me. Being with a kid all weekend—it can get repetitive. But when I'm dancing, in the dark, I'm me."

It's deeply exposing to move your body in front of strangers who don't have a vested interest in said body; this is why dancing with strangers can feel more intimate than sex with someone you care about. Then there's the uncomfortable contrast between the silence of the people and the beat of the music. The rule against talking, which makes the experience uninterruptable and almost meditative, is actually the hardest rule for people to obey, says Blank. Some people come but they can't handle it and flee. "It's fascinating to communicate nonverbally.

I feel like it's a lost art. But by not talking, we're all communally focused on the music, and each individual expression of it. It's unifying. It's a unique ceremony of sorts."

Silence and ceremony seem in keeping with the mood of an early Sunday morning, and Blank observes that the Wednesday night dances just *feel* different; the darkness makes everyone stay longer, the dance is deeper. Sunday is light, and Sunday feels sacred. "There's a different feeling when you wake up to dance," says Blank. "People are starting on the same page, fresh out of sleep, and everyone is more awake. Sunday morning is eyes open. We all see each other. It's a more positive vibe."

The popularity of ecstatic dance is a product of the very specific time and place in which it exists: privileged, playful San Francisco, mid-2000s; culturally and generationally diverse; a place where the main industry is technology, which should be—in its most romantic terms—about expanding experience. But dance is also ancient, the reflection of a primal urge to transcend the body and strive for the spiritual; an expression of something unchoreographed, unknown. The Sufis spin to celebrate God. The Bible is filled with passages urging dance in worship and tribute, as in Exodus: "Then Miriam the prophetess, the sister of Aaron, took a tambourine in her hand, and all the women went out after her with tambourines and dancing." They dance to celebrate their freedom, when the slaves are emancipated from Pharaoh's relentless brick making. They're dancing because they're not at work.

Ecstatic dance is infectious. On the floor, we are all following each other, even if not literally; one person's joy in dance gives the next person permission to feel as deeply. It's a strange kind of camaraderie: together but apart. Yet it doesn't *feel* separate, dancing next to someone; it feels like togetherness. I get the appeal: eyes closed, repetitive beat digging down, pushing me into a kind of trance state. A constant thrum of awareness that others are nearby too, and we are sharing the room, and the moment, at once carefree and careful, looking out for each other.

That intimacy translates off the dance floor. All through the morning, people are spilling into the halls, talking, laughing, and making plans. Later, my friends will meet other dancer friends in the park, and kids and parents will gather in the big Victorian house for pizza. This genuine togetherness cuts through my easterner's skepticism, and my inborn hatred of rainbow textiles.

It is, however, exhausting. I pack it in at the two-hour mark, and I don't know if I'll ever do ecstatic dance again. But I do know that all Sundays should start in celebration, connected to something primal and holy, and to other human bodies, moving through space.

FEEL-GOOD ACTIVITIES FOR THE SPIRITUALLY CHALLENGED

My parents were strictly secular, United Church dropouts and spawn of the freak-flag '60s. Growing up, I was envious of my Jewish friends with their requisite summer camps and Friday nights that included two of the best things ever: candles and bread. They had a built-in rhythm to their weeks. Then there were the Christian kids who we'd meet up with in the park after Sunday School, which apparently took place in a basement and involved insane stories of virgin births (!) and boatloads of animals. "It's boring," I'd hear from Jews and Christians alike, about their weekend classes. Clearly they were liars.

I should admit up front that while I've always been curious about the unknowable shapes behind the curtain, and that ephemeral tissue that connects us to each other and to larger invisible forces, it doesn't really translate into God for me. I'm the kind of spiritual dabbler that totally irritates devout people who have made clear choices and don't dwell in the gray areas. At nineteen, I stayed for a couple of months at a Buddhist temple in Thailand; at thirty, I did the same at a Hindu ashram in India. In between, I've meditated, yoga-ed, sat in a few churches, and stood at the Wailing Wall. I've been moved by beauty enough to endow those moments with otherworldly meaning. I mean, I get it. The rage for order. I respect the leap of faith and the amazing good works done in the name of God. But in daylight, I can't really fault Christopher Hitchens–style atheism. I don't care for magic usurping science, and I'm no fan of the odious attitudes and bloodbaths undertaken in the name of dusty texts. I'm not alone with my atheism: the world is becoming increasingly secular. The number of Americans who don't identify with any organized religion is rising, and the number of Christians, as a share of the U.S. population, is falling. Trust in religious institutions has been declining for at least three decades.

With that decline, the scaffolding of the weekend crumbles. While many Americans, particularly African Americans and

Southerners, do still hew to the Sunday morning church ritual, for others, work has replaced religion on the weekends. Work doesn't only occupy the time once given to religious practice; work has become a locus for devotion and identity, as religion once was. In the eighteenth century, as Benjamin Hunnicutt has pointed out, work was a way to venerate God, the true and highest calling. Now work itself is the calling. It's also the deepest investigation of our week, filling even our Sundays, the time once set aside to ask the big questions of our lives. Hunnicutt said in an interview at OfSpirit.com, "Some people still go to houses of worship including Catholics and Jews. However, work becomes a drug that replaces the struggles of prior generations around deeper questions: 'We're born from infinity and we'll go back to infinity—what does it mean?' Work is the placebo, the unexamined answer. We don't have to think about the deeper things . . . Work is a passive religion. We don't think about it, but it soothes us into spiritual paralysis where we don't have to worry about these things."

Spiritual paralysis is undoubtedly a piece of social isolation; if we can't join other people pursuing the same questions, we are alone. It takes a hearty dose of yay-me individualism to support a work-centric culture like the one we're in now, and it's no wonder that our feelings of social connectedness and belonging have dropped since the 1980s, too. There's a practical reason for this isolation: public policies that have cut funding for many social gathering sites like libraries and community centers, meaning fewer places free to the public that aren't about consumption. We desperately need these vanishing zones that urban sociologist Ray Oldenburg calls "third places," defined as neutral spaces for people to gather beyond home (the first place) and work (the second place). Those are the spaces in which to get connected, and the Women's Center in the Mission, where the ecstatic dancers meet, felt like exactly that.

A large study of forty communities across twenty-nine states showed that personal happiness is tied more closely to perceived levels of social connectedness and trust than it is to education or wealth, echoing the conclusions of the Harvard Grant Study. But a culture of long work hours makes meeting in third places increasingly difficult, for the simple reason that there's no time. When politicians blow the bullhorn about the erosion of the social fabric, they need to acknowledge that a society weakens when its members are no longer able, or willing, to come together outside work. Work-life balance isn't simply something to be negotiated in the workplace; it's a public interest issue.

A hundred years ago, Durkheim wrote that when citizens feel alienated from their community, suicide rates rise. He believed that each of us possesses a kind of dual conscience: the individual and the social self. If the balance is off—a pursuit of personal wants eclipsing collective needs—people become alienated from their communities. Society descends into a state of "anomie"—purposelessness, estrangement. But religion isn't the only recourse for that kind of social isolation. A growing number of Americans who consider themselves secularist—atheists, free-thinkers, skeptics—are gathering regularly, forming their own communities and averting anomie, even without God.

Saturday nights, around 6:00 p.m., at a Panera Bread café in a strip mall in southern San Diego, Jason pushes two tables together. Jason is the organizer of Coffee and Conversation, a Saturday night event sponsored by the Humanist Association of San Diego, though you don't even have to know what humanism is to attend. Sometimes five people show up, sometimes twenty-five. Jason, a law student, spends the days before circulating the URLs of news clips to discuss, and preparing an agenda, which he finds helps wrangle the conversation, avoiding free-for-all chaos. As described by Jason, the meetings have the energy of the first day of school. When everyone is seated, beverages in hand, they go around the table and give their names. The agenda circulates. Then they talk, giving each person an opportunity to say his or her piece (silence is okay, too). Jason is predisposed to topics along philosophical and political lines, but he throws in some fluff, too; a newsworthy Kardashian has been known to make an appearance. "Some serious people don't care for this type of thing: 'Why are we talking about the woman who had seventeen children?' They want to talk about Putin annexing Crimea. Then other people are like, 'I don't even know where that is on the map,'" he says. Once in a while the subject is actually a tenet of humanism, as in "Can we be good without God?" The conversation moves in a circle, an invisible talking stick passing from hand to hand. "It allows everyone to be able to shine as an expert. It's validating," says Jason.

The Ancient Greeks gathered in *symposia* in each other's houses to debate, recite poetry, sing, and drink copious amounts of water-diluted wine (full wine was for barbarians). Only a few pertinent details and centuries separate the caramel lattes in the strip mall Panera Bread and Aristophanes's descriptions of the symposium with "tables . . . laid and loaded with the most exquisite dishes; the couches are covered with the softest of cushions." Of course, the *symposia* weren't exactly "All Welcome": as Aristophanes continued, "the slaves are standing in a row and waiting to pour scent over the guests." That's clearly the worst catering job in history. Nor were women invited to weigh in on the future of democracy, though they did get to play flute or fan the dudes in their roles as *hetaera* (high-end prostitutes). Flash forward to the seventeenth and eighteenth centuries and wealthy noblewomen were often the organizers and participants in the French salons of the *ancien régime*. This era of artists and aristocrats mingling in debate was called "The Age of Conversation," which pulls us back to Sherry Turkle's call for talk—the intimate exchange of ideas, face to face.

Leisure has often been about talking. In the early twentieth century, New York "It Girl" Mabel Dodge hosted Wednesday night salons in her Greenwich village flat. Margaret Sanger might drop by to discuss birth control in a room that included photographer Alfred Stieglitz, psychoanalysts, and union leaders. The conversation would turn to art, sex, politics, while Pinch scotch, Gorgonzola sandwiches, and ham circulated. "Dodge's salon was where black Harlem first met Greenwich Village bohemia," writes historian Andrea Barnet. "And, conversely, where white bohemia got its first taste of a parallel black culture that it would soon not only glorify but actively try to emulate." In the best conversations, social and class lines crisscross; bodies and ideas integrate. Communities form from words.

Humanists share a belief in reason over religion and the supernatural; they believe that moral and ethical decisions can be based on reason and empathy for fellow humans, not doctrine. Jason has an inborn skepticism that seemed to point him in this direction—i.e., he's a bit of a shit disturber. When he was seventeen, he attended a Pentecostal retreat in a small town in Nebraska. He describes himself as "a corrupting influence." After the ministers staged an elaborate nighttime show for the kids—singing, dancing, God—he put up his hand and asked, "Quick question: If God is so powerful, why do you spend so much money on the music and lights?"

As a kid, Jason moved a lot, too. Never in history has the world's population been so peripatetic. The world is in motion, and this makes the quest for stable community even more difficult. Jason jokes that the first question most Americans ask each other is "What do you do?" but in San Diego, it's "Where are you from?" The city is a way station, the south-southwestern-most point of the contiguous United States. Jason himself is from Nebraska, but he's lived in Massachusetts, Colorado, Mexico. And on Saturday nights at Coffee and Conversation, the diaspora comes together. "When everybody is from somewhere else, our group has a particular role that we play. We connect people, and people build close associations, analogous to family. We're stepping in for those deeper relationships, the extended family role."

Jason's smart-assery has been tempered—or has morphed—into a pursuit of social justice. Often, the Humanists of San

Diego will come together in activist causes, like last year, at an anti–Prop 8 rally in support of same-sex marriage. After two hours of talking, some members of the group will go for a walk together, or to a bar. Sometimes they've stayed together until three or four in the morning.

These kinds of secular gatherings are anecdotally popular (no data seems to exist to measure the numbers). At the non-denominational Sunday Assembly in London, England, people gather on Sunday mornings for philosophical discussions, music, and the motto "Live better. Help often. Wonder more." It's casual. On the Facebook page of my local chapter, a recent scheduled meeting in a library was moved to the food court of a mall. After only a few years, Sunday Assembly chapters have come together in eight different countries where people sing songs, hear inspiring talks, and create community.

As organized religion recedes, recent surveys suggest a rise in the number of people who identify as "spiritual not religious"—my box! A 2016 Pew Research Center study found a notable increase in the share of people, including those who do and do not identify as religious, who say they "often feel a deep sense of spiritual peace and well-being as well as a deep sense of wonder about the universe." This could be sneered at as the rise of self-help masquerading as community—replacing God with Deepak—but regardless, secular pursuit is reshaping our weekends. Meetup.com (a website that lists community activities by interest) and bulletin boards in coffee shops in most cities offer weekend yoga retreats, groups like Jason's, meditation classes. Without religion, "secular spirituality" pursuits are clearly satisfying an untended part of people, and creating connections that the faux-familial dynamics of work can't replicate.

"I see these people become friends, and people's lives become better," says Jason. "People who are lonely are less lonely. People get sick and they need someone to bring over some food and we do that." He is succinct about what talking and gathering actually creates: "We make people's lives better."

For those without the framework of religion, community is a bit of work. We aren't born into tribes, but have to seek and create them. From there, without a guidebook, on the weekend, it's possible to forge new ritual comforts.

A FAITHFUL WEEKEND

Even with a societal tilt toward the secular, worship still sculpts the weekend for many. The numbers may have declined, but 37 percent of Americans claim to attend religious services once a week. (Of course, the stat is self-reported, and the reality— at least according to data collected from church leaders at The American Church Project—may be less than half that.) Those who do use the weekend to enter a house of worship are following an ancient tradition, one that's sustained human connection and built community for centuries. In the decades after Christ, early Christians gathered in private households on Sundays— the first day of the week—sharing a communal meal, followed by some preaching and prophesying, wine and singing.

For Muslims, Friday prayers mark the beginning of the weekend.

The Orland Park Prayer Center, about forty-five minutes by commuter train southwest of Chicago, comes into view the way a mountain rises out of flatlands, surprising and beautiful. The mosque is modeled on Jerusalem's Dome of the Rock, gleaming like a polished golden egg. It sits among the markers of suburbia: strip malls, highways, and gated communities with their faux-nature names in curlicue font ("Welcome to Mallard Landings!"). The Prayer Center is actually two buildings joined by a walkway, and it looks out over a Catholic cemetery and soybean fields. In all that vastness, the mosque feels accidental, like a crash-landed spaceship.

In 2004, when local Muslim leaders proposed building the Prayer Center, heated town meetings erupted, the kind where Osama bin Laden and 9/11 get name-checked. But the area around Chicago has a large, growing Arab American population that needs places to gather. Chicago and its environs are home to one of the largest Arab communities in the United States, around 100,000 people, mostly of Palestinian and Egyptian origin. The former are not newcomers: the first wave came in the late nineteenth century, often setting up shop among inner city African American communities. One hundred years later, many are in suburbs near Orland Park.

Middle Eastern grocery stores and restaurants serving excellent falafel and hummus are easy to find, but when I visit on a Friday night, my guide, a mosque volunteer named Suzanne, asks if I want to do a Dunkin' Donuts drive-through before sitting in on the activities at the mosque. We are in her SUV, with one of her three kids in the backseat, a thirteen-year-old boy talking video games. Suzanne is elegant and tall and somehow taller still in her hijab and abaya (a long black prayer dress), her face immaculately made-up. She wears the hijab in public, but has to change out of her office-wear after commuting from her job at a financial firm in downtown Chicago. Giant coffees in hand, we drive across the highway toward the mosque. I ask her about the rise of Islamophobia, and an alarming incident in 2015 when bullets went through the dome during a morning prayer service. The crime has never been solved. Suzanne talks a mile a minute, with a lightheartedness that's at odds with the subject: "Oh, well," she says. "It's our turn. It happened during the Civil Rights movement. There always has to be somebody. All we can do is be excellent neighbors to them." "Them" is confusing: Suzanne was born in Chicago and raised in Orland Park. She's an American, whose parents came from Palestine. She is devout, and her weekends are structured by her faith.

Churches have long provided sanctuary for immigrants, offering instant community to newcomers. For Muslims, the mosque is sanctuary during a time when their religion is often maligned by outsiders, and abused by zealots. In fact, less than 1 percent of the American population is Muslim; 70 percent of Americans identify as Christian. Almost 70 percent of Muslim Americans say religion is very important in their lives, and two-thirds pray daily. Almost half pray five times per day, as dictated by the Koran.

Friday is their most holy day. During the afternoon, the parking lot at The Prayer Center is overflowing for Jumu'ah prayers. Men fill the downstairs prayer hall (Friday prayers are obligatory for men only) while women pray in the balcony space above.

We arrive post-Jumu'ah, in early evening, when parents are dropping off their kids as if for a school dance. The event is called Friday Night Live, aimed at kids between thirteen and college age, and it says on the website, "A teen's spiritual hangout stuffed with inspiration and good times. Eat, laugh, pray and learn!"

Sheikh Kifah Mustapha, the imam at the mosque, speaks quietly; he doesn't shake my hand, and he leaves the door to his office open as we talk. He tells me that, on average, the Muslim American population is much younger than the non-Muslim population, and the numbers of youth are growing. The Prayer Center wanted to offer programming to engage the youngest members of the community, a demographic boom in under-thirties. "We needed to create a safe zone against the bullying and stress they were experiencing," he tells me. "But kids have attention spans of about fifteen minutes, so we needed to make it appealing."

The result is an evening led by the older teens, often college students, brandishing cordless microphones. The boys sit on one side of the room; the girls on the other. Their shoes are on racks by the door. The girls wear the hijab and loose clothes; most of the boys are in jeans and track pants, with sports-team and corporate logos on their shirts and baseball hats. Many of the girls' headscarves are brightly colored and patterned, signaling their personalities the way other teens might do by dyeing their hair purple or wearing tube tops. The boys, Suzanne explains, must approach the parents of the girls if they want to date, and for the most part, the boys and girls don't look at each other.

Other than that prominent gender divide, it's pretty typical community center programming—Q and A, videos, snacks—but with a religious streak. There's an element of confession as the microphone goes around the room. One girl stands up and talks about being bullied, the victim of rumors. She sounds like any teenager, her speech a tumble of "likes" and mutterings, and the youth leaders throw some supportive stories from the Koran back at her. The moral lessons are cleanly delivered, and usually fall along the lines of: Do the right thing. The kids ask questions: one question, submitted anonymously, is from a boy who wants to know what to do about watching too much porn. Then the teen leaders project a news clip of an eight-year-old with a gun and debate the ethics of children bearing arms. The discussion involves more whooping and cheering, some high-fiving.

The sea of kids is in constant motion, getting up and walking around, sucking on their giant sodas, checking their phones. Engaging and disengaging, they cluster around the edges of the room, giggling.

At 5:50, there's a call to prayer over the loudspeakers. The boys go together into the prayer hall, and the girls walk upstairs to an elevated balcony, looking down on them. I follow, and they pray, sitting and standing, to the musical sounds of the prayer. Other teens don't pray at all, but lounge on the wall-to-wall carpet, doing their homework.

A boy named Mohammed, fifteen, tells me that this is what he does most Friday evenings. "I know a bunch of kids who used to play sports on Friday night, but now they come here," he says. An eighteen-year-old girl named Diana says, "I started volunteering in high school. It's my second home. When I was in high school, I was really separate, afraid of not blending in and not liking how I looked with my headscarf. But this is my family." She tells me about the volunteering that the mosque does: a fun run for burn victims; cleaning the park by the housing development that was most opposed to the presence of the mosque. This kind of community engagement is not just philanthropic but also a way to integrate, according to the imam: "We can't be in a bubble."

It's an ordinary scene; churches and community centers are always trying to corral kids to hang out and "rap." But it's remarkable, too, that with the typical suburban temptations of adolescence all around, dozens of teenagers are in a place of worship on a Friday night, thinking and talking. Suzanne is proud of this. "They're such good kids," she says, several times. The plan is to keep them close and connected, and safely get them through these years, which is what all parents want. Each kid will decide what to take into adulthood from these formative Friday nights; and each will decide, also, what to shed.

WHY DO-GOODERS HAVE MORE TIME

In high school, I admit that I raised an eyebrow at the cluster of Tracy Flicks whose every lunch hour was taken up by bake sales for African children and every weekend filled with car washes for Amnesty International. Yay to the causes, but boo to the showmanship: "We get it—you're better than us!" Some of these kids were transparently CV-buffing, their self-promotion leaking through the altruistic scrim.

Yet I also knew, even then, that anytime I was goaded into lifting a sponge or standing behind a table of cinnamon buns, I felt pretty damn good. I'd count the profits, imagining the small difference those dollars might make for someone, somewhere, far from my easy life. So I tamed my cynicism, and for several years in my twenties I volunteered at a sexual health clinic for women. We were trained in "empathic listening" and sat across from people at the highest and lowest moments of their lives: in love and in search of birth control to be ready for the first time; facing an unwanted pregnancy with a toddler and a boyfriend in the waiting area. Those weekly three-hour shifts defined my post-college years, and probably changed me more than any of the jobs that paid my bills. I'd go in during the late afternoon, after my day job (waitress, intern, grad student), and lift my head to find darkness outside. I didn't know what had happened to the day. Volunteering placed me in an entirely different relationship to time.

That sensation, which I'd always attributed to a kind of "flow" state—being lost in the work—may be something else entirely. A 2012 study published in *Psychological Science* found that people who gave away their time felt they had more of it.

One group of subjects was assigned a meaningful task, like writing a note to a gravely ill child, or editing the essay of an at-risk student. In one experiment, the other group was instructed to waste time by counting "e"s in a block of Latin text. In another, the second group did something that benefited only themselves. And in a third experiment, they were permitted to leave the lab early, thereby gaining free time. In each case, those who had done the activity that benefited someone else reported feeling that they had more time than the other groups, even though, of course, they had lost time in doing their charitable act. Researchers chalked up this sensation to "self-efficacy." The authors wrote that "spending time on others makes people feel highly effective and capable and . . . the same duration of time is perceived as longer when more has been accomplished—when it is 'fuller.'" Volunteering on the weekend may actually make your weekend longer—or at least it will make it seem longer.

Americans do some volunteer work on weekends already: Sunday is the biggest volunteer day of the week, with 7.5 percent of the population participating. But Saturday is the second lowest, at 5.8 percent (Americans volunteer least on Mondays). And overall, the number of Americans who volunteer hit a ten-year low in 2015. Lack of time is the main reason people give for failing to volunteer. If we barely have time to take care of our own and our family's needs, and work continues to drift into leisure, then how many hours are left over to give to anyone else?

But here's an argument in favor of making time for others on the weekend: it's good for you. Volunteers experience lower depression rates and an increased sense of well-being. Volunteering may even help you live longer. And volunteer work is a fast track to social connectedness, pulling people into their communities—and beyond—as well as improving the quality of life in the place where we live. Volunteering has also been shown to promote empathy, the ability to step into someone else's shoes with the intention of understanding her worldview, and—the most important part—altering our own behavior accordingly.

We may be neurologically wired to be compassionate: during a brain-imaging study headed by cognitive neuroscientist Jordan Grafman at Northwestern University Medical School, subjects were placed in a fMRI machine and asked to decide which charities on a list should receive their monetary donation. Scientists assumed the frontal lobes, those sites of reason and logic, would start popping, and they did. But they were surprised to find the more active parts of the brain were the same ones that light up during sex and eating—our pleasure centers. Even more surprisingly, the subjects' pleasure centers were as active when they were giving money away as when they received money themselves. Helping others actually feels really good—sex and chocolate good.

THERE IS ONE PLACE in the United States where volunteering thrives: Utah. Year after year, Utah beats all the other states in volunteer hours. The majority of the volunteer work is done through a religious affiliation, which makes sense in the Mormon state.But when I talk to Danielle, a frequent volunteer and student at the University of Utah in Salt Lake City, she says, "Actually, we're Catholic, but religion never played a humungous role in my life."

That life is ridiculously busy, but Danielle says she doesn't *feel* busy. She's a full-time college student at the University of Utah with an eye on medical school. She works at a Nike factory

store at least twenty hours a week. She also has Crohn's disease, which has been in remission for a few years. And on weekends, through the Lowell Bennion Community Service Center
at school, she does "community engagement stuff," an under-
statement considering the dozens of hours she logs each month
organizing Saturday service projects for armies of student volunteers. Last Earth Day, she led crews of students to the Jordan
River Parkway, on the west side of Salt Lake, for a mass cleanup.
They pulled invasive weeds from the shores and filled garbage
bags with refuse and a few dirty needles. On another weekend,
she went with a group to a long-term housing center for the
homeless and scrubbed hallways and bathrooms.

Danielle grew up doing charity work (most people who volunteer have it in their family, like brown eyes). She remembers
her mother accompanying her to the dollar store and buying
Barbies (or Barbie knockoffs, because that's what they could
afford) to distribute at a local shelter. In high school, she was a
Big Sister, and watched a girl grow from fourth grade straight
through graduation. "I love my volunteer work. It provides a
sense of family and support. I'm Type A. I don't really know
what my life would be like without it." Well, what *would* it be
like? "I'd have a lot more free time," she says. And what would
she do with all that extra time? She pauses. "I really don't know.
I'm doing what I want to do already."

In other words, for her, volunteering is leisure; it's not an
act that depletes leisure. For people like Danielle, there's been
a mind shift away from the assumption of time famine. She
sees volunteering as time-expanding and happiness-inducing,

which makes it entirely possible to find space on the weekend to do it.

But volunteering doesn't have to be sustained or continuous, and often it isn't anymore: there's been a rise in "event" volunteering—the one-off; the Earth Day grab. If that's all you can do, then do that.

For a few hours on the third Saturday of the month, the Panhandle park in San Francisco draws a group of volunteers to help it out. The skinny, long strip of green is surrounded by ornamental San Francisco apartments on the edge of Haight-Ashbury. Despite the pretty homes, the park used to have a slightly sketchy image (drug detritus and patchy, scabby grass) according to Dale, who leads the Panhandle Volunteer Project. "Our mandate is the simplest: we work together once a month to make the park more beautiful and more accessible to people."

He and the handful of neighbors and strangers who show up rake and scrape mud, installing drought-tolerant plants and fixing the basketball courts. It's a social occasion where old neighbors catch up, and new ones have a first encounter. In a neighborhood as diverse as the Panhandle, and as in flux as the city, the park project gets people out of their silos. For a while, a small group of men in their forties who were part of a substance abuse recovery placement showed up and pitched in. "By getting to know them, we got to know people we might not have otherwise spoken with. Just by being out there in the community, you're lowering barriers. It makes life much richer," says Dale.

Dale, it turns out, is also a Danielle-style overachiever: he works long hours as a medical researcher but still finds time to volunteer at another park, the Presidio (where he gets to "geek out about plants and animals"), and in the Lesbian/Gay Chorus of San Francisco, where he sings and sits on the board of directors. Volunteering seems to beget volunteering: he feels like he has more time, so he fills it. "It's important for me to have a sense of balance in life, so it's not all about work. I have a feeling of accomplishment every time I visit and see the results. The singing is healing, but the parks—it brings me such pleasure," says Dale. "There are some sacrifices: I'm less likely to go on those spontaneous weekend road trips or a huge bike ride. But for me it's totally worth it for the pleasure I get. It's how I want to spend my weekends."

DALE AND DANIELLE are clearly saints sent here to make us feel bad about ourselves, but sainthood isn't actually a prerequisite for volunteering. Surveys show that most volunteers are motivated by some form of self-interest; they may be altruistic, but that's not the only reason they volunteer. Some cite work experience, or their own self-growth. Fine. It doesn't really matter *why* you do, just that you do.

Until my kids are older, and I'm less of a commitment-phobe, I can't imagine volunteering every single weekend. But I'm open to the one-off. Part of my weekend fatigue, I'm certain, is the feeling that even the time I do have isn't well spent. There seems to be so little to show for a weekend come Sunday night; just barely surviving the busy-ness doesn't feel like enough.

For years, I've been wanting to introduce the kids to the idea that Christmas isn't just a grotesque money grab—i.e., blow their minds. I heard about a project where families come together to gift-wrap donated presents for low-income families. I'm a little wary of the idea that acquiring more stuff is a cure for poverty, but the families are vetted by social agencies, and their need is undeniable: newly arrived refugees; people out of work and looking or returning to school; women leaving bad relationships. People in transition.

On a Saturday in December, we drive to the suburbs. My ten-year-old daughter is ecstatic, a kid with a natural philanthropic streak who also loves gift-wrapping. She's felled by a terrible cold but she's been looking forward to this for weeks and refuses to hang back. My husband and son are more perplexed: "Will there be ribbons?" asks my husband. "I can't wrap," my son keeps repeating. "I suck at wrapping."

We arrive at a massive empty office space and join a group for an information session. Seated with us are several families and clusters of work buddies, as well as a large group of women in smock dresses who appear to be Mennonites. We share a table with a mother-daughter team from a part of the city I've never been to.

The first family we are gift-wrapping for is a single mom with three kids of varying ages. Together, our group divides up the goods that have been donated. There are toys and games, but many of the items are poignantly practical. Snowsuits and mittens, imperative in below-zero temperatures. Pots and pans. Toothpaste. All of these items have been specifically requested by the families who applied to the program.

I think of good intentions as I wrap. After the Haitian

earthquake, tons of donated broken bicycles and secondhand household goods took up precious space in hangars needed by emergency crews, depleting volunteer time as they were discarded. What people want in a crisis, more than anything, is agency; they want to be able to make a decision about what to buy to replace what's been lost. These parents have given lists, and so there are pajamas and binders, soap and towels. Each family gets a $100 gift card to a supermarket, as well as a plastic, decorated tree. I know that we aren't solving poverty, but there's satisfaction in imagining the moment of unwrapping. Some needs will be met, some respite felt.

We stay for three hours, wrapping and chatting with the mother-daughter team at our table. I'll admit that the afternoon doesn't engender the same lasting hedonic rewards of long-term volunteer work—what sociologists call "serious leisure." Researchers have found that "voluntourism"—when people do a one-off volunteer activity in a remote location—appears to lack the same lasting psychosocial benefits as lending a hand in one's own community. But here's the thing about the weekend: you can't always craft a perfect experience. In forty-eight hours, the goals have to be realistic for you at that moment, in your life. We can't all live like Dale and Danielle. But if we find a little time now and then to give back, our weekends do feel longer and better spent.

It's a most unusual Saturday. Even my son and husband are exhilarated by the end of the day. All of us, from our position of great good fortune, have been reminded of the needs of strangers. We'll remember that. We agree to do it again next year.

◇◇◇◇

SEXY TIME

There are some sweet, reflective songs about the power of the weekend, like Morrissey's pleasingly mopey "Everyday Is Like Sunday," or Neil Young's heartfelt "Out on the Weekend." But mostly, in pop music, the weekend serves a very specific purpose: sexy time. A weekend playlist could start with Katy Perry's "Last Friday Night (TGIF)," where Friday night involves skinny-dipping and a ménage à trois, then Coldplay's more red-rose-and-candles-inflected "Hymn for the Weekend." Perhaps add a little Earth Wind & Fire with the grind-along "Saturday Nite," a song too sexy to bother with correct spelling.

Yes, songs that refer to the weekend tend to err on the cheesy side of the musical spectrum, but they do try to capture the giddy anticipation of two nights unencumbered by work or obligation. The weekend should mean indulgence: the slow unbuttoning versus the Wednesday night quickie, one eye on the clock. The weekend is the five-day-deferred opportunity to give one's undivided attention to that special someone (that line is best read in the voice of Barry White, who should narrate all sexy weekends).

But are we making the most of our weekends? In the United States, 10 to 20 percent of romantic relationships can be described as "sexless" (a couple that has sex less than once a month or fewer than ten times per year). Some couples make peace with this life—good on them—but research suggests that people in sexless marriages report being more likely to consider divorce, and are more likely to be unhappy. On the flip side, having sex at least once a week correlates with increased happiness. Yet when we're stressed, rushed, and tired, sex can feel like yet another addition to the To-Do list. A pair of British therapists blogged about the sudden and surprising spike in clients complaining about their nose-diving sex lives. Successful and work-centric, their clients attributed their weekly sex deficit to exhaustion from the long-hours culture. Stress about their jobs had spilled over into the bedroom; they just weren't in the mood.

Theoretically, we defer sex to the weekend because the weekend means open time, away from work. But what if we're never not-working? Cynthia, a blogger and journalist in London, England, admits that her smartphone was killing her sex life. Cynthia's relationship with her phone is both personal and professional, though you might have a hard time distinguishing between the two. For work (or is it fun?), she's online all day fishing for stories and monitoring her news feeds. For fun (or is it work?), she's on social media and texting with friends. A while ago, she found herself on her phone from the moment she woke until the moment she went to bed, clicking away during dinner while her husband and five-year-old ate. "Fork in one hand, phone in the other," she says. I ask her when she turns it off and she laughs. "That would be never."

The prospect of being disconnected from her smartphone felt scary, so much so that Cynthia started carrying a portable battery-charger with her. "I worried I was missing out on something," she says, which is actually a phrase psychologists use to describe the compulsion to always be online: FOMO, "Fear of Missing Out."

Cynthia's not alone with this anxiety. A University of Missouri study identified "iPhone separation anxiety" as a significant experience for many. Participants in the study had blood pressure cuffs strapped to their arms, and were given word searches to work through. Then researchers removed their iPhones, claiming they were causing "Bluetooth interference" with the cuffs. Device-free, the subjects were undertaking a second puzzle when their phones began ringing a room away. Unable to answer, their heart rates and blood pressure rose, and they did worse on the puzzle, suggesting that the absence of smartphones actually impaired their cognition. Researchers wrote that heavy cellphone users are "capable of perceiving their iPhone as an object of their extended self, which can be negatively impacted (i.e., lessening of self) during separation." It's understandable that we take our cellphones into the bedroom if they feel like an extension of our very beings. But when we do, what we're saying to our partners is: *My time and attention is elsewhere, not on you.* Presence is the most important requisite for good sex. And if both partners are on separate devices in the same place, then they seem together, but they're not. Digital researcher Paul Levy coined a perfect phrase to describe the phenomenon of couples being physically together but mentally elsewhere on devices: "wretched contentment."

The phone was in bed with Cynthia and her husband even on weekend nights when their son went to sleep, a space in the schedule that might have been filled with sex. Cynthia has an objective, clear eye on the situation: "I'm in bed, going through my apps and posts, and I'm so engrossed in what I'm reading and the pictures that I kind of forget that I'm in a marriage. The time when the child goes to sleep, that should really be time to communicate with my husband, maybe even get intimate. I can sense from his body language that he knows I'm being dismissive. He's trying to talk to me, or more, but I'm distracted. It's like I'm in a world of my own when I'm online," she says.

Michele Weiner-Davis has been a sex therapist for over thirty years. From her office in Boulder, Colorado, she runs weekend boot camps for couples on the edge of divorce. In 2003 she published a best-selling, Oprah-approved book called *The Sex-Starved Marriage*. At the time, on media rounds, she was asked over and over to identify the number-one cause of breakdowns in relationships. She recalls now that she would answer: "Couples aren't prioritizing their time together. They don't carve out sacred time." She often recommended the weekend as the time of the week when busy couples could commit to a sexual encounter; a restorative, unbreakable date for intimacy.

Over a decade later, she observes that time has become ever scarcer for her clients. "What I see with couples nowadays is they aren't necessarily working Monday through Friday, nine to five. Technology makes it so much easier to take your office home, so either they're working or they're exhausted. Either way, couples are not taking advantage of the weekend."

Weiner-Davis describes her clients as leading "separate but parallel lives"—shepherding the kids; trading off errands and activities; half-attentive. Even if they're not working, they're anticipating working, glancing at devices to see if they're needed and never fully present in the relationship. In that dynamic, little resentments start to pile up and anger moves in. The mundane usurps the romantic, weakening the connection that brought you to your partner in the first place. Weiner-Davis advises couples to approach the weekend with the same stark efficiency with which we approach work. Don't feel you have time for sex? Enter it in your iCal. Sex with your partner needs to be a non-negotiable date, as immovable from your schedule as a conference call.

If the price of intimacy is vigilance, then it goes beyond booking sex to making time to simply be together. Therapist Mira Kirshenbaum argues in her book *The Weekend Marriage* that relationships suffer a version of Murphy's Law: "The less time you have together, the more things go wrong in your relationship." My neighbors Lindsay and Corey have two careers and three kids, but they run together. Several times, I've seen them out on the streets on a Saturday, side by side, talking and running in their shiny gear, and I like to shout, "Where are the kids, you bad parents?" It's a joke, but I have wanted to know how they do it. When our kids were little, a public appearance by Julian and me as a solo couple was as rare as a J. D. Salinger sighting. Lindsay explained that they made a decision as soon as the eldest was old enough to plunk them in front on a movie and take off, phones in pocket, and refuse to feel guilty about it. With that kind of admirably ruthless attention to their own relationship, I don't think it's a coincidence that Lindsay and Corey are a little bit PDA-ish. Their closeness is palpable.

Other couples I know trade off child care for nights out. I like this solution: leaning on other people to protect together time. Sustaining the relationship becomes a shared value, a community endeavor.

I point out Kirshenbaum's Law when I lobby Julian for a "date night," a cringe-y, retro phrase I am now choosing to embrace. During a period where we haven't seen much of each other on weeknights—he was marking; I was on deadline—we book a sitter and a night out for a Friday when we're in the clear, work-wise. We see a play, an Irish ghost story, and go out for dinner afterward, following the rule that we won't talk about kids, home, or work. With Weiner-Davis's boundaries in place, we're forced to engage on a different level. We unpack the play, and I listen to his stories about Ireland, a country I've never visited. I like him, which, a decade-plus on, is much harder than love. Being reminded why you chose that person—the poetic insight; the sharp eye—requires time and attention.

But our next date night might take a different shape. It seems that it may be better to block some time on the weekend to take a beer-making class together rather than return, yet again, to your favorite restaurant. Researchers at the State University of New York discovered that when couples participated in a new activity together, they rated their marital satisfaction level higher than couples who participated in something familiar. When trying something new, our brains release dopamine and norepinephrine, igniting the brain's reward system. The same chemicals rush those circuits during the passionate courtship phase of a relationship. Undertaking a novel activity together might just help recreate those initial feelings of falling in love.

The worst thing you can do is use the weekend to get to

the bottom of your relationship issues, Weiner-Davis says. "No fighting when you have rare face-to-face time," she advises her time-crunched clients. Instead, schedule weekly meetings about domestic issues or fight over email or in notes. "Sometimes waiting to express your needs can give you the distance you need to avoid a fight," she says.

I found great relief in this advice nugget. I've felt the pressure to use that rare time with my husband—perhaps that surprise moment on a Saturday where we find each other at home, in a quiet pocket, kids delightfully elsewhere—to unpack the relationship. *Ah-hah!* I'll think. *Time to "work through" the issues of the week!* I now recognize this push toward productivity as part of a deeply held anxiety about leisure: free time must be utilitarian. An open hour on a Saturday is an hour to improve and better the marriage, in between that dry-cleaning run and yoga class. In a culture that values work so highly, we have a remarkable ability to turn even our relationships into labor.

Better, say the experts, to use that hour for sex. But what if, you know, you're just too tired, or too busy, or not in the mood on the weekend? Weiner-Davis has no time for you (okay, me). She has a fake-it-till-you-make-it attitude and lobs a phrase from Nike at her clients: "Just do it."

"I think feelings often misguide us," she says. "I teach people to be more pragmatic. If what you're saying is you want more passion, or a better connection, or more friendship from your partner, then you have to behave in ways that are consistent with that, even if you don't feel like it. Your actions have to be aligned with your values."

This sounds a little like an edict from on high, which, in fact, it is. The Talmud asserts that it's God's will that husband and wife have sex on Friday night (another very cool mitzvah: the woman must climax first). Thinking of sex as a divine commitment that must be honored at least once a week, even if you're not particularly religious (the commitment could be to the marriage, not God), is kind of a perfect rescue strategy for an undersexed relationship. There's no worry about mismatched desire levels or imposing your needs on a less-than-enthused partner. Jess, a Toronto magazine editor, and her husband, an academic, did this when their kids were small. In an email, she wrote about their pact to always have sex on Friday nights: "If you don't deliberately make time out for each other you can get caught up in the minutiae of daily life and ignore what's important. I think we learned from that experience that if you are always exhausted, as you always are when you have young kids, you have to conspire with your partner to identify time for sex. Fridays happened to be the night we absolutely weren't going to work or binge-watch TV so it became the perfect night to fuck—now we don't have a weekly date but we retained from that period the idea of planned sex rather than just waiting around for spontaneous rom com sex." If every Friday night is sex night, the weekend then begins with an act that fortifies connection.

When Cynthia was lying in bed one night with her phone, her husband turned to her with two questions: "What about me? What about family time?" It wasn't a full-on blowout, but it was a wake-up call. This wasn't the relationship she wanted, the life she wanted.

She put the phone in a drawer. Now, she schedules specific times to check her email. On weekends, she puts her phone in her bag and tries not to take it out if she's with her family. She keeps devices out of the bedroom, and her sex life has improved vastly. But it's an ongoing battle, she admits, to keep that sacred time. There are so many forces keeping us from the relationships that matter. Protecting our weekends for intimacy is the first line of attack against them.

CHAPTER 4

BINGE, BUY, BRUNCH, BASKETBALL: BETTER RECREATION

I MENTIONED TO a friend in New York that in parts of Sweden, people take a three-day weekend. My friend is that breed of New York–successful that works ten-hour days running her own company while raising two kids and somehow always has her hair parted to the side in a perfect flip slightly elevated above her head, like the extended wing of a bird (this actually looks amazing and cannot be reproduced by mortals so don't bother trying). She raised an eyebrow: "But what would you do with all that time?"

I was taken aback at first, but then I struggled to answer. "Read?" I suggested lamely. "Netflix?" It isn't a crazy question: If we are able to protect those forty-eight hours on the weekend (or a few of them), then what? How do we pass the time outside work in a way that's not merely diverting, but fulfilling? To find oneself wrestling with this question suggests that the ability to enjoy recreation is a muscle that softens from lack of use. We don't seem to be very good at leisure. According to the Bureau of Labor Statistics, the most common waking activity on the weekend is watching TV. We spend more money on weekends, too. Watching and shopping—is that all there is?

So I decide to call Sweden. I know that everyone is sick of hearing how good they have it in Scandinavia. Swedes are some of the happiest people in the world and university is free and the sun shines for twenty hours a day in summer—blah, blah, blah. Every time I'm trying on boots while my daughter whines, I think about the fact that some shoe shops in Sweden provide daycare. Sure, there's a downside—the high taxes, a fishy diet, the widening gap between rich and poor—but Sweden is also moving forward on this three-day weekend. How does that work exactly?

I call a woman named Ametist who works a four-day week at an organization that provides support services for people with mental illness in downtown Stockholm. I ask her what she does with her three-day weekend. She seems to find the question strange. "Well, what do you mean—*do*?" she asks in her excellent English. Break it down for me, sister, I urge. So she walks me through the weekend like she is explaining the days of the week to a toddler. "We have a summer house—lots of people have summer houses in Sweden." (This is both jealousy-inducing and impressive.) "I can take the train there in the afternoon on

Thursday. In the winter, if I don't go to the house, I take a ceramics class for three or four hours on Friday. On Saturday or Sunday I might go to a coffee shop with a friend or for a long walk. I try not to cook or clean on the weekend because that's not fun. I will do the washing if it means just pushing a button." There is a downside, she admits, to the four-day workweek and it's simple: she makes less money than she used to. But she makes enough for what sounds like a pretty good weekend. The money part is the trade-off. She chooses time instead.

The Ancient Greeks viewed leisure as holding the highest value in life, and work the lowest. The word "leisure" comes from the Latin *licere*, "to be allowed." This idea of permission is ingrained in free time: it's the allotted space in which to go forth in pursuit of the spiritual, the intellectual, even enlightenment. Of course, leisure was not available at all social levels in Ancient Greece; the upper classes sat around contemplating the universe on the backs of slaves (where, presumably, they balanced their grapes). For those of us somewhere between slave and CEO—people with jobs—a good weekend is one that breaks the continuum of a week shaped by labor. As a 1926 editorial in *The Nation* put it, free time is the definitive split from the money-making drive of the workweek: "Leisure means free time—when activities are not determined by economic compulsion, but by native impulse. Recreation means free play, what we do from desire, not necessity."

But for people like my New York friend, who work all the time and take pleasure in work, it can be tough to separate desire from necessity. Our professional selves so inform our private selves that it's hard to switch off the burner beneath the former and spark up the latter; the workplay fire is a uniform burn.

SPECTATORITIS

British philosopher Bertrand Russell believed that too much work acted as a veil over pleasure, making it hard to recognize, obscuring its shape. Writing after World War I, he noted that British workers had logged shorter days during the war in an effort to stabilize the economy. Russell thought he'd witnessed the new normal, and that short workdays would be a postwar holdover; it was a new age, and the way people worked and lived would never be the same.

Yet once the war ended, to his dismay, full workdays and workweeks became the norm again. Writing two years after John Maynard Keynes, Russell, too, wondered if workers had lost the ability to be at leisure:

> It will be said that, while a little leisure is pleasant, men would not know how to fill their days if they had only four hours of work out of the twenty-four. In so far as this is true in the modern world, it is a condemnation of our civilization; it would not have been true at any earlier period. There was formerly a capacity for light-heartedness and play which has been to some extent inhibited by the cult of efficiency. . . . The pleasures of urban populations have become mainly passive: seeing cinemas, watching football matches, listening to the radio, and so on. This results from the fact that their active

energies are fully taken up with work; if they had more lei-
sure, they would again enjoy pleasures in which they took an
active part.

In a world of total work, there's no energy for anything but
the most inert, docile weekend pastimes, Russell suggests. He
was, in essence, predicting Netflix.

University of Calgary sociologist Robert Stebbins defines
two main categories of leisure: serious and casual. Serious leisure
pursuits provide deeper fulfillment, and, to bring back a 1970s
word, "self-actualization." These pursuits require the regular
refinement of skills learned in earnest: your barbershop quartet
singing, your stamp collecting. Serious leisure is that which is
returned to again and again with the tenor of the professional,
even if the pursuit is amateur. In contrast, casual leisure is
short-lived, immediately gratifying, and often passive—Russell's
nightmare. Watching sports events and binge-watching TV fit
under this umbrella; even the average megachurch, with bite-
sized chunks of scripture distributed across stadium seating, is
less church service than entertainment spectacle.

Russell's suspicion of casual leisure is something we instinctively feel; it's the rumble that caused our parents to say "Turn
off the TV and get outside!" which has been updated to "One
device at a time!" But casual leisure has dominated our free time
in the past hundred years. In the first third of the twentieth
century, stadiums were built and newspapers began to devote
space to following teams and stats in sports pages. The phrase
"spectatoritis" came to the same pages soon after. In a book

from 1915 called *Christianity and Amusements*, the author sniffed about the phenomenon, "Here and there appears the aggravated case, completely infected, the fan who is nothing but a fan—a flabby creature, symbolic of the multitude, a parasite upon the play of others, the least athletic of all men, never playing himself at anything, a spectacle hunter, not a sportsman."

But the lines between passive and active entertainment aren't always so neatly drawn, and the pearl-clutching over the flabby super-fan can sometimes elide the major upside of the spectacle: the shared experience. As cities boomed in the twentieth century, a new entertainment culture arose, uniting people across class and ethnic boundaries. In the social history *Going Out: The Rise and Fall of Public Amusements*, American historian David Nasaw describes a sudden proliferation of entertainment venues like movie palaces, amusement parks, and inner-city baseball parks. Glamorous public spaces were lit up at night by this new invention "electricity," luring people out of their houses like moths. These weekend nights did spark spectatoritis, yes, but also a new kind of socializing. In those public spaces, people who would never have otherwise met did so, conversing and interacting in the public square. "Unlike the landsmen's lodges and union halls, the saloons and church social, and the front stoops, parlors and kitchens, the new entertainment centers held more strangers than friends," writes Nasaw. These gatherings occurred in part because incomes rose for urban workers at the turn of the nineteenth century, and free time increased. Vacations and Saturday holidays were a dividing line between old, Victorian ways of being and the new: the peasant class worked; new-model urban Americans went out at night and burned it up on weekends—together.

IF WEEKEND FUN is often a combo of spectatoritis and more social, active leisure, there's no better example than the tailgate party. The first tailgaters gathered in Virginia in 1861, during the Civil War. At the Battle of Bull Run, hundreds of people, including local citizens, government officials, and press, set up picnics with food and wine, then kicked back to the enjoy the spectacle (Union blue retreated that day, but eventually triumphed). It was a Sunday.Modern tailgate parties, also a weekend phenomenon, are gatherings of football fans in parking lots near the stadium, almost always cannon-free. "It's highly social," says Amanda, who lives in Dallas, Texas. "It's all about loving the team together."

Amanda's Twitter description is "I bleed orange," the color of the Longhorns, the football team of her school, the University of Texas at Austin. She grew up on football. Friday nights at her high school in San Marcos, near Austin, followed a schedule: a pep rally at school, then home to dinner, then back to school for the football game. "I remember one time being in a restaurant on a Friday night as a teenager, looking around, and thinking: 'Is it possible there are people in this restaurant who are *not* going to a football game?' The thought of it blew my mind."

A couple of decades later, Amanda, her husband, and their two preteen sons spend almost every weekend of the football season driving three and a half hours from Houston to Austin to watch games at her alma mater. A few hours before the game, they often tailgate, like nearly 70 million Americans each year. By the stadium, fans set up tarps and tables, and TVs attached to generators broadcast other games. Bigger parties are big money, with beer sponsors or caterers. There are actual, non-football related activities, too: Amanda's kids like the "cornhole games" (this very troubling phrase means "bean bag toss"). Someone usually brings a football, and music blares. At the more elaborate tailgates, fans create living areas, with dens and bedrooms in the zones around their cars. John Sherry, a marketing professor and cultural anthropologist at the University of Notre Dame, calls this phenomenon of recreating warm, domestic spaces in public "vestavals," in honor of Vesta, the Roman goddess of hearth and home.

"It's camaraderie," Amanda says. "We talk about the team, but we talk about other things, too. We talk about our lives." Tailgating is a chance to connect with friends and family, and for Amanda, football is emotional and nostalgic, hearkening back to her childhood memories of being with her father at games.

Of course, the negative interpretation of tailgating—and other kinds of sports fandom—is that it's just whipping up the bloodlust before the gladiators go out to concuss each other. Sherry rejects this perception of tailgates as beer-fueled high-five-fests. He sees the parties as akin to harvest festivals, when the end of the summer's bounty is celebrated before winter halts the communal gathering. Tailgating also infuses a passive experience—football watching—with something collective and alive, says Sherry: the fans themselves actually give the teams their meaning, co-creating the brand. Mostly, it's about community building. "People have tailgated in the same place for years, they have tailgated through generations, they have encountered strangers who have passed through and adopted them to their families and became fast friends," he's said in *Wired* magazine.

For Amanda, football is a homecoming. Her mother still lives in Austin, and she and her family will try, whenever possible, to make a weekend out of it. "They're the only weekends I've known," she says.

THE BINGE WEEKEND

That collective experience of entertainment finds a twisted new shape in the age of "the binge weekend." The new mode of entertainment delivery is the marathon, and marathons are a solo endeavor. The video game industry has eclipsed film and music in profitability, a factoid that conjures an image of basement-dwelling mushroom men (mostly men, we imagine) missing out on light and life while shooting at each other over headsets. Yet gaming isn't always a passive form of entertainment. Partners of diehard gamers may complain of being turned into gaming widows or widowers, but interestingly, research shows that if both people in a couple play, then gaming may actually be good for a marriage—a fortifying shared pastime, say digital researchers. Most games are interactive, and played with other people, even if the connection is (literally) remote. What's different about video games—and apps, and the Internet—from the amusements of a century ago is their relationship to time: video games don't have to end. A book has a final chapter; a baseball game, a final inning. With video games, it's entirely possible that you'll never reach the credits. Because of their open-ended nature, games can sneakily suck up a weekend, or a life.

Of course, a lot of this was once said about TV, the intellect-depleting "boob tube" with which, as Neil Postman warned in 1985, we are "amusing ourselves to death." I submit that binge-watching TV is even worse than the broadcast-teat we gulped at for decades. It's more passive, stealing nights and days with the sensation that no time has passed at all. If you sat in a chair in front of your TV or computer and did nothing but watch every season of *The Good Wife*, it would take three full days. All seven seasons of *The West Wing* would suck up five days of your life. The physiological effects of sitting for hours on end include sluggishness and weight gain.

It can also turn you into a bit of a jerk. I watched *Happy Valley*, an eight-part British series about a policewoman in a drug-addled Yorkshire town. For five days—including one weekend—I became mentally and physically consumed. I got snarky with my kids when they didn't go to bed early enough to allow me to get back to it. I feigned illness at a family brunch, attempting to appear casual: "I just need to lie down in a cool dark place, such as the basement, on a comfortable piece of furniture, such as the couch, across from that, what do you call it? The television, I think?" It was ugly, and then—unlike addiction—it was over, and I spent the rest of the week mourning the end of my one-way relationship with that cocky Cockney police chief.

Subjects in one research trial about binge-watching reported feeling depressed when a series ended. Where's the return on this investment of time? The friends who you were hanging with have abandoned you. On the upside, *Happy Valley* was really good. This golden age of TV makes it pretty easy to float away for six hours without consuming the brainless pabulum of older TV. An entire Saturday could vanish while I watched blocks of *Brady Bunch–Love Boat–Happy Days–Fantasy Island* back in the 1970s, binges dictated by the scheduling whims of broadcast executives.

I'll take up Bertrand Russell's mantle and say that a weekend of purely passive entertainment is a wasted weekend. Of course, once in a while, we all need to heed the call of that Blue Jays series, or the entire run of *Portlandia*. There's fleeting pleasure in being a spectator, a sugar rush that's one of life's visceral thrills and can't be denied. But too much passivity breeds absence in lives already starved for presence. An overdose of passive leisure is solipsism, lacking the human contact—bodies sharing space—that brings the benefits of true community.

Solitary pursuits can get lonely, yet our lives are more designed for a solitary experience of the world than ever before. It can feel like technology is pushing us deeper into our own aesthetic caves, where we're surrounded by our interests, listening to our own music, reading the articles recommended by our phones, and viewing the world entirely through our own singular lens. We become entrenched in our social and taste niches, our inclinations and experiences confirmed, not necessarily expanded. So binge well, is the advice of experts. Pick and choose the ones you must see, and don't ever try to keep up. FOMOTV (Fear of Missing Out on TV) is guaranteed to steal your weekend. Only watch after a good meal and not near bedtime (which may disrupt sleep). Invite human beings over and talk (!) while watching. The more social one can make passive entertainment, the better the weekend.

GETTING AND SPENDING

Bergen County, New Jersey, has malls like a beach has shells. Across the George Washington Bridge from Manhattan, in the borough of Paramus, three highways funnel shoppers into mall after strip mall after mall after strip mall: 26,000 stores, give or take. Some of these are slightly low-end discount joints, but at the Westfield Garden State Plaza the offerings are decidedly upscale, and after parking in one of 11,000 parking spaces, you can visit Apple, Gucci, and Fashionable Pets with a Shake Shack shake in your hand. Sixty thousand visitors pop by daily. New Yorkers cross the bridge for the low-tax bounty, as do Quebecers, Pennsylvanians, and most of eastern New Jersey. On Saturday, the gridlock is the stuff of nightmares, a hellacious start-stop journey through vehicular quicksand that turns a fifteen-minute drive into two hours in an unmoving car, like some Zen monk midterm. One couple complained on local news that exiting a covered car park during the post-Christmas sales took them four hours.

But on Sunday, it all shuts down. The malls are closed, and the parking lots stand empty. On the drive down mall-laden

Route 4, one empty parking lot gives way to another, and it's unnervingly post-apocalyptic, as if an evacuation order had just been issued. The moonscape emptiness is broken by the occasional teenager learning to drive, slowly turning and lurching between the stalls.

Rose, who lives in Ridgewood, New Jersey, taught both of her kids to drive in those parking lots. She's a former HR employee who now, in her fifties, works in the men's department at Lord & Taylor. Her son works at Best Buy and her daughter, who's in college, has a job in a bakery chain. Bergen County is one of the most affluent areas in New Jersey, but it also has a lot of citizens who work in retail; retail is to Bergen County what fishing is to Maine. Originally from the Bronx, Rose moved to Ridgewood in the late 1980s with her husband, who has since passed away. Ridgewood, with its cobblestoned downtown and tree-lined yards, seemed like a nice place to start a family. But on her first weekend in her new home, the New Yorker in her was horrified to learn that she had moved to the one place in the United States that still obeys "blue laws," those vestiges from the Puritans that prohibit most "trading" on the Sabbath. In Bergen County, it's almost as if, because the shopping is so outsized the other six days of the week, the counter-response on Sundays has to match. "I was like: There's a shopping mecca outside my door and no taxes on my clothes and you're telling me I can't shop on Sunday?" she remembers thinking. "But it didn't take me more than a couple of weeks to realize what a gift it is."

The Fourth Commandment says "Remember the Sabbath

day, to keep it holy," and the Puritans were a by-the-letter, punitive lot: on Sunday, anyone who showed up too soon or too late to church—or on "too showy a horse"—could be punished. As one early history of Connecticut reminds, in 1869 "no woman shall kiss her child on the Sabbath." These rules of good Sabbath-keeping were printed on blue paper, and referred to as "blue laws" (some scholars dispute this, insisting the phrase comes from an eighteenth-century meaning of the word "blue": rigidly moral, in a pejorative sense).

In 1854, New Jersey enacted strict Sunday laws: "No traveling, worldly employment or business, ordinary or servile work on lawn or water, (works of charity or necessity alone excepted) shall be done or performed on the Christian Sabbath." But by 1957, Bergen County had become home to the largest shopping mall in the country. State legislators gave individual counties the right to enact or repeal the blue laws, but small business owners, wanting to stanch the loss of customers migrating to the malls, joined with the Church (who liked a Sabbath) and residents (who hated cars) to keep stores shut on Sunday. Bergen County became the only county in New Jersey to refuse to repeal the blue laws, and as the rest of the country gradually eased up on Sunday shopping prohibitions, this one place kept ye olde laws intact. There's no other county in the United States that prohibits Sunday shopping (some municipalities make their own decisions), which means that Bergen County is a funny paradox: a man-built temple to our most materialist impulses and a vigilant, old-fashioned—almost Puritan—rejection of that same shopaholic mentality. In the borough of Paramus, the laws are even stricter. Every few years, after grumblings from newbie politicians and business people that it's time to bring this very twenty-first-century place into the twenty-first century on Sundays, too, the county holds referendums on the blue laws. These efforts are always soundly defeated.

"They'll never win. The quality of life is too good here," says Rose. Ridgewood on a Sunday is, as Rose describes it, the America of storybooks. There's a palpable quiet as the roar of cars is quelled. People walk on the streets and play baseball and soccer in the parks. The rowing team might be practicing in the river. Restaurants are open, and people line up for brunch (restaurant workers don't get the day off). Rose's son meets with other sports car enthusiasts in those empty mall parking lots. They drink coffee and show each other their cars. (That even flat gray parking lots can become mixed-use community zones speaks to our primal need to gather. I mention this and Rose points out another reason: "People make a lot of money here and most kids in Bergen County get cars when they turn sixteen.")

Every Sunday morning, Rose goes to church. "You have christenings and weddings on Sundays and you can commit to attending. There's nowhere else where I could work in retail and plan my weekends like I can here."

The lack of Sunday shopping has made her shop less, and smarter. If she needs to buy things, she makes a plan to do so on the other six days. Living in Ridgewood has also removed recreational purchasing from her leisure menu: she almost never shops for fun. Perhaps shopping loses its appeal when the place you live and work is all about shopping, the same way my friend who teaches toddlers once asked me, "If I come over on Sunday, do your children absolutely have to be there?"

Rose chimes in regularly to a Facebook page called We Support the blue laws of Bergen County, NJ. The host is Mattias, who lives in Paramus. Now in his early twenties, he has a job as a recruiter in marketing, but for six years he worked in the malls in Bergen County, at brand-name stores selling kids' clothes, women's fashion, home decor—you name it, he sold it. In retail, Mattias was incredibly grateful for Sundays off, which is the time of the week when he visits with his family, and buckles down to study. The campaign to keep Paramus free of Sunday shopping is one of his hobbies, and funnily, he often spends Sundays sending emails to civic leaders making his case against Sunday shopping. He has met with the mayor, and sent here's-how-it-is letters to the developers of a new mall. He speaks breathlessly in defense of the blue laws, pointing out that despite the Sunday closing, Bergen County has the highest annual retail sales of any zip code in the nation. Stores are open until 9:30 most nights so there's plenty of time for people who work long hours to shop during the week, too. In fact, there's little to suggest that Sunday closures have a negative economic impact. In 2015, Hungary banned Sunday shopping, and overall retail sales remained steady, with no major layoffs or closures. The economic hit that business owners had nervously predicted simply never came.It's possible that Sunday laws don't actually make people shop less, they just encourage consumers to spread out their spending over the course of a week, or cram it into Saturday.

Mattias also attends church on Sundays, but his interest in protecting Sunday isn't religiously motivated. "If you frame it in religious terms, then it becomes exclusionary and maybe illegal," he says. "And it's not just Christians that want a day off. We have Jews and Muslims who back the blue laws."

Around this point in our conversation, it emerges that Mattias is Swedish, which is very exciting to someone researching leisure. He and his family moved to Paramus in 2007, when he was sixteen years old. Clearly, this is the root of his sensible attitudes toward shopping. Alas, he bursts my bubble.

"Stockholm is very clean, but it's very boring," he says. "It gets dark by 2:00 p.m." And on Sundays? "They love to shop. There's a big new Mall of Scandinavia that's open ten to eight, even on Sundays. It's more Americanized than America." I try to take this in, and have the terrible thought that perhaps Swedes are circling the three-day weekend solely in order to *have more time to shop*. Then he adds, as if to make me feel better, "But you know, Sweden does still have five weeks of paid vacation."

What's unusual about Bergen County is that leisure isn't an issue to be hammered out in mediation; these are citizens protecting quality of life by protecting their weekends from shopping, and for now, business has been forced to go along.

"People go to the zoo. They might go skiing. But really, there's nothing to do in Bergen County on Sunday," Mattias says. "Which is what I love about it. We can all be doing nothing together. There is a real sense of a weekend."

Some weekend shopping is obligatory; for those who work Monday to Friday, the weekend is time to stock up on groceries and household necessities. But the shopping that goes down at malls isn't usually urgent (is that Urban Outfitters soy sauce bottle-print crop-T really a necessity of life?); it's recreation. Around the world, shopping has become one of the most common leisure activities. Down the street from me, in Chinatown, hordes of people climb on Friday night buses to outlet malls beyond the city for daylong excursions or weekend shopping "retreats." Around the world, tourist boards frequently promote a destination's shopping assets first, well before the delights of historical plaques and natural attractions. That shopping and culture are now regarded as qualitatively equal pastimes is evident in the rise of "museum malls," like the Cleveland Hungarian Museum, located in the Galleria at Erieview.

Spending the weekend shopping is a relatively new phenomenon, one tied to the liberation of women—and their bladders. In *Shopping for Pleasure*, Erika Rappaport, a professor in the Department of History at the University of California, Santa Barbara, charts a transformation in the way Victorian and Edwardian women lived in London. Until then, the downtown public sphere of London's West End was largely a lady-free zone of business and pleasure. Only women of the upper classes could lead a public life, moving freely between shops and streets. But they couldn't hang out too long: there were no women's washrooms, making a day of shopping a grueling affair. Those women who did go out weren't welcome in restaurants, either, so they would return home with bladders bursting and stomachs empty. One working-class mother told her daughter that shopping was impossible: "Either ladies didn't go out or ladies didn't 'go.'" In the 1870s, a campaign to bring women's lavatories to stores succeeded, and soon there were tearooms and women's clubs—places designed to keep those upper-class, wealthy women in and near the stores, rarin' to purchase. Selfridges even installed reading and writing rooms with soft lights. Shopping became a pleasurable pastime, and women, out in public at last, inched toward equal participation in society.

For better or worse, all that social progress led straight to the mall. The covered mall was the 1950s dream of a Vienna-born socialist architect named Victor Gruen. Gruen dreamed of the Greek agora in the American suburbs: a marketplace where goods and ideas would flow between local citizens. Those of us raised in the 1980s, at the height of the mall boom, didn't have quite that experience—Orange Julius flowed more freely than conversations about democracy—but the mall did shape the teen weekend. In my early teens, hours (days) could pass under the glass roof of the Pacific Centre Mall in downtown Vancouver. We traveled in groups, and it felt—this amazes me now—like freedom: free of parents and high school rules; free of weather and natural light. The mall was at once a place of total anonymity and a public catwalk. Complicated social rituals were encoded: the mall was where I learned which movies to see, which stores were cool (Le Chateau) and which ones were totally lame (next week: Le Chateau). We went for the fast food and cheap clothing and beloved records. But mostly, we went to be together, in a neutral space, because there seemed to never be anywhere where teenagers were allowed to just *be*. Even with the sticky consumerist patina, it did feel like a public square—except the plants were plastic and the air recycled. We didn't mind.

Today, covered suburban malls are a money pit for businesses, who are fleeing along with the customers. Consequently, my generation's nostalgia fuels the Internet's porny interest in photographs of vacant "dead malls." Old school retail malls have been killed by a combination of overbuilding and e-commerce, but their decline is mostly about the widening income gap. High-end shopping centers, as in Paramus, are doing pretty well, but middle-class malls are fading along with the middle class. Cheaper big boxes like Wal-Mart and Target do the job without a lot of expensive real estate. Meanwhile, teenagers are less likely to hit the mall. It's not just that kids are getting their social fix via devices, but many American malls now have a "parental escort policy" on weekends. A bunch of teens in a mall on a Friday these days are likely to get busted by a mall cop. This embarrassing proposition appears to be driving them back home.

Yet Gruen's dream isn't entirely forgotten. Some dead malls are being repurposed, their huge empty spaces turned into hospitals, churches, colleges. In Vancouver, one of the malls where I used to slink—Oakridge Centre—is being redeveloped into an entirely new city. Parks will be surrounded by residential high-rises and community-friendly sites like a Tai Chi pavilion, and a water park for kids. Shopping is still a draw, but these reanimated, mixed-used spaces are designed to sustain actual communities even when the shops are closed.

People want more than just shopping from their malls. In place of the Muzak-filled behemoth mall, consumers are gravitating toward the one type of mall that's in demand by retailers and being built by developers: the "lifestyle center." Anchored by a specialty store (Barnes & Noble, Pottery Barn) rather than a department store, these smaller malls are designed as a kind of simulacrum of the urban downtown that their ilk once supplanted. Walkways are vast and maybe cobblestoned. Some feature farmers' markets and food trucks; the vibe is nostalgic Main Street. They're malls that call forth the yearning for a pre-mall way of life. Maybe these malls soften the sharp consumerist edges of the old malls, or maybe they're just same old, same old dressed up in hipster clothing. But their success is evidence that people want to spend their time—and especially their weekends—in places that aren't hermetically sealed and shot through with nosebleed-inducing chemical cinnamon smells. "By affording opportunities for social life and recreation in a protected pedestrian environment, by incorporating civic and educational facilities, shopping centers can fill an existing void," wrote Gruen a half century ago. "They can provide the needed place and opportunity for participation in modern community life that the ancient Greek Agora, the Medieval Market Place and our own Town Squares provided in the past." And perhaps in the future.

WHY DO WE SPEND the weekends shopping at all? Is it entertainment? Is it reward? Is it to stave off our fear of death?

It's a given that shopping is ingrained in our culture: an unavoidable, normalized experience. We live in times of high consumption, with record debt levels and nonstop advertising

migrating from billboards to intimate spaces like our text messages and Facebook posts. Juliet Schor argues that today's workers are trapped in a "work and spend cycle" that's both a product
of our long hours and a perpetuator of them. Work-and-spend
is the idea that if you work long hours, you make more money.
If you make more, you spend more. The more you spend, the
longer you have to work to support the consumerist lifestyle.
Long hours mean less time for leisure and the pursuit of what
matters: family, community, pleasure. But there's no finish line.
No amount of spending will make us feel complete, says Schor,
because we are forever glancing at our neighbors' bounty,
choking on inadequacy: "What if our desires keep pace with
our incomes, so that getting richer doesn't make us more satisfied? Or what if satisfaction depends not on absolute levels of
consumption, but on one's level relative to others (such as the
Joneses)? Then no matter how much you possess you won't feel
well off if Jones next door possesses more."

This is an old idea: the term "conspicuous consumption" was
coined in 1899 by economist and sociologist Thorstein Veblen
to describe consuming in order to accrue status. To reclaim our
weekends for something besides shopping would mean reclaiming our time—but we don't want time; we want stuff. The leisure class of earlier modernity was truly at leisure, whiling away
the days in ennui and crustless sandwiches brought to them on
trays, like Daisy in *The Great Gatsby*. To do nothing was a sign
of status. Now doing nothing is a sign of underemployment.
Shopping feeds a social mania for movement: constant acquisition, constant motion, keeping up not just with the Joneses

but with the whole, exploding global economy—David Levy's "more, better, faster." There's some evidence that shopping—or even the anticipation of shopping—activates the brain chemical dopamine, firing up our pleasure centers.

Even if you're completely cool with living in a material world, there's a price for that: shopping takes time, and time is limited. Almost two thousand years ago, the Greek philosopher Seneca wrote a perfect little treatise called "On the Shortness of Life: Life Is Long if You Know How to Use It." Really, it's the only self-help book anyone needs, filled with chastising, motivating wisdom that feels utterly contemporary. It's a reminder, too, that the struggle for leisure is an old one, as when he schools the citizens on the time-suck that is the work-spend model: "It is inevitable that life will be not just very short but very miserable for those who acquire by great toil what they must keep by greater toil. They achieve what they want laboriously; they possess what they have achieved anxiously; and meanwhile they take no account of time that will never more return. New preoccupations take the place of the old, hope excites more hope and ambition more ambition. They do not look for an end to their misery, but simply change the reason for it."

Seneca was right: shopping doesn't actually make us feel great. Materialism and loneliness are caught in a self-propagating cycle. The "loneliness loop" is the name for the idea that materialism makes people lonely, and loneliness makes people shop, despite knowing that human contact is actually a better remedy for isolation than more stuff. But a study out of the University of Chicago following 2,500 consumers over six years found the kinds of people who value material possessions are not all the same. Two types of shoppers are prone to the loneliness loop: those who are "position defined"—the Joneses-watchers—and those who shop as a form of therapy, to assuage unhappiness. Valuing material possessions as a measure of success and as medicine for unhappiness was associated with increases in loneliness over time; both types of materialists felt lonely from shopping. But interestingly, a third category of materialist doesn't struggle with loneliness in the same way. He shops for fun and pleasure, and because he likes nice things. Shopping for "material mirth" can actually decrease loneliness, researchers concluded.

This feels right to me. Not all shopping is pernicious or stupid, turning us into pawns in the capitalist game. There can be beauty in the things we acquire, and the act of acquiring them. We respond to the texture and sensation of the object; we want to be sensually moved. Reporter Virginia Postrel documented how the women of Kabul, once liberated from the Taliban, quickly began expressing themselves through material possessions, yearning for the comfort of decoration, even beauty. They painted their nails and bought colorful burkas, seeking the finer embroidery and fabrics they'd been so long denied.

Paul Bloom, a professor of psychology and cognitive science at Yale, writes that there's something beyond the sensual in our seeking of pleasure through acquisition of material objects: we want to understand the story of the thing. If a Rolex costs $100,000 and is virtually identical to a watch that costs $1,500, some people will still buy the more expensive one even though there's no way it could signal any kind of superiority; even the Joneses wouldn't know. It's the "hidden nature" of the object that provides pleasure; provenance speaks deeply—if silently— of craftsmanship, history. Bloom, an evolutionary theorist, believes we honed this skill of essentialism a while back when our ancestors' survival depended on the ability to tell the difference between yummy plants and animals and the ones that could kill them.

Some people shop with this kind of attention, and love, as if the wrong choice could kill them. I have a friend, M., who is a careful and meticulous shopper. She can work a vintage store with such care that, frankly, it's a bit exhausting. I remember one Saturday years ago, moving through a Chelsea flea market with her as she sifted through piles of clothes and stopped every few feet to contemplate. Once she picked up a brooch, stared at it silently, then put her fist around it, closing her eyes like she was receiving a message from the brooch's home planet. Naturally, she works in fashion.

But there's something to be learned here, and not just about my impatience. Shopping isn't necessarily evil. It's a problem when consumption becomes the driving force of your life— when you work to shop, losing your precious, fleeting time to the purchase, thinking that will fill the hole. Shopping carefully and thoughtfully, for pleasure, not self-worth, isn't the worst weekend pastime. The worst weekend pastime is brunch.

◇◇◇◇

BEST BRUNCH? NO BRUNCH

Around the corner from my house is a small restaurant with less than a dozen tables called Saving Grace. Each table is usually graced with a single flower in a small vase, and the china is sweetly mismatched. They make very nice Rajasthani eggs and French toast with caramelized bananas, and I once saw Michael Cera having brunch with Aubrey Plaza there. Mostly, Saving Grace is known for the lineups, which stretch out the door and onto the sidewalk and can last, on a Sunday morning, about two hours. This is, needless to say, ridiculous. Two hours of a Sunday waiting in line, hoping to imbibe your iced Vietnamese coffee in the presence of Michael Cera, is two hours you will never get back.

But brunch is very much about our relationship to time. It's a declaration of leisure, an act associated almost entirely with the weekend. No one meets for a business brunch. It's a stake planted in leisure time, and the stake makes a hole and drains it, expensively.

Brunch is a British invention, and the word first appeared in an 1895 *Hunter's Weekly* article called "Brunch: A Plea": "Brunch is cheerful, sociable and inciting," wrote the article's author, Guy Beringer. "It is talk-compelling. It puts you in a good temper, it makes you satisfied with yourself and your fellow beings, it sweeps away the worries and cobwebs of the week."

It is one of the most robust secular rituals in cities, and a point of human contact that really can be "talk-compelling." It existed prior to the boom of the 2000s, and other cultures have variations: there's the Chinese dim sum and the French *le grand petit déjeuner*. The present-day urban brunch is a group outing organized over endless chains of texts, marked by lineups and the Instagramming of waffles and coulis. The specifics get reinvented as we age through the hungover twenties into the young parenthood of our thirties (it's the one meal out where kids can be disruptive without judgment).

It can feel, in other words, like community and connection—those things we need to carefully cultivate on our weekends—yet writer Shawn Micallef, in his book *The Trouble with Brunch*, calls out the meal as an act of conspicuous consumption and an epic time-waster. Micallef's little book is actually about class; fourteen-dollar eggs, he contends, are a serious signifier of disposable income. Micallef notes that the pricey food is usually just the restaurant's leftovers from the week before, buried under rich sauces. The queues like the one I witness every Sunday around the corner present a Hobbesian dynamic of careless, gluttonous diners ignoring the hungry outsiders pressing their faces against the glass. "Empathy," Micallef writes, "does not exist at brunch."

The brunch backlash is almost as widespread as the brunch invite. In 2012, New York's *Daily News* declared: "Brunch is America sticking a maple-syrup slathered finger up at the concerns of the real world." In 2014, Julian Casablancas, the lead singer of The Strokes, explained in an interview in *GQ* magazine why he moved away from New York City: "I don't know how many, like, white people having brunch I can deal with on a Saturday afternoon." This notion that brunch is a fatuous weekend wank-off for the privileged hipster set inspired yet another rash of articles with headlines like "Brunch Is for Jerks."

Micallef still eats brunch, he admits (though, not surprisingly, he's not invited very often). In his twenties, he
moved to Toronto from his hometown of Windsor, Ontario,
the working-class city across the lake from Detroit. Brunch
had been a special occasion growing up, an event reserved
for Mother's Day at a banquet hall or a golf club. In Toronto,
among a downtown stratum of educated knowledge workers—
Micallef's peers—he was dragged to brunch week after week,
without deriving much pleasure. Brunch in a big city is often
crowded, and digestively as well as acoustically abrasive. The
aesthetic sameness from one brunch restaurant to the next is
striking, with minor variances: the achingly "authentic" farm
tables and Feist music; the white walls and vintage *objets* of a
simpler time. We've had hipster brunch in many cities, and in
Detroit, London, and Toronto, the rusty milk tin has appeared
as a decor focal point. Why does this exercise in such joyless
conformity endure?

In a library café, I sit with Micallef—who has the dark-
rimmed glasses and fedora of the very specimens he examines—
and ask him how we manage to find time for two-hour drunken
brunches when everyone is so busy and overworked (make that
four hours, with lineup and windbag server making for add-on
time). "I wonder if brunch is a kind of conspicuous leisure
that's a really defiant acting out against that busy-ness. We're
declaring: work is off limits now. It's like the bailing out of a
leaking boat," he says. "They're showing everyone that nine-to-
five, twenty-four-hour busy-ness has not totally consumed their
experience." In this take, brunch is kind of poignant: a sincere

attempt to stake out leisure on the weekend, and pleasure. The problem is, it's often not that pleasurable.

Micallef came to read brunch as a class marker, a way for creative-class people to demonstrate their success, even if that success is spurious. Many creative-class workers are hopping from contract to contract and working long hours with no stability; their footing on the ladder of upward mobility is precarious at best. While they may have creative agency in their lives, they don't have financial agency. Brunch requires both money and time, and many brunchers actually have little of either, which makes brunch something of an illusion—play-acting at middle-class stability. "It's a grand performance of leisure that is not, in itself, all that leisurely," Micallef writes.

But it does provide social cohesion at a time when community is fractured, and so many people feel isolated. At its best, brunch is human, non-digital contact (except for the Instagram part). Especially in cities, where we often don't live near family, brunch is a time for *chosen* family, and so it takes place on Sunday, traditionally the day for gathering with one's tribe. The idea of holding tight to the non-biological family that understands you better than your biological one was codified on *Sex and the City*, the show whose cornerstones are brunch and cupcakes—yummy interactions with a slightly bitter aftertaste.

COMING TOGETHER around food on a weekend is a legitimate leisure pursuit that doesn't have to mean a costly, gut-busting brunch. Anh-Thu, an attorney who lives in Park Slope, has spent three mornings in the kitchens of immigrant women, learning how to cook Uzbek, Lebanese, and Japanese food.

The League of Kitchens offers cooking classes in the homes of New York immigrant women. Its founder, Lisa Gross, grew up surrounded by delicious food on both sides, with a Hungarian father of Jewish descent and a Korean mother. Her Korean grandmother lived with her family, and the smells and tastes of Korean food permeated her childhood, but she never learned to cook it. When she grew up, and yearned for those tastes, her grandmother had already died. She didn't want to learn from cookbooks, but from real women, as if at the side of her grandmother. The League of Kitchens sprang from that yearning.

Gross found New York women who were talented cooks willing to let foodies and tourists into their homes for a day of cooking and teaching. The League of Kitchens now facilitates courses in Trinidadian, Indian, Afghani cooking and more, paying the home cooks a decent wage of $25 an hour (and reimbursement for supplies). "A lot of these women are in their fifties and sixties and they have expertise, but might not have a place in our society where they can be respected for what they know," she says. Most of the classes are five and a half hours, which is a major outlay of time, especially for work-addicted New Yorkers. "I guess you could say that New Yorkers are especially busy and overscheduled but also especially interested in who lives in their city," says Gross. She suggests that, in a way, the lengthy immersion each class requires gives participants the sensation of more time, not less. "This kind of experience immediately creates the 'time out of time' experience you have when you're traveling, when you allow yourself to meet people you wouldn't normally meet. You're in someone's home, so it's intimate. It has that magical feeling."

To learn Uzbek cooking, Anh-Thu took the subway to Flatbush, an area of the city she'd never visited, and trekked up to the apartment of Damira, a former doctor from Samarkand, an ancient city on the Silk Road. Anh-Thu and the five other participants chopped vegetables and took instruction, but mostly they tasted and watched, learning the history of the region as well as the food, which is a kind of Turkish and Central Asian mash-up, with dumplings and halva. At the end of the session, they sat down with Damira's family, talking politics and history. "It was like a graduate seminar," she says.

Anh-Thu's parents came from Vietnam as refugees, and she's acutely aware of how segregated immigrants can become in a big city. For her, entering a stranger's home—the invitation to have a dialogue between citizens of the same city who may never otherwise meet—feels as significant as the food. "I always had a lot of my cultural identification tied up with food and storytelling around the dinner table. In most cultures, cooking is the opportunity for individuals of multi-generations to bond," she says. "To be in this context, invited into someone's home, invited in to talk about history and culture and politics—it's really incredible. It's not just going out to brunch in a public place. It's the privacy, the exchange that makes it such a unique experience."

To me, this feels like the opposite of brunch: the collapsing of difference, rather than the highlighting of it. Of course, I don't have The League of Kitchens in my city, and you probably don't either. But no matter where you live, there's inspiration in the endeavor. You could cook with neighbors or friends; hook up with a local organization that welcomes newcomers.

What The League of Kitchens reminds us is that the best weekends contain multitudes—new experiences; new people; activities that place a new eye on the place where you live. This particular cooking class requires presence, and empathy; the understanding of another person's experience of the world. Plus—food!

Once in a while, brunch might give you all that good stuff. But probably, next time you're tempted to spend another Sunday lining up, and the hours following it lulled into a food coma during the only free time you have during the week, it might be good to think of Annie Dillard's words in *The Writing Life*: "How we spend our days is, of course, how we spend our lives." How you spend your breakfast is how you spend your weekend.

HOBBIES VS. JOBBIES

A few years ago, my family and I lived at an international school in a cliffside Italian village overlooking the Adriatic. My husband was teaching, and I was writing. I was also in charge of ushering our two shell-shocked kids to and from their village schools, trying to put a positive spin on the fact that they spoke zero Italian as I backed away from the gate: "They will give you *mozzarella di bufala* at lunch! *Ciao!*"

Faculty at Julian's school came from around the world—a mini-UN of teachers. Right away, I noticed something different about them. When I made get-to-know-you small talk, they didn't immediately turn to their professional lives; there was no CV rundown in response to the question "What do you do?" Instead, they talked about what they actually *did*, as in, during the time they weren't working. It turned out that the Scottish science teacher also competed in decathlons, and the Dutch economics prof was always appearing in shiny bicycling clothes and helmet, heading off to the mountains. By Friday at 5:00 p.m., other residents of our village were card sharks, sketchers, gardeners, and hikers. Consequently, I was asked more than once, in a range of fetching European accents, "So, what is your hobby?" Good question, and one I had literally never been asked in Toronto. What had I been doing all these years? Ingesting social media and occasionally hitting museums were not sustained passions; they were fleeting diversions. Did the odd yoga class count? How about trading sassy pop culture barbs over wine with friends? Good times, but also not a hobby.

A hobby is an interest practiced for pleasure, rather than reward, and in a work-centric culture, it's no surprise that the concept has faded from the vernacular. The Puritans warned of the "descent into idleness," and Victorian-era women's magazines instructed women that crafting and musical pursuits must be "useful." We may not say it out loud, but the idea of just following pleasure week after week, fervently, feels a little . . . lazy. Are we any different from those prissy Puritans?

Perhaps not coincidentally, the old-fashioned hobbies of the crafting and gathering type—model railroad making; mineral collecting—appear to be in decline. One British paper reports a survey showing that one in four Brits describes "watching TV" as his or her favorite hobby; Americans spend thirty-three hours per week doing the same. The British survey showed that practicing a musical instrument was a pastime for only 4 percent, while fishing was enjoyed by only 2 percent. Local papers periodically revisit the mournful feature that reads like an obituary when yet another beloved hobby store closes down. Of course, fetishists who can't afford bricks and mortar set up online, and some niche hobbies thrive on the Internet (at Bagophily.com, one can commune with other collectors of airline barf bags). But our nostalgia for the craft store is not just for homeless model ship kits, but also for the free time they once inhabited. RIP, weekends. It's no coincidence that hobbies boomed in popularity in the United States in the 1930s when the eight-hour workday was finally legislated, and more people than ever before had weekends off.

Hobbies exist in a gray area of our free time; they're supposed to be the opposite of work, but they can be laborious. Steven M. Gelber, a history professor at Santa Clara University, has written that hobbies "take work, turn it into leisure; take leisure, turn it into work." By definition, hobbies are freely chosen, but Gelber argues that many of them are repetitive and goal-oriented, imitations of work that we invite into our home (thus reinforcing capitalist values and keeping us cheerful cogs in the machine, he notes). Hobbies can also feel inherently conservative, cementing gender roles. Gelber writes how 1950s women were encouraged to sew and make music, while men were supposed to flex their DIY muscles in the garage with very big tools, or exercise their man-science brains with model kits.

But even if some hobbies follow the contours of work, there's one significant, liberating difference: nobody cares how good you are at your hobby but you. In amped-up, high-stakes, economically anxious times, hobbies are a deliciously low-stakes pursuit. Yes, there may be spectatorship and competitiveness within the insular world of a particular hobby (in Utah a few years ago, a Dungeons & Dragons hobbyist, displeased with his friend's behavior as Dungeon Master, snuck into the Master's house and beat him with a hammer). But most hobbies are personal refuges, a private space in the week where we can explore mastery for its own sake. Collecting every inverted stamp ever is surely some urge to make order out of the chaos of life. Cataloguing and counting are comforting acts.

My husband's parents have become bird-watchers in their later years. At first, I admit, I didn't totally get it. Bird-watching is a type of collecting, really, with its checklists and insider lingo. It's also one of the fastest-growing hobbies in North America. They wear funny hats and keep binoculars with them at all times; it is, like so many hobbies, supremely uncool. But the pleasure bird-watching brings my in-laws is palpable. It transforms their holidays, shaping their weekends and changing the meaning of the landscape that they're in. It's also something that bonds them as a couple. When I picture them, I see them side by side on the edge of a road, necks craned, binoculars tilted to the heavens. My father-in-law, Brian, describes it as "a pair of matched minds pursuing the same end." But he also likes the solitude of bird-watching alone. He speaks of the mental exercise: the patience required on the long wait for the bird that may or may not emerge; the rise to the surface of all his senses. He has what positive psychologist Mihaly Csikszentmihalyi calls an "autotelic personality," someone with an innate curiosity to master things just for their own sake and the ability to concentrate on those things for long periods of time (collectors and catalogue hobbyists). Brian admits to having taken over 75,000 photos (he whittled one trip to Mexico from 10,000 photos to 10). "Birds have this power, this spiritual power, to bring us to ourselves, to tame our distracted mind. Their appearance can feel like grace, and their disappearance contributes to the magic," he says.

Hobbies are also incredibly good for you physiologically. Hobbies can boost social interaction, which reduces stress—and loneliness. They may even make you less susceptible to dementia. Researchers at the Mayo Clinic interviewed 256 seniors about their leisure habits. At the start of the survey, none of the group—average age eighty-seven—displayed any impairment of memory or thought. Approximately four years later, 121 of the subjects had developed mild cognitive issues. Researchers discovered that certain activities indicated a lower likelihood of impairment, such as socializing and using the computer for surfing and games. But by far, the best way to stave off mental decline was to participate in artistic hobbies. Subjects who had regularly taken part in artistic endeavors in middle or old age— like painting, sculpting, or drawing—were 73 percent less likely to develop mild cognitive impairment than those who hadn't.

Crafters (pottery, woodworking, quilting, sewing) were 45 percent less likely to develop memory issues.

And if you really need to think of everything in terms of work, hobbies breed professional success, too: Nobel prize-winners are more likely than other scientists or members of the public to have had long-standing hobbies. A recent study found that those who practiced creative hobbies in their free time were better equipped to recover from the demands of work after hours, more likely to help others, and likely to be more creative when they returned to the office.

All of this productivity stuff is well and good, but a hobby's real value is in its purposelessness. In 1932, Bertrand Russell wrote that "play" had been crippled "by the cult of efficiency." The idea that every activity must be useful takes on a new cast in the Internet age: the web can make an entrepreneur out of anyone with a mouse. There's a lure to monetize what we become good at, to turn the amateur into the professional. Uber started as a hobby! Maybe my idea to _____ will grab the world by storm! This is what's been called a "jobby," not a "hobby": a pursuit with an agenda. But hobby as side-hustle kind of misses the point: a hobby is something that's not about winning, it's about doing one thing deeply.

So often, the self feels inescapable; privately, we cultivate our self online all day, posting versions on social media; professionally, many of us work at jobs with an online dimension, broadcasting every beat of our day. Here's what we need in a weekend: flow. Csikszentmihalyi describes the "flow state" as total immersion in an activity for its own sake (this is why paid work doesn't count, though flow at work is an incredible experience). It's the feeling of being out of self, and out of time: "Every action, movement, and thought follows inevitably from the previous one, like playing jazz. Your whole being is involved, and you're using your skills to the utmost."

In 1776, while riding in a coach from Henley to Birmingham, James Boswell sought Samuel Johnson's advice about a creeping feeling of melancholia. Dr. Johnson had an answer for him: "When you have a place in the country, lay out twenty pounds a year upon a laboratory. It will be an amusement to you. . . . Take a course of chemistry or a course of rope-dancing, or a course of anything to which you are inclined at the time. Contrive to have as many retreats for your mind as you can, as many things to which it can fly from itself."

So, Johnson was advising Boswell that the best way to manage his depression was to get a hobby (even though "rope- dancing" means tightrope walking, which sounds a little sarcastic). "Retreats for your mind"—don't we all need those, and isn't that just flow? Hobbies are the way of unalloyed pleasure, which we so desperately need after those long hours and nights, tethered to our devices and our jobs. The tasks that make up the responsibilities of our lives have end points, but the hobby is boundless. It can be a site of rejuvenation, and preparation for epiphanies to come.

ON SATURDAY MORNING at 10:00 in Tucson, Arizona, an adult coloring club meets. They bring their own books and colored pencils and sit down at a long table in a quiet room. Jamar runs the group, booking the space, posting the location (library, community center, retirement home) online on Meetup.com; he walks around the room quietly, murmuring encouragement as everyone colors.

A few winters ago, Jamar was living in Montana, bored and housebound by snow, and he began drawing mandalas. Then he started mirroring them, creating elaborate Escher-esque patterns, complex line drawings that begged to be colored. This was before the adult coloring book trend took off, as it has: roughly 12 million adult coloring books were sold in 2015, up about 1 million from 2014. Jamar decided to self-publish and sell his drawings online. Then he read that people were gathering and coloring together, and he decided to start a group. "I realized pretty quickly that it's not about the coloring, it's about bringing people together."

It's odd, really: a group of adults with their heads bowed, silently coloring. Sometimes there's small talk and laughter, and once, someone was being "disrespectful" and Jamar had to ask him to leave. It's easy to sniff at this trend, which has the faddish feel of Cabbage Patch Kids and Tae Bo. Adults coloring, grumble the grumblers, is a form of mass infantilization, and the packaging of mindfulness for profit. It's not even creative! Sheeple, put down the crayons!

But this tut-tutting means nothing in the room at the Tucson coloring club. Different people come every week, and friendships have been forged. Those who love it describe a mental shift that feels entirely different from other kinds of weekend hobbies. "It's the neatest experience, your mind goes into a place where it hasn't been. It's like it's structured and it's free," says

Robin, who works in medical publishing. She lived in New York and St. Louis before moving to Arizona and relishes the quiet of the desert. She never really had a hobby before. Painting and pottery classes didn't yield much pleasure. She and her husband know Jamar from their regular nights at the restaurant where he waits tables, and at his invitation, she decided to come out one Saturday. She was apprehensive, but she enjoyed the ritual of preparation: the fresh pack of pencils and the crisp new book, like a kid on the first day of school. And once she sat down and started coloring, she was engrossed.

The rhythmic repetition sounds exactly like flow: the loss of time, the world falling away. The positive effects of coloring are well documented. In one study, the anxiety levels of subjects were measured in a baseline test. Then, researchers described a scary experience, increasing participants' anxiety. In that heightened state, they were randomly assigned to color a blank page or a patterned page. The blank page people showed no decrease in anxiety levels, but those who colored were significantly less anxious.

"It gets you out of a very busy, frantic pace," says Robin. "It's like your circuits slow down. When you were a kid, you could sit in the corner and play with dolls or cars or coloring books; you did it for hours and that was all that existed in the world. This is like that. I've never felt that as an adult."

SOMETIMES A HOBBY can save a life.

Tyler is a young software developer in Portland, Oregon. He got into origami on a road trip with his family when his mother gave him the Klutz guide to origami. Soon, he was folding constantly, leaving his creations around town. When he went into restaurants, he would leave pieces behind; in one Thai restaurant, his objects accrued at the counter until they formed a pile. The manager asked him to make a koi fish out of a hundred-dollar bill, based on an Internet sensation, "Wan Park's dollar koi," where the hands of an origamist take a dollar bill and fold it into a beautiful scaled fish with whiskers and eyes in the exact right place. The patterns didn't quite line up on the hundred, but Tyler did finish, staying several hours after closing.

On weekends, he often does origami at home, alone, but on the second Sunday of each month, he attends a group at a Portland library. He's not the most social person, so this can be a struggle for him, but he makes a conscious point of going. The group that gathers isn't uniform, with people from ages eight to sixty-ish. It's equal parts male and female, culturally diverse, with many older Japanese people. There's no instruction. Tyler wants to see what other people are making and get inspired, and also (he admits) show off his own work, which is spectacular: long braids that look sculpted out of marble; a row of delicate birds linked at the wings, facing different directions, as if breaking out of one continuous piece of paper.

Even as it shares some of the qualities of his paid work— the logic and patterning of software—origami is an escape from what he does during the week. "Software is endless, and each piece of origami has a beginning and an end," he says. It isn't, he notes, meditative: it can actually be a bit of an adrenaline rush, as he pushes to the finish.

A few years ago, Tyler suffered serious depression, and found that one way to get out of it was to use his hands. Repetitive motions release serotonin, and origami felt like a way to manage the pain. He's doing better now, but he worries about the depression returning; he works to keep it at bay. In a poignant email, he described how important this hobby is to his life. It provides a sense of purpose, and at the Saturday club, it puts him inside a larger community:

> My worldview shifted from being in so much pain for so long. I'm terrified that something will happen again and I'll be trapped in this body suffering for years. A lot of life seems to be a great deal of effort just so you have somewhere to sleep until you put in a great deal of effort tomorrow so you have somewhere to sleep until you put in a great deal of effort tomorrow. And on and on it goes. The kicker, of course, is eventually you die anyway. My best guess is that after death there's nothing. No consciousness. Most importantly no pain. So that's my silver lining, sad as it is. (Though to be fair, I really don't know anything about death for sure . . . it might just be wishful thinking.) But, one good thing is that our creations and contributions can stick around for people to enjoy for at least a little while after we make them. And that doesn't necessarily stop when we die. For whatever reason I seem wired to find at least some meaning in sharing the things I find meaningful with other people. Sharing origami designs and helping someone learn to fold is a good way to do that.

◇◇◇◇

THE SPORTING LIFE

According to *The New York Times* "Sunday Routine," everyone is working out on Sunday. I love-hate this weekly feature, and my own Sunday routine includes devouring it, a hilariously rarefied diary of the average Sunday of completely non-average people wherein the vast majority of subjects profiled claim to exercise. Many are merely going to the gym but some are doing much more appealing activities: DJ Ruckus wears special compression pants to box; designer Cynthia Rowley goes to an exercise class where an instructor leads her and her kids through a class on stationary surfboards.

The "Sunday Routine" is a delicious hit of aspirational journalism that's both enchanting and appalling for its privilege and obliviousness. Week after week, New York executives, wedding planners, actors, and pediatric neurologists diarize a Sunday that's brimming with meditation, brunch, and always, always, always exercise. They work frequently, too, but somehow this is a virtue: "Sunday is a phenomenal day for work," architect Rafael Viñoly said. Many Sunday Routiners check emails, take calls, or visit the office. Biographer Robert Caro puts on a suit and tie and heads to his office on 57th Street.

The feature's popularity speaks to a lacuna: we need a weekend prescription because we don't really know what to do with our leisure time. With our own weekends so compromised, why not take a voyeuristic interest in what other, more important people do with theirs? In that way, *The New York Times* "Sunday Routine" is beyond mere rubbernecking; it's like a Victorian etiquette book. And the instruction is: work out on the weekend. Whether or not you, like Cynthia Rowley, are actually exercising on Sunday (everyone is probably also not going to Central Park, either, which so many Sunday Routiners report), you know that you *should*. The benefits of exercise are well documented: stress reduction, longer life, increased happiness—no news flashes here.

Americans do exercise more on the weekend than during the week. For many people, it's the only time in a busy work schedule that allows for fitness, and so they play weekend warrior and pack it all into the week's sole workout. Nothing wrong with that: weekend exercise will, research suggests, make you a better worker on the other five days. One long-term study showed that over nine years, those who used their leisure time for physical activities felt they had better control of their careers and less strain at work than those who were physically inactive over the same period of time. A *Forbes* article titled "14 Things Successful People Do on Weekends" suggests that "networking is a lifestyle" and if you're a hedge fund manager who wants to go riding on the weekend, don't miss the opportunity to bring other hedge fund managers along.

Unless, of course, your idea of fun is riding a horse while talking hedge funds, this is depressing. The melding of exercise and work—the need to justify the time spent exercising in terms of productivity—is one of the ways in which exercise has been leached of fun. Even the word "exercise" feels sort of punitive and dated, like "calisthenics." And the weekend is supposed to be fun. So if you know you should exercise, but you struggle to get to the gym because you don't want to use up your precious weekend time hamster-ing along a mechanical belt watching CNN, perhaps it's time to change it up. People who really love working out on the weekend don't usually call it "exercise." They say, "I have a regular tennis game." Or, "I play pickup basketball." The best reason to get active on the weekend is simple: play.

The drive to play is nestled in the brain stem, the ancient survival centers, and has endured as the brain has evolved, according to Dr. Stuart Brown, founder of the National Institute for Play and the author of the book *Play: How It Shapes the Brain, Opens the Imagination and Invigorates the Soul.* We play, like all social mammals, to survive. The consequences of not playing are dire. As Brown points out, the opposite of play isn't work, it's depression. He's examined the "play histories" of men who grew up to be murderers, and concluded that in this population one shared characteristic is a childhood devoid of play. He's an advocate of "remedial play therapy"—early intervention for kids who may not be getting enough play, a reality with long-term social consequences. Play must be voluntary, purposeless, and done for its own sake. The player loses the sensation of time passing and self-consciousness recedes. Real play also has "improvisational potential"—the outcome is unknown, and you want to keep on going to see where it leads.

Kids are deeply, intuitively in touch with play. My son, Jude, now twelve, loves sports, all of them. If there is a sport on offer, he is there. This is a kid who comes home from school and says happily, "I signed up for volleyball even though I suck at it!" In this past year of experimenting with better weekends, we've been trying to make sure our kids have more free time on Saturday and Sunday, and no one takes more advantage of this than our son. When he has a block of free time, he calls (texts) a friend, and then packs a shopping bag with a basketball, a soccer ball, and a glove, tucking a bat under his arm, as if anything could happen. He goes to the park and he plays and plays, returning home for water and food, like our outdoor cat. Then he exits again. He is all smiles, sweaty and a bit disgusting by the end of the day. He sleeps deeply. He's a kid who rarely gets lost in a book, but easily gets lost in a game. I hope he never grows out of this.

For some of us, the benefits of play can arise at a yoga or fitness class (though there's certainly more control in a gym workout, and less improvisation), but it's sports that are truly playful. It's sports that encourage abandon.

EVERY SATURDAY, Neal plays pickup ultimate Frisbee in a park in Pasadena, California. He moved to California for the reason everyone does, and now he works as a production assistant in film and TV, and acts, too. Film and TV workers have notoriously unreliable schedules: a shoot can sometimes average seventy hours a week. It's a feast-or-famine game and highly competitive; if you can't work a fourteen-hour day, someone else will. Weekends don't exist. In many productions, the directors, writers, and producers—"above the line"—are well compensated, but for those below the line, it's a middle-class pay scale with very long hours, sleep deprivation, and health risks. Fifteen years ago, an assistant cameraman on the set of the film *Pleasantville* worked a nineteen-hour day, and crashed his car while driving home. This event spurred veteran cinematographer Haskell Wexler to start a movement for shorter days and more humane schedules in the industry called 12 On 12 Off (a backwards step from the century-old plea for "Eight Hours for Work, Eight Hours for Rest, Eight Hours for What We Will!"). It had little effect. Wexler died in 2015, and the movement continues, as do the torturous hours.

Neal notices the work obsession around him, and he sees what he doesn't want to become. "I see people who get sucked into their careers and they never take a breather," he says. "They seem wrecked. I look and I don't see a single smile. Their eyes don't light up. It's like, 'Are you enjoying your work? Your life?' It's like, if they're not always busy, then they're failing." So he tries to get people to come out with him for ultimate. He posts about the weekly game online, and when he's on a set, he urges people he meets to join in.

No matter what his work life looks like, Neal does his best to keep his Sundays free. He's been in California for only three years, growing up in St. Louis and moving west after a stint in the air force. He had played ultimate only once before, but he's tall and athletic and immediately loved how the game is physical but technical, too. A win or loss is at the mercy of distance, angles, and wind, not just strength. When he plays, he is completely immersed in the game. "It's just fun," he says. "It's a friendly and competitive way for me to relieve my stress. It's a complete venting process." It's social, too; players have barbecues together or go out afterward. It's an unmovable date on his calendar.

One person who doesn't join in is his girlfriend. She's doing yoga, or getting a massage, he says. According to the Pew Research Center, men spend about 5 hours per week more than women on leisure activities; it's a big umbrella that includes games, sports, and TV. That's an average for all men (between eighteen and sixty-four), while men with children under eighteen are getting only 2.7 hours more per week.

My husband is much better than I am at protecting play. One night a week, he plays pickup basketball; he's in a Fantasy Baseball League. For women, those kinds of personal pleasures seem to be the first to go, sacrificed for work or family. When asked, in a survey, why they don't exercise, women answered: too tired. The reason women have less time (and maybe more stress) is because they do more of the domestic work than men.

But domestic work is not all equal: "child care" falls under the umbrella of domestic labor in most research. For many working mothers the weekend can feel like the only slot in the week when it's possible to spend time with their kids. This makes it hard to throw the gym bag over the shoulder and say "See you this afternoon!"; those pie-eyed progeny at the window miss you, and you miss them, too. All of which leads to no exercise, or something like "the 5:00 a.m. club": women rising before the kids wake up, exercising in the dark, alone.

This is fine, but it's not play. When women do exercise, it's more likely to be in a class or at a gym than as part of an actual sport—the option to play is rarely on the menu. Why (many) women don't play sports is a question that's tangled in some sticky old ideas about masculinity and femininity. In adolescence, there's the gym class feeling of your body changing in public, under scrutiny; the volleyball smashing your period-swollen belly; playing with boys who never passed, or made fun of you for how you ran. Aggression and competitiveness—the stuff of sports—remain lauded traits in men; the same behavior is often deemed "bitchiness" in women. Even with all the progress of past decades, girls still receive a screwed-up message about what they're supposed to be doing with their bodies: women and girls are more likely to be seen in the media pruning and cultivating and displaying, à la the Kardashians, than sweating and triumphing on the pitch, à la Abby Wambach. If girls rarely see women playing professional sports on TV or in the media, there's little to—pardon the pun—shoot for. It's no surprise that the organization Keep Her in the Game notes that at around age fourteen, girls start to drop out of sports.

At ten, my daughter is hyper-social, and she and her friends do play: they build dollhouses out of cardboard and scrap fabric, and dress up and dance around the house. She shot a seriously touching stop-motion movie about two estranged rocks that find each other at last. But her play is often about hobbies and crafts, rarely about sports, despite being an athletic kid, fast and long-limbed. She seems to play—cheerfully—only in the organized games we pay for. The love of sport doesn't drive her to play in her free time the way it does my son.

It's not that she's playing "wrong," but I worry that the sports ambivalence is my fault. For me, exercise has always been about controlling the body, managing weight and stress—

checkmarks on the To-Do list. I do lots of different workouts—yoga, fitness classes, running—but the point is just to get them done. I'd really rather not.

My relationship to sports is stranger than most. As an adolescent, I stepped into all the traps that keep girls away: self-conscious, oddly shaped, and picked last. But my other problem is more unusual: I grew up with a high-level athlete in my house, and so I backed away, hands up, ceding that territory. At a young age, my preposterously athletic brother was on the path toward professional soccer. This meant growing up in a house that was clutched by his games and tournaments and travel schedule. His career, even as a teenager, had a presence in our home, and while my parents did their best to keep things equal, a family's time is limited, and ours usually funneled his way. On top of that sting, I didn't have the same physical prowess. Every September, I'd watch as the new gym teacher, at first excited to learn there was another Onstad in the ranks, grew quickly disappointed as I fumbled the ball, or deked around the cones with the dexterity of someone wearing snowshoes on her feet.

So I've always chosen forms of physical activity that don't involve teams: I got into hiking in the outdoors; I ran; I joined a gym when I was fourteen. When exercise is in service of something else—thinness, and impossible beauty standards burned deep into the neural pathways around, say, age fourteen—then it feels like obligation. Occasional conversation by the StairMaster notwithstanding, it's not all that social. I don't get to go to a barbecue with my fellow classmates after hot yoga.

Too many women have internalized the idea that every second must be filled with obligation and utility. To give up our weekends for games would mean exhaling; it might seem greedy, and not self-sacrificing enough. When my husband takes off for basketball, I have the distinct impression that he is not looking back. He simply takes the time he wants, plucks it from the branch without a thought. I know there are many women who do this, too: full applause. But if I go for a run, I am too often half present, thinking about all the things I could be doing instead during that one hour, and all the things I'll be doing in the next one. What's fun about that?

EXERCISE AS PLAY is something I wanted to understand better, and in sports, playing pickup games is probably, in the hierarchy of great things to do on the weekend, at the very top. They're social, fun, local, free (or cost a nominal fee). One study found that kids who spend hours engaged in organized sports might become less creative adults than kids who play unstructured sports.

I Skyped a woman who grew up playing pickup basketball in Harlem to see what a life of pickup might look like. Niki grew up in Spanish Harlem in the late 1990s. Her brother, Virgil, was a year and a half older, and everywhere he went, she went, too. It was a neighborhood of parks and playgrounds, and Niki got good fast, playing both football and basketball. In pickup basketball, two captains pick ten players from the crowd of people who show up. By the time she was ten years old, Niki was getting picked first.

She would come home from school to Franklin Plaza, on 106th Street between 2nd and 3rd, and head straight to the nearby courts, playing nonstop until the lights came on, the signal that it was time to go home. (She jokes that perhaps she should have used some of that time for homework.) On weekends, basketball would go all day, until either the lights came on or her mother showed up on a bicycle calling for her kids.

Niki succeeded because she was unexpected: she's not especially tall, and she's pretty, upending stereotypes and sending all kinds of mixed signals that threw off her opponents. "Because of the way I looked, the guys would think, 'Oh, she has to be the weak link.' That was my trick. So they would leave me a bit open, thinking they could. Then when I got the ball, I would shoot and I would score every time. I had a good shot! That's how I developed my shot to be so fast because I'd see them coming."

By the time she was fourteen, Niki was playing organized ball (with boys), but she still popped by the parks most weekends to play pickup. "Pickup is tougher, it's more competitive," she says. "There's no rules really. With pickup, everyone does what they want, they have to earn their respect. Once you're on the court, you're going to be on the court with four other strangers, you don't know who does what, what someone's good at—then everyone will begin to reveal themselves. You can see, 'Oh, this guy is the scorer, and he's the aggressive one.' But it does develop into a family. The game is something that you have in common. You can all see the same thing at one point in time, regardless of background. I can pull four complete strangers from different parts of New York City and we can all understand the same thing."

She has made a career out of basketball, playing in college at Eastern Kentucky University, and going on to play professionally in four different countries. She's an NYC Expert on the Nike website. When we talk, via Skype, Niki is in an apartment in the mountains in Poland, having just started as a point guard for the team PEAC-Pécs.

Sociologist Robert Stebbins calls this kind of professionalization of the amateur pursuit "devotee work," belonging to those who are lucky—and gifted—enough to turn a hobby into a paid career. Niki's "occupational devotion" illustrates Stebbins's point that leisure and work aren't always entirely separate spheres. It's possible to find such joy in a leisure activity that it becomes work, and vice versa. "Basketball gave me everything. A lot of people don't get out of my neighborhood, but I've been able to do so much," Niki says.

And it all started with the possibility of an empty court. "What separates ballers that play under the whistle, or with teams, from street ballers is they're more controlled: 'Let me go here and cut or do whatever the coach told me.' It's not as free as pickup," she says. "I miss that." She is often in New York in the off-season, mentoring younger players and visiting the park next to Franklin Plaza. On a Saturday morning, she still looks for that empty court, and plays.

REST ASSURED, this chapter is not going to end with the author engaged in a cheerful Sunday morning game of pickup basketball. I need another, say, three years of therapy to get there. But the notion of a more engaged, group experience of exercise is something I know will better my weekend; in my year of weekend-improvement, it's top of the list. I crave community and protected time; an unassailable slot that's for my body, and for me, religiously protected. So I joined a running club.

This club has been meeting for years in a leafy neighborhood near a large park. I'd briefly been in a group years ago, while training for a half marathon, but I'd never run with people without a goal in mind. That purposelessness feels new; this will be only for pleasure, not a finish line, which is the kind of leisure my weekends have sorely lacked.

On a Sunday morning, everyone gathers in the running store, a sea of spandex, geared to the gills. They all seem to know each other, which brings an initial rush of gym class last-picked terror. Then the owner of the store stands up and tells everyone of upcoming races while I hover near the back, trying to give off friendly-not-creepy vibes.

One of the reasons people gather to run is what psychologists call "social facilitation": one's performance of a task improves when it's done with others, or in front of an audience. But the runner has to be skilled for social facilitation to work. If not, then the audience or co-runner actually creates "social inhibition," and speed and accuracy decrease.

I'm not so concerned with going fast, but I don't want to be lagging behind either. The big group splits into smaller groups, and I choose one that's distinctly middle speed, and we set off for a 14K run. At first, no one really talks to me. The guy leading the group is goofy and telling jokes that seem a little insider. I do get the patented PE feeling, but it's okay: I'm learning to be alone in a group, which is actually a skill—even in a restaurant, we pull out phones and magazines, always defending ourselves from solitude. It's naked to be silent in a group, but the running works its lulling magic and I follow along, inspired to go a little faster than I usually am when alone.

A few people struggle on a nasty hill, and the better runners wait at the top, cheering them on. I'm surprised how much this helps, like a hand extended. A runner announces she's tired and wants to turn back; the leader asks who will accompany her. I realize then that even in its informal looseness, and lacking jerseys or a mascot, this particular run feels like a team sport.

Finally, a woman talks to me, asking my name. We chat about the city, the river that's snaking along next to us. She introduces me to other runners, and I begin to move through the crowd, making small talk. There's not a lot of eye contact, which is somehow a relief; we're like spies, speaking out of the sides of our mouths. All of us sweating and breathing heavily, without self-consciousness.

I see things I haven't seen before; a neighborhood I didn't know existed; a park filled with kite-fliers. I hadn't looked at the map in advance, wanting to fully give up control. I don't look at my watch either. Close to the end of the 14 kilometers, the socializing stops, and people are tired, quiet. Then there is another body next to me, a woman I don't know, and she's struggling a bit. I move ahead, but her success is somehow my success. So I wait at the top of the final hill, and cheer her on, as if to victory.

CHAPTER 5

DO LESS AND BE
MORE AT HOME

T HERE ARE A COUPLE of equal, coexisting truths about
our homes.

One: Home is a source of pleasure, a site of sanctuary and
security that speaks for us, declaring our aesthetics and our
histories.

Two: Our homes are major time-sucks that are destroying
our weekends.

Repairing, cleaning, designing, cleaning some more—
houses and apartments are *takers*. Time-use surveys show that
people spend most of their waking time on weekends cultivating the domestic sphere, cleaning and shopping. I suspect we are
shopping for cleaning products to clean the crap we just bought,
or tools to fix the crap we brought last year. Then it's time for

a major household purge, which means taking all the worn-out and unfixable crap to the Goodwill. On the way home, perhaps it's time to stop and buy some more crap to replace the absent crap. And then—Monday!

We can't be too hard on ourselves. Weekends seem like the perfect time to tie up the loose ends of housework not completed during the week. For families, the weekend brings the added pressure to achieve maximum togetherness. One British survey suggests that during the week, parents are spending about thirty-six minutes per weekday with their kids in a manner they consider "quality time," and that time is often spent in front of the TV, silently. So the pressure's on to pack the weekend with enriching activities and hanging out. In my twenties, I had a friend I (in my inner voice) called Ms. High Expectations. Every movie we'd attend or bar we'd enter was going to be "the best." At the doorway of a party, just before the door opened, she'd announce: "This is going to be the best party EVER. You are going to love these people MORE THAN ANY OTHER PEOPLE EVER!" My heart would sink. The expectations were too high, and the party would be agony and the people unbearable.

You are similarly doomed if you look to the weekend as a remedial makeup session for life unlived during the week. By thinking we can do everything in two days, we set ourselves up to fail. The Sunday blues aren't just anxiety about work approaching, but guilt about a weekend of unfulfilled expectations.

But there are ways to let go of the fantasy of the perfect weekend and live an actual weekend that benefits all members of a home. It starts with asking a question: What gives my weekend value? My own list, from that long-ago audit, includes play, community, altruism. Second question: What prevents those things from happening? My list: shopping, cleaning, house-primping, kid commitments. The small obligations tend to swarm the only significant obligation that matters: living a life that's meaningful.

The formula that seems to work for people who have good weekends is simple: doing more of the former—The Big Stuff—and less of the latter—The Little Stuff. On some weekends, of course, the value you need most is having a clean bathroom and doing laundry. But the rest of the time, the best weekends are about ducking around the obligatory domestic management that eats away our leisure. Doing less—and having less—on all fronts may be the best way to make those forty-eight hours feel like a true reprieve. You can't do all the things, so you have to do what matters.

HAPPY HOME

So much of our feeling harried and time-starved is because the weekends are the only two days where we can attack the domestic flotsam that our grandmothers probably finished (invisibly, and possibly thanklessly) during the weekdays. I imagine that as a kid during the 1940s, my dad and his siblings were in school while their mother, who didn't work outside the home, knocked off the household tasks. Surely the family's weekends weren't consumed by zipping around town with a chore list. I, on the other hand, sometimes line up the children on a Saturday morning and say the word "Costco" just to hear them moan in a very specific, farm-animal-giving-birth way. It's amusing, if tragic.

Women now make up 47 percent of the American workforce, and nearly 70 percent of women with children work outside the home. Both numbers have been climbing for decades, yet even with so many of their hours taken up by paid work, women still shoulder the bulk of domestic labor. A 2012 report from the Pew Research Center found that American mothers are spending nearly double the time on unpaid work than fathers do, devoting thirty-one hours a week to child care and chores versus seventeen hours for fathers. (Time for a joke from comedian Ali Wong: "I don't want to lean in. I want to *lie down.*") This means fathers have more free time, and they're making the most of their weekends. On weekends, fathers average 5.5 hours of leisure time per day, while working mothers average 4.3. Working moms may be doing a little less child care (down from 1.7 hours per day during the week to 1.3 on the weekend) but the amount of housework they do over those two days goes up significantly, from 1.8 hours per day to 2.7. The resulting inequity has been labeled "the gender leisure gap."

This lousy reality is, sadly, nothing new. Historically, with the exception of upper-crusters like *Downton Abbey*'s Crawleys, most women have never enjoyed much leisure. Unfettered time for reflection or respite has usually been the domain of privileged men, facilitated by someone else's labor, often women's.

Women have always worked. Rural medieval women undertook agrarian labor, tending livestock and spinning flax and wool, while urban women ran shops and inns. Even noblewomen helped manage their husbands' estates. And regardless of class, the women ran the home. The Victorian era might have lionized "the angel in the house"—the submissive domestic goddess, and moral center of the family—but most Victorian women still brought in income. In fact, in the U.K., female employment in the 1850s, '60s, and '70s reached highs not seen again until after World War II. Over a third of working-class women contributed to household incomes in the mid-Victorian years, working in domestic service or trades like brewing and laundering. In the Industrial Revolution, women joined the factory lines.

So this image of the "housewife" puttering for long, empty days inside that house she married is a modern invention, a product of postwar prosperity. And even that lady of leisure was a fantasy. On Saturdays and Sundays in the 1950s, women's weekends might have been filled with church obligations and the social caretaking of family, close and extended. The home was the center of life, and women of the new middle class shopped and prepped for entertaining. Even on the weekends, women have rarely been "off."

With that backwards glance, the domestic labor division looks better now than it's ever been. Opposite-sex couples are creeping—if slowly—toward equity; not yet at fifty-fifty, but getting closer. So why, then, do so many women feel overtaxed on the weekends?

When I ask people what they do on weekends, I'm surprised how often I hear "housework." It's a nasty truth—some might say conspiracy—that as women joined the workforce in the 1980s, losing that time at home, the industry of retro homemaking took off. We're three decades into the Martha Stewart era, and the pressure to create the perfect home has migrated from magazines to our Internet feeds. From Martha Stewart to GOOP, women are bombarded with aspirational images of modern "lifestyles" that are impossible to attain. NBC's TODAY Moms website feature found that 42 percent of seven thousand American mothers surveyed say they suffer from "Pinterest stress": anxiety that they can't live up to the images of domestic perfection posted on Pinterest. Already saddled with the double burden of work and parenting, domestic labor becomes a third tier of tyranny: the house as prison, precisely cultivated and cleaned.

Obviously the single most important way for women to be relieved of these pressures and grab some leisure is for men to do more work and give up some of their free time. Social change is the key to reclaiming the time that women lose when they struggle to balance work and family. Better public policies around child care and better work practices like job sharing—practices that reflect the realities of people's lives—will ease the time crunch that families experience. Our weekends will become better when our weeks do.

There is, of course, another, simpler band-aid solution: refuse the domestic time-suck. Ametist, my Swedish friend, simply does not clean on weekends because her weekends are for living, not cleaning. Many other families spread the cleaning and chores into bite-sized chunks over the course of the week. Even if they don't exactly upend gender inequality, I like these practical tips; they feel like a pragmatic way to get time back.

Blogger Erin Doland subscribes to a "One day, one room" regimen: "Dedicate half an hour to cleaning one room every day instead of cleaning the whole house on the weekend." If you can't get to the cleaning during the week, give yourself a closed period of time on the weekend (nine to noon, Saturday, say), and if you can't finish in that time period—walk away. Your house is clean enough. As novelist Lucy Cavendish told BBC Radio 4's *Woman's Hour*, after explaining why she minimizes housework: "A general level of mess doesn't bother me in the way it bothers other people. My house isn't my castle, it does not define me. I can understand why tidying makes some people feel in control—and I do keep things clean—but I have no intention of spending hours cleaning my oven. Trying to keep a tidy house could drive you to dementia. Life is too short, I'd rather read a book or go to the cinema."

If you have children, then you have the tools you need to get to the cinema next weekend. Enlisting kids in chores and errands isn't just a very nice way to fob off certain tasks and steal back some time, it's excellent parenting. Chores are key to developing self-mastery and self-reliance, yet one 2014 survey showed that while 82 percent of adults reported doing regular chores when they were kids, only 28 percent required the same of their own children. We don't want to deprive them of self-sufficiency, right? Tell them that's what you're thinking when you hand over the mop.

The other strategy is a little less Cinderella-esque: do the chores together. A friend who's a single mom spends Saturday morning with her son—he vacuums the apartment while she dusts (then he plays Lego while she cleans the kitchen, but it's a start—he's seven!). Tackling domestic drudgery together makes it less boring for everyone and imparts a message about the values of the home: "We all help out to make this a place that's comfortable for all of us." What kids are capable of will be determined by their age, and their competency, but some of the more fun tasks of the household are, in fact, opportunities for quality time, a reframing of labor as leisure. Years ago, my husband was building a fence in our yard, and my son, then four, stood there silently with a tool belt around his waist, handing him nails as requested, one by one. We still joke about how long this went on; how focused and in the zone the little boy was, proud and totally in sync with his dad. Was he too young to be handling nails? Quite possibly. Did it make for a nice afternoon? Yes.

In honor of this memory, one Saturday, I pull Mia off Minecraft and into our tiny, patchy backyard. She's a little grumbly during the weed pulling; the bonding is minimal. Then we take a trip to the gardening center, where I basically bribe her with ladybug gloves and the choice of a plant to fill a space between shrubs. The girl contains multitudes—she loves ice hockey and hamsters and unicorns and fart jokes. She chooses the pretty plant: a bleeding heart, on sale, drooping with pink buds.

When we get back, the sun is hot, but she doesn't seem to notice, crouched and digging a deep hole. She looks up at me, her face streaked with dirt, grinning. What started as a one-hit gig turns into an afternoon. We circle the little garden together, shearing the overgrown rose of Sharon and attacking dandelions between the stones. We don't say much but our bodies are close. We brush against each other's backs.

Here's the dark twist ending: the bleeding heart died. Our dog lay on top of it, and I don't think we planted it right anyway. But I still remember that afternoon, the quiet and the sting of heat; my daughter's pride at the end of the day as we looked upon our labor.

A NOTE ON CAREGIVING

For those with aging relatives, or people in their lives who aren't entirely independent, care is often the axis around which the weekend spins. For years, my neighbor Eric spent part of every Saturday and Sunday driving across town to his mother's house. They would go together to a movie, or the library. He accompanied her on errands or to get her hair done. On Sunday, they went to church. He married and had a child of his own, and his mother grew older. Outings weren't as easy, but still he went to be with her every weekend, often with his own family in tow. He organized respite care and a personal home worker, and came when called to deal with emergencies. He is the definition of a good son.

A few years ago, she died. I saw him on the street one weekend a while later, and rather clumsily, I asked him what it was like to have so much free time now. "I loved my time with her," he told me. "I wouldn't have missed a minute."

Eric's lucky; caregiving isn't easy. People who have fraught relationships with their parents may look upon such visits as obligation and injustice. Even the most loving relationships can be tested by illness and infirmity. Yet each year about 44 million Americans provide unpaid care to an adult with limited abilities, adding up to about 37 billion hours. The typical caregiver is not actually Eric, but a working woman, average age forty-six, and she spends twenty hours a week caring for her mother. The financial and emotional strain of duty is significant, and so is the drain on the weekend.

For both devoted offspring like Eric and more wary caregivers, there are strategies to protect at least some time for other activities: share the labor with other members of the family; if you can afford help, get it; monitor your own health closely, protecting your body from the exhaustion, emotional and physical, of caring for someone else.

It's likely, however, that most caregivers are well aware of all such tips and tricks. What might be more useful, if you're feeling that your weekend is shrunk by the needs of others, is a reminder that caring for someone else may provide the scaffolding for the most meaningful weekend there is: the kind that informs a meaningful life.

Jean Vanier is the Canadian Catholic philosopher whose life's work has been building communities for people with intellectual disabilities. In his twenties, he visited a mental institution in a southern suburb of Paris and was horrified by what he saw: violence and overcrowding; an assault on the dignity of the people inside. So he bought a house in a village near the Compiègne forest in Trosly-Breuil and moved in, bringing two of the institutionalized men with him. It was the beginning of L'Arche, now a network of 147 homes in five countries where the disabled cohabitate with the healthy, sharing living space and meals, as well as the responsibilities of daily life.

Vanier has written extensively—beautifully—on the meaning of a life among those he calls "the weak and the poor." Time with those less-abled changes perception, he writes, bringing forth the best of our humanity. The care flows both ways, and alters the giver, too. "The weak teach the strong to accept and integrate the weakness and brokenness of their own lives," he writes.

Aging and illness can be messy and ugly; we are only able to give as much as is bearable. But when it is bearable, those caregiver visits can call upon the best in us. They change time, too, taking us out of the rush and striving of the week, away from the hurried pace that dominates the days of the "healthy" and "able." There's no getting or spending while holding the hand of someone who is ill, or lonely. There's no striving for perfection or acquisition. But there is a quieting of that weekday panic. A current passes between the hands, and just for now, we occupy the same moment of time, slowly and together.

THE MINIMUM IS ENOUGH

In the film *sex, lies, and videotape*, Graham, the prodigal college friend, returns to his hometown, stopping by his old room-mate's suburban mansion to describe his philosophy of One Key Living, explaining that everything he owns is in his car. An apartment would mean two keys; a job, possibly another key to open and close. "Buy some stuff, I'm afraid it's gonna get ripped off or something, and I get more keys," he says. "I just like having the one key: it's clean."

Graham is a spiritual ancestor of the "minimalist movement." Minimalists shed their possessions and other signposts of status and adopt a life focused not on acquisition but on experience, relationships, and—of course—time. There's no official registry so it's hard to know how many people are living minimally (by choice) in North America, but blogs and books have proliferated in the past few years, and the converts are zealous. They feel really good about breaking free. Websites like missminimalist.com are filled with first-person accounts like that of Kate (who runs her own minimalist website, cohesivehome.com):

> We dusted off old dreams and quit any activities or responsibilities that didn't add value to our lives or support our vision for our family's future. Kirk began playing and writing music again, and I began writing my first children's chapter book, both long-time dreams of ours. We then sold or gave away about 90% of our possessions, including our first house, and then packed all of the remaining belongings for our family of four into a 6' x 12" U-Haul trailer. In June 2015 we moved cross-country to pursue our new life.

The arc becomes familiar after a while on these sites: we were salary slaves; we acquired a lot of stuff; it didn't make us happy; we shed the stuff; we are now happier with less. Stuff gone equals time regained.

Courtney Carver is one of the better-known online min-imalists, running a "simplicity" website called Be More with Less. In the early 2000s, she was working a high-powered sales job in Salt Lake City, Utah. Whatever she made, she spent immediately, and then she racked up credit card debt and took loans to cover the extra spending. "The harder I worked, the more I thought I deserved," she says. "I'd work late into the evenings and through the weekends, and then I'd shop to make myself feel better. I was shopping for sport." Raising a kid and tending a big suburban house became exhausting, and she was experiencing migraines and vertigo, which only made her think, "I don't have time to be sick."

In 2006, she got what she now considers a wake-up call in the form of a diagnosis of multiple sclerosis. "I don't think the stress necessarily caused the MS, but I do believe it exacerbated it. I had to weed it out." For her, that meant cutting out meat, and examining sources of stress. The biggest one was debt. Every day she was fielding collection calls and bills in the mail. She began to tackle the finances, consolidating debt and making payments. She started thinking about money in terms of time: a new pair of shoes didn't cost a hundred dollars, but rather, ten hours. This immediately cut back on her shopping.

Other life changes followed: after barely avoiding a car acci-dent while checking her phone in the car with her daughter in the backseat, she put it away. She turned the phone off in the car, and kept it off after working hours and on weekends.

"Nobody noticed," she says. "My sales went up. We think we have to be so busy, so available, but if we pull back a bit, often there are no ramifications."

Then she began shedding stuff. There was a lot of stuff in their big house, but most of it wasn't in use, and it was distracting her as she paid off her credit cards: "It was a reminder of our debt and discontent." So she gave a lot of things away: clothes, books, and decorative objects. Eighty percent of what she owns left the house, and she says she hasn't missed anything: "Not even the whisk."

"Decluttering" is a trendy pursuit, with decluttering consultants and online "decluttering challenges." Professional organizer Marie Kondo is the trend alpha; her book *The Life-Changing Magic of Tidying Up* has sold millions of copies around the world. Kondo's directive to her cluttered readers is to hold each object in your hand, determine if it "sparks joy," and if not, then toss it. She has a slightly mystical approach, endowing possessions with a vague (and sometimes sinister) spirituality. She's tapping into the unease so many people feel about how simple it is to accrue things in an era of cheap manufacturing and disposable goods. But her message is really a stern admonishment about time: You don't have time to read those books, so get rid of them. You will never again look at that instruction manual for the camera you don't use—get rid of it. That box of photos and letters that you plan to gaze upon in old age—a lie. It's an ascetic—and ironically, joyless—approach to living, a little tinged with sadness. Anyone who feels truly connected to her books or enjoys getting lost in a box of old letters may find a coldness in Kondo's plan that can't be abided. But there's no doubt that the positive reception to her message speaks to a deeply felt cultural anxiety about time.

Once Courtney had shed large amounts of stuff, the next thing to go was the container. She and her husband sold it, downsizing from a huge 2,000-square-foot home with a garage to a 750-square-foot house. "For the first six months, not a weekend would go by where I wouldn't think: 'Guess what I'm not doing this weekend? I'm not painting a fence!'"

Now they spend their weekends moving slowly. She is a fan of two-hour walks, with no technology. When her family eats dinner, she wants to linger, letting her fork sit on the plate between bites. It is, to buzz a buzzword, a mindful existence, and her health has improved significantly. There was a gap between the life she wanted to live and the life she was living, and she closed it.

ENTERTAINING

I don't know if I've ever been invited for dinner at Liz and Scott's, but I've eaten there many times. Usually it happens because I'm just sort of already there, sitting at the island in their kitchen on a Saturday afternoon, when Liz starts cooking. Soon it's evening and I have a drink, and then a plate of food, and there is chaos around us as the kids play and the dog barks. They don't have a dining-room table, so it's always buffet style. Other passersby may be lucky enough to join, but sometimes it's just me and my family. It is always delicious, and seemingly effortless. So I was surprised when I asked Liz about it and she revealed a strategy.

It turns out that Liz once used entertaining as a tool to break loneliness. Moving to Toronto from Calgary several years ago, she didn't know anyone, so she would ask people she met over to eat. "I basically made friends by entertaining. It gave me social capital. People had to invite me over once I'd fed them," she says. So she perfected a few signature dishes and opened the doors. Her mother had always been an excellent entertainer, and she took her cues from her. "She always told me that people's requirements are way less complicated than you think they are: people want a warm greeting at the door, they want a drink in their hand, and they want to feel you've gone to a little trouble, but not too much." She purposely doesn't have a dining-room table because she thinks it makes guests skittish: "No one wants to sit next to the vicar's wife."

I thought about Liz and Scott when our family attended a more formal Friday night get-together, at the home of some friends who hold a Shabbat dinner every week. It was a spectacular four-course meal, with a beautifully laid table, and water in a crystal pitcher that literally sparkled. They are hardly Orthodox: my friend's husband lit the candles though the woman of the house is supposed to do it, and this happened after the sun had gone down, so not eighteen minutes before sunset, just as the world sinks into the twilight, inviting Sabbath. There was a little prayer, and we passed the challah (which my son gobbled down, "Like a carb-loving atheist," I muttered to my husband). But then we talked a lot about baseball, and our city's crazy mayor, and work. These friends are impeccable hosts, warm and generous. It's an entirely different vibe than at Liz's, but they, too, make it seem effortless. After we finished eating, we sat around that table, drinking as the kids ran in and out from the yard, and the candles flickered.

Eating together with friends and family is an age-old ritual. In Ancient Egypt, guests wore cones of scented fat on their heads that melted as they ate, contributing a nice smell to the evening, which is way more original than bringing a bottle of Merlot. It's a social act to eat side by side: the word "companion" comes from the Latin for "with whom one eats bread." We gather at a table, or on the floor, or around a mat, and eat not just for sustenance, but for conviviality—to sate each other's needs, body and mind. We eat to transmit love in the food we prepare and share, and take other people's love into our bodies through the food they've made for us. When we eat marks our culture and heritage, and the weekend underscores those identities. Jews have Shabbat. Catholics give up flesh on Fridays, setting themselves apart from Protestants. Some Indian families eat bread during the week and rice on weekends.

Growing up, my family didn't go to church, but we were very devoted to the eating part of the traditionally Christian post-church Sunday meal. On Sunday nights, our family moved from the kitchen, where we ate the other nights, to the dining room. Our family of four often grew to include my grandparents, or other relatives or friends. There was classical music on the turntable, and a formality that our hippie house lacked the other nights of the week: cloth placemats, candles. There, we sat down on Sunday nights to a British-style dinner of roast beef and Yorkshire pudding, the traditional "Sunday roast," which began in medieval times when the lord would reward his serfs once a week with a meal after church.

In a 1994 column in *The Independent*, food critic Jane Jackman railed against the family dinner, an upper-class construct "which saw the dinner table as a battleground for discipline and a means of enforcing codes of behaviour." She's right that any invitation to eat excludes someone, and there's power in deciding who does and doesn't sit at the table. But the democratizing truth is that everyone eats; those working below stairs gather for dinner, too. Yet as she continues her rant against eating, her most alarming pronouncement is this: "Eating in a group surrounded by family and friends has not suited human beings throughout most of history. It no longer even suits our working habits."

I don't think I want to live in a world where we allow "working habits" to subsume all other experiences, including two of the best: eating, and connecting with other human beings. What's depressing is that, writing in 1994, Jackman was prescient. Twenty years later, we eat together less than we used to; we are turning into a nation of grazers who chow down vertically, leaning against walls and islands. Sales of dining-room tables have declined, as have sales of plates. The average American eats one out of five meals in her car. Work and technology habits are absolutely at odds with a rambling evening around a table with friends and family, but there are repercussions when families don't eat together. Researchers have found that children who don't eat dinner with their parents twice a week are nearly twice as likely to be overweight compared to kids in families who do eat together. According to a study by the National Center on Addiction and Substance Abuse at Columbia University, kids who eat with their parents five or more days a week do better in school and are less likely to abuse drugs and alcohol.

My parents had a firm belief that Sunday dinner mattered. When I was sixteen, I was at the house of a boy I liked desperately on a Sunday afternoon, and his parents invited me for dinner. I called home and my mother shut it down. "It's Sunday. Your grandparents are coming," she said, as if that were an explanation. I'm sure I yelled into the phone, "SO?" before sulking all the way home.

I couldn't understand why my generally chill parents were suddenly turning into sphincter-clenched bourgeois killjoys. Now I look back and realize that those Sundays were when I got to know my grandparents, and was forced to listen to my brother and see him as a person and not just a sweaty nuisance. Around that circular table, I heard my parents talk politics and run through the more trivial news of our lives. It was quiet, and darkly lit, a ritual in a family with few rituals, the one sure thing of each week. I know now why my mother protected those nights. They were a secular kid's first experience of the sacred.

WE'RE NOT JUST EATING together less; we're partying less, too. The number of Americans hosting and attending social events on a typical day has been on a steady decline, down 48 percent between 2003 and 2014. People in their twenties appear to be especially cool about entertaining. In a 2015 article in *The New York Times* called "The Death of the Party," Millennials complain that exorbitant rent and real estate prices keep them too poor to host. Some fear rejection because a bunch of "Yes" responses to a Facebook invitation doesn't necessarily mean anyone will show. Or perhaps they can't keep up with a rabid foodie culture, paralyzed by expectations of organic wine and Vacherin Mont d'Or cheese wrapped in spruce bark. One twenty-seven-year-old woman from Brooklyn said that she and her roommates tried throwing parties, and gave up. "We decided it was more effort than it was worth."

That is, of course, the point of eating together: effort. The surge of TV cooking shows and celebrity chefs suggest that we actually do want to use the parts of our minds that are neglected in the flitting and skimming encouraged by devices. To cook requires attention, mindfulness, detail, discretion. Cooking a special meal for guests takes time, and the time to do it is the weekend.

The upside of foodie culture is a growing acceptance that prepackaged foods are bad for us and the planet. A return to real food found in nature feels and tastes better. For some, executing these ideals in a five-course, nose-to-tail, farm-to-table dinner for twelve is a great pleasure; for others, it's a source of stress, or worse, so daunting that it's never attempted. Liz and I snicker unkindly about the "weekend chef," the phenomenon of people who cook only on the weekends, videos and full-color cookbooks on hand. This kind of performance cooking is like a one-man *MasterChef* episode and therefore consumes an entire

Saturday (and an entire Sunday to clean up, which may be the partner's problem).

The great pleasure of preparing food shouldn't be lost to this all-or-nothing attitude. Liz is certain that the bigger the kitchen, the worse the cook. She is fierce about simplicity. "All you need is one flourish of jazz hands and everything else can be basic," she says. For example: a pot of simple chili, but with the flourish of a cherry margarita. I've had this particular combination at Liz's and I can tell you that the chili is hardly army fare, with crème fraîche and roasted tortillas on top. And I still remember the margarita. Jazz hands!

Perhaps what I like best about those dinners is the spontaneity. We don't plan them; they spring up, like that neighborhood friend when you were little who would show up on the doorstep with a mischievous look in her eye. You knew nothing about what was about to transpire except that it was going to be a good day.

A study out of Washington University's Olin Business School found that scheduling leisure activities changes how we experience them: if the date and time are strictly assigned, then the activity comes to feel more like a chore—more like work—than like leisure. I love an invitation, but when the calendar is full, locking down dinner dates and entertainment on those precious weekends translates into stress. Perhaps we entertain less because we schedule too much, a work habit that's leaked over into our weekends. Making dates and appointments in our private time is an echo of the goals-oriented and "milestone" thinking of the modern workplace.

What is this drive to overplan? Journalist Oliver Burkeman, in his book *The Antidote: Happiness for People Who Can't Stand Positive Thinking*, chalks it up to anxiety about the unknown. If we plan every moment, then we can vanquish our fear of the unfixed future. Of goal-setting and overplanning, he writes: "We invest ever more fiercely in our preferred vision of that future—not because it will help us achieve it, but because it helps rid us of feelings of uncertainty in the present."But all that planning tends to make us more stressed. An open-ended weekend embraces life's uncertainty, rather than fighting it. Fun is hard to schedule, easy to stumble upon. Forget the perfect party, or the impeccable dinner table. Open the doors, and the fridge. The best weekends are agile.

UNLEASH THE KIDS

I live, like many of us, in a city where kids' lives are stuffed with activities. From the moment they're born, savvy marketers present new parents with cradle-to-grad options: baby yoga; kiddie salsa; animation class; coding for teens. The sports aren't just open-to-all house league, but higher-level "Select" or "Rep." The tutors are many. In suburban and rural communities, the menu of activities may not be as twee as it is in my downtown neighborhood, but the kids are still busy. One survey found that over half of suburban American boys between third grade and fifth grade will play on three or more teams. Sports are gener-ally a good thing, teaching teamwork and athleticism, and coun-tering creeping obesity rates and the lumpen device-centered

life. But sports—like any other extracurricular done to excess—
can also change the shape of a family's week. With parents driving kids to and fro, sitting in the arena or at the edge of dance
class—the weekend is in jeopardy.

Christina has a five-year-old daughter. She and her husband both work long hours in media in Toronto, and because
of their jobs, they can't schedule classes for her on weeknights
so the weekend is activity time. They try to keep it simple:
dance on Saturday and swimming on Sunday. Swimming is
non-negotiable—a survival skill, like shoelace-tying. But with
a five-year-old, a single activity has the ability to take over a full
day (tights—in what workshop in Hades were tights for toddlers invented?), and by Sunday night, the family is exhausted.
So last summer, they dropped dance for the season and discovered a more mellow type of weekend. There was some sleeping in, some unplanned, meandering afternoons. Christina felt
less wiped out on Sunday night.

Then fall came, and Christina asked her daughter if she
wanted to do dance; she said yes. But within a few weeks back
on the full weekend schedule, her daughter started complaining. "She actually said, 'I don't get a weekend like other kids!
I don't have one day where I don't have to do something!' I
started arguing with her: 'You asked to go back go dance!' In my
mind I was like, 'I paid $300 for this dance class.' It was on me.
She was cognizant of the fact that she did not have a day off and
she's five years old. It stopped me in my tracks. My instinct was:
This is crazy. Let's just stop."

Christina says that her "cheapness took over" and they're

seeing the class through to the end of the year. I don't think it's cheapness (refusing to throw away $300 seems pretty sane), but her revelation raises a real question: Do we have to put our kids in classes and sports on the weekend? Well, for those of us lucky enough to afford them, there are some seriously awesome offerings out there now. There were no filmmaking courses or girls rock camp when I was a kid. One sport on the weekend, and piano on Mondays—that was the general diet for most kids I knew in the 1980s, and most of us abandoned one or both by middle school.

But as charming as this influx of enrichment activities might be, they often seem to arise from a dark, oily place: from the fear that our children's futures are fragile, and global competition is going to annihilate their opportunities. Surely French choir will arm them for the coming economic apocalypse! Michael Thompson, a clinical psychologist and author of *The Pressured Child*, has said, "When I was growing up it was clean your plate because they're starving in China. Now it's go practice your instrument because kids in China are learning violin."

A wealth of research on the downside of overscheduled kids tells us what we intuitively know: kids with no time to meander are prone to stress and anxiety, and out of touch with their creative instincts. Thompson admits that no one knows exactly where the line is between healthy enrichment and overscheduled, stressed-out kids, but if we, too, are feeling exhausted and burned out facilitating our kids' schedules, then that's probably the line.

A couple of years ago, Mia played for a Select soccer team. We asked her if she wanted to try out, and while I had a feeling we were setting ourselves up for a time-suck, of course I was secretly a little giddy when she went for it (she has drive!), and giddier when she made the team (a star is born!). But several months later, I saw the reality of Select soccer. It cost a boatload, and seemed to mean little more than extra practices and weekends spent in car trips to tournaments in faraway suburbs.

The last practice was on a school night in late September, long after the season should have ended, and everyone seemed tired—well, the parents did, anyway. In the dark, the girls sat on the field in a circle, eating pink cupcakes brought by some mother who wasn't me. Hovering around the edges were the parents, as ever. A dad asked me if Mia would continue to play indoor soccer through the winter. I told him no, she plays hockey in the school year, and we try to keep it to one activity per season. He looked alarmed. "But aren't you worried that she'll fall behind?" Behind what? I wondered.

Much as I love my daughter, I highly doubt that soccer will be the dominating force of her future, except (and I hope this is true) as a fun activity she can do with a group of friends throughout her life. Yet many parents are actually harboring fantasies that spending every weekend on the court or the ice is an investment. According to a poll from NPR, the Robert Wood Johnson Foundation, and the Harvard T. H. Chan School of Public Health, 26 percent of U.S. parents whose children play high school sports actually hope that their child will one day go pro. Among families with annual household incomes of less than $50,000, the number is 39 percent. In fact, the odds of your talented high school athlete making a living in professional sports are infinitesimal: 1 in 2,451 boys playing high school basketball will eventually get drafted by a National Basketball Association team.

Coaches have noticed that when parents hear about these bad odds, they don't think, "Well, I'm out." Instead, they think, "Well, we'll start my kid earlier, and work harder!" The ten-thousand-hour rule—an expert requires ten thousand hours of "deliberate practice" to reach expertise in any field—that Malcolm Gladwell put forward in *Outliers* has been a real bitch for parents. I can feel that factoid lurking at the edges of the ice rink on Sundays. Much has been written about how kids in university today exhibit increasing anxiety levels and decreasing creativity. They're barely able to look after themselves after years of helicopter parents ushering them through their busy lives. When would they have had time to cultivate their human selves, to develop those basic survival skills, as they're shuttled from activity to activity?

Of course, no one wants their kids locked in the kind of boredom that creates a vacuum for drugs or badassery; all this childhood programming is, at its best, a genuine effort to keep them stimulated and off the street corner. But the pendulum may have swung too far if they no longer get to experience boredom. Boredom is powerful; it's the trigger for creative epiphanies, and it might even save society. A paper out of the University of Limerick analyzed research that suggests bored people are likely to become "prosocial," driven to selfless, altruistic activities and considerate of the needs of others. If they're bored, feeling their actions are meaningless, they then become motivated to do something meaningful. Subjects experiencing deep boredom became motivated to give blood, and donate to charity.

Remember the supreme power of boredom, and all the weird thoughts you turned over during those long, boring Sundays of your youth? This was the space in which to wander the corridors of your own mind, discovering what makes you uniquely you, far from the agenda of parents and teachers. Boredom can be agony, but it forces independence and self-reliance. Boredom puts kids on buses, and in parks, and makes them pick up cameras and paintbrushes and hammers. It coaxes the self out of the shadows.

But boredom requires unoccupied time. So here, then, is the message to stressed families wondering how to get their weekends back. It's a familiar refrain: Do less. Do less. Do less.

Margaret Rafferty, of Sydney, Australia, decided to stop the madness. She has a full-time job and three kids (one is in college now), and for a decade, she spent her weekends driving everyone to sports. She did a little coaching; she brought the orange slices. And the weekends slipped away. "I had a dawning realization that I didn't have a life anymore," she says. When the soccer season ended, there was a month of downtime where everything slowed. Margaret and her husband were less stressed; her kids seemed more rested. At the end of that month, as the new season loomed, she and her husband talked about how nice it had been, and landed on a "What if . . . ?" They discussed ending the sports, and presented the possibility to the kids. To her surprise, they were fine with it. So she pulled them out, and wrote an article for a blog: "Why My Kids Don't Play Organised Sport." She immediately received hate mail, calling the decision selfish and unfair. "Someone commented that it was parents like me who were responsible for Australia's poor showing at the Olympics," she recalls. But she kept checking in with the kids, and they kept saying they didn't miss soccer.

Meanwhile, their weekends transformed. "Our family has a tiny little property in the country and we'd hardly visit it because six months of the year the weekends would be filled with sports. Removing that from our timetable meant we could get back there once a month. The kids were puttering around on the farm and playing down at the creek—those traditional childhood activities that we had had no time for."

At first, taking care of the house rose to the forefront of the weekend; she did some serious cleaning, she admits. But then, her own needs emerged. She got engaged with hobbies: she's training for a half marathon and researching her family history, an activity that her youngest kids have joined in on. Her husband has time to run and swim. As for her kids, their lives are full. In the wide-open space of the weekend, they began to follow their own pursuits and lead their own childhoods. One son is heavily into comic books, another into music—their own desires emerged, without prodding.

"They're not waiting for me to set their agenda," she says. Being hands-off is something that parents are increasingly scared to do, Margaret tells me, "because they worry if they do it they'll end up with loser children who play video games all the day—that cliché. It doesn't have to be like that. The more you try to make your kids conform to the accepted wisdom of what they should be doing and achieving, the less likely they are to stand out in the world, and find a unique identity and skill set that equips them to make a mark."

It's interesting that this cultivation of enriched, distinct childhoods has wound its way back to a place of sameness; all this grooming of our children actually delivers a cookie-cutter experience of childhood from parents who have fought so hard to avoid it.

But even if total withdrawal isn't possible, declaring an "OFF DAY" on the weekend from time to time reaps benefits. I'm not as good at this, but my husband has no problem waking up on a Saturday and calling for an "OFF DAY," classes, practices, and games be-damned. Obviously, we don't do this if the kids don't want the break, or it's a pivotal game where an absence affects others. But I want to live in a world where a ten-year-old missing a house league hockey game to go on a hike with his family is entirely possible. Still, it can feel like an incredibly rebellious act: What will they miss? What if this is the day they pass out the secret key to the universe at dance class? The reality is that they probably won't miss much; the activity will still be there the next week. They're committed to their activities all those other Saturdays in the year, but now they're learning something else. Flexibility. Leisure. What it feels like to open up time. Anything could happen.

Tom Hanks, in an NPR interview, told a hilarious story about the 1960s brand of parenting, the kind of divorce-generation benign neglect that characterized many '60s and '70s childhoods:

There was one time in high school I had the flu and I spent
two weeks at a friend's house and when I finally came home
my dad said, "Where've you been?" I said, "Oh I had the flu,
I slept at Kirk's house." He said, "I figured you'd take care of
yourself." So that brand of freedom, it wasn't a cruel brand
of disinterest, but they were just very busy doing other things.
. . . That along with attention deficit disorder made me what
I am today.

Since then, the culture has done a 180 toward attachment
parenting, and most of us have been told we need to make up
for lost time on the weekends. For parents, this creates a hotbox
of expectations, and only possible outcome is failure. Miranda,
a magazine editor, lives in Brooklyn. Her husband is a lawyer in
Manhattan. On Friday, the promise of a weekend gets her mood
up, but by Sunday, she's left with letdown, the sensation of a
promise unmet.

"I would love to be able to achieve one semi-significant home
repair, have one culturally important experience, and have time
with the children where I felt we were being creative together in
childhood mode," she says. "The contradiction of the weekend
is that I imbue it with all the American self-improvement do-it-
yourself-ism while simultaneously expecting it to hold infinite
relaxation and no time pressure—and I can never get it right."

Everyone suffers from high expectations for the weekend,
but for working parents, the weekend can feel like two days
of apologizing for the absence, emotional and physical, of the
week. Scott Schieman, a sociologist at the University of Toronto,

is engaged in a longitudinal study of dual-earner families with kids, examining stressors in work-family interactions. "One of the interesting findings is that when people feel like they don't have enough time with their kids, it's one of the biggest predicators of feeling anxious or tense or off," he says. "There's a nostalgic sense that weekends were protected time."

But it's exhausting to shift identities so quickly, to step out of our work skins and into our parental selves. The competing needs that stress us out during the week—the personal and the professional—don't actually vanish just because it's Saturday, and we end up feeling we satisfy none of the roles, always uncomfortable in the self we're wearing.

Miranda tries to find amazing things to do with her kids, and she's really good at it. They've made paper butterflies on the High Line, and seen Matisse's cutouts at the Met. They go to the farmers' market early on Saturday to get fresh eggs. All of these family rituals bring joy. But when everyone is too tired and unmotivated, and they stay home, she feels guilty about the emptiness of her time: good mothers cultivate good childhoods at every juncture, don't they?

The reality is that togetherness is not going to happen every single weekend, and we are killing ourselves trying to get it. Researchers at the University of Maryland expected to find that the entry of women into the workforce over the past four decades would be reflected in a drop in the amount of time they spend with kids. Instead, to their surprise, they learned that today's working mothers are spending as much time with their kids as they did forty years ago, even though only a fraction of women had full-time jobs then. What women are giving up is sleep and leisure; they're experiencing "leisure deficits"—declining their own pleasure to spend more time with their children.

But for what? Researchers closely examining diary data found that the number of hours a mother spends with her kids between the ages of three and eleven may not matter. More hours didn't actually affect children's academic success or psychological well-being. (Interestingly, mothers spending more time with their kids during adolescence may have a more positive effect, leading to less smoking, drinking, and sex.) "The quality of mothers' interaction with children—warmth, sensitivity, or focus—may be more important than the amount of time mothers spend with children," writes Professor Melissa Milkie and her colleagues. But guess what: parents who are overworked and preoccupied are often not present even when they're present. The working moms who feel the best about their parenting describe abandoning intensive mothering—the helicoptering of overscheduled kids—in favor of "extensive" mothering, being in charge of the overall well-being without necessarily being present for every moment. I like this idea of thinking big picture: Are my kids loved? Are they engaged with the world? Will they feel more loved and engaged if I stand at the side of their soccer practice every single Saturday instead of every third Saturday?

The big picture requires protecting. This gets easier as they get older, but in all likelihood, you don't have to be there for every single practice and game. You can, you know, just *leave*. While they're doing their thing, do yours. Bring a book. Go for a walk. Practice this phrase: "I'll see you in two hours." In fact, you can buy an extra hour by teaching them to take public transportation to their activities. My son was ten when we taught him how to take the streetcar and subway to baseball. We bought him a cheap, 7-Eleven burner phone (like the kind on *The Wire*) and off he went. Now he's a twelve-year-old who takes the streetcar to school and knows the entire subway map of the city. This is what psychologists call "self-efficacy"; we call it a confident, happy kid who will (God willing) do okay in the world when he enters it on his own in a few years.

OF COURSE, all these ideas about how a family can protect the weekend become much less convincing when you're faced with the tear-swollen eyes of a twelve-year-old.

As fall approaches, my son announces that he wants to play Select hockey. "Please," he says, those big eyes expanding. (He said "please"!) Playing at this higher level means two more games and/or practices a week on top of the two games he already plays, and these extra games take place in the north end of the city, about forty-five minutes away in rush hour traffic, on school nights. Plus possibly some weekend tournaments. Plus an extra $700, and we've already paid $500. This is actually cheap; not to us, but to the real hockey parents. At the AA level of Toronto kids' hockey, a family can easily pay $20,000 per year in fees, equipment, tournaments, and skills sessions.

As Jude is making his case, I immediately picture a family we know who rise most days at 5:00 a.m. to get their three kids to different rinks all over the city. Still, Julian and I nod and murmur,

"We'll discuss it." When our son leaves the kitchen, we look at each other and exhale. It isn't *exactly* a violation of our one-sport-per-season rule. Until our daughter's Select soccer experience, we'd always kept our kids in house league, which felt manageable: one or two hour-long games a week.

Now here's the tricky part, which Australia's Margaret Rafferty didn't have to contend with: Jude loves hockey. For weeks, he religiously wore a Montreal Canadiens shirt that's several sizes too small—Hulkily straining the seams—with a giant hole in the chest as a kind of mourning garb, to grieve P. K. Subban being traded. He has binders of hockey cards that he rearranges over and over for hours at a time. And he's only recently become good enough to even consider playing Select. Did I mention that he said "please"?

So my husband takes him to the tryout. He looks good out there, a contender, and Julian admits to a certain pride.

We talk long and hard, balancing his excitement and love of the game against the picture of the life we want our family to lead on weekends. Let me interject: I am aware that this scenario is the definition of a First World Problem. Yet we are about to bruise our son, and it doesn't feel small to us.

Back in the kitchen, Jude leans and we hover, and Julian tells him: "Your mother's been writing a book about weekends for the last year, and we've decided we want our weekends to be open, at least one of the two days. You're getting older, and you'll have homework, and you'll get interested in other things. But if the hockey takes up four days of free time a week, there's no room for anything else."

This is the part where the eyes well up. "Is it the money?" he asks quietly.

"It is a lot of money for us right now, but more than that, it's the time," Julian says. "We want to be able to do things spontaneously. If our Sundays are open, maybe we can go skiing one day—"

"Or for a walk!" I pipe up (I'm a terrible skier).

"Or for a walk. The point is, we have to make choices, and right now, as your parents, we think it's more important to choose to keep the weekend open."

I am not good with a sad-faced child and start rambling: "And you can play shinny on the weekend, if you still want to play hockey. Or we can all go to a museum. Or lounge around and do nothing." It's the last one that perks him up a little.

The campaign for Select went on for a few weeks, but as I write this, we are on the precipice of the first weekend in years with one full day open: Sunday is officially free of kiddie activities. And our son has learned that sometimes the needs of our family, the collective, matter more than the needs of the individual, him. It's a lesson we wanted to impart anyway; now we have.

And as a bonus, we've taken back the weekend—well, half of it. It's a start.

A NOTE ON HOMEWORK

A mother of two middle-schoolers recently complained to me about how much homework she had to do on the weekend. "Oh, did you go back to school?" I asked. She shook her head no. "Good news, then—you don't actually have homework!" She was irritated, I think.

But I meant it: all that homework—and there is too much homework—is not yours. That means you don't have to do it. There—you just got a few hours back.

Yes, there will be Sunday afternoons when your offspring needs you to go over an assignment, and some kids require more guidance. But this trend of parents and kids sitting down together like peers to hash through the algebra and civics—this is madness. It disempowers kids, and sets them up for anxiety about their own skills and scholarship. It stops them from problem solving and managing their own time. It prevents teachers from knowing where the kid is at academically. And one more thing: it's a weekend killer.

Next weekend, tell yourself what your kid is wishing someone would say to him: Ditch the homework and go have fun.

CHAPTER 6

THE POWER OF BEAUTY

A WEEKEND WITHOUT beauty is hardly a weekend at all. This doesn't necessarily mean lining up for the blockbuster exhibit at the local museum (though that could be pretty cool). Beauty is in gardens, on buildings, and in public sculptures. Don't get hung up on the intimidating question "What is beautiful?" We know beauty through a kind of sense memory. Sometime, somewhere, a song made you cry. A photograph stopped you in your tracks. Maybe it was a really bad song; maybe it was by Milli Vanilli or Twenty One Pilots. Maybe it was the orange cast of that strange moon. Something shifted, opened up inside—and that's a feeling to chase on the weekend. The late Irish poet John O'Donohue wrote that we instinctively understand beauty: "We find that we slip into the Beautiful with the same ease as we slip into the seamless embrace of water; something ancient within us already trusts that this embrace will hold us." Beauty is comfort; a salve atop the harshness of our days, our own mistakes and burdens.

Perhaps you're thinking, "There's no beauty where I live, lady." But nature and art are available to everyone in some variation; it may take a little looking, a little reframing. Some people will locate their nature fix in wakeboarding or parachuting, but even the most diehard urban dweller can find her way to a tree for a half hour. A relationship to nature can increase happiness and restore our bodies and minds.

Restoration doesn't arise only from experiencing art, but from making it. In an experiment, thirty-nine adults were given a set of preschoolers' art supplies, including pencils, glue, and clay. After forty-five minutes of arts and crafts, cortisol levels—markers of stress—had dropped significantly in 75 percent of the subjects. These people were not artists; no one will purchase their scribbles. But the quality of the work doesn't matter, it seems; the very act of creating something can measurably change how you feel.

What links art and nature is "awe," an experience that breaks the monotonous rhythms of the week. According to researchers Dacher Keltner and Jonathan Haidt, "awe" is the underexamined emotion "in the upper reaches of pleasure and on the boundary of fear." Awe encompasses two experiences: vastness and accommodation. Vastness is perceiving what's greater than us—the waterfall, the tornado, childbirth—and accommodation is how we assimilate that vastness into our current mental structures, how we make sense of it.

Just as volunteering can create the feeling that time has expanded, experiencing awe may be another way to find more time on the weekend. A working paper led by a researcher from Stanford explains how "awe" can anchor one in the now: "Experiences of awe bring people into the present moment, which underlies awe's capacity to adjust time perception, influence decisions, and make life feel more satisfying than it would otherwise." So if you say, "I don't have time on the weekend for beauty," the act of seeking it out may actually get that time back for you.

NATURE CALLS

I am a city mouse, or to be more anatomically correct, at six feet tall, a city giraffe. I can conquer subway systems in any country and currency, but I grow ungainly when the substance beneath my feet isn't concrete. On a hike, I fall a lot, missing the grooves in the dirt that bred-in-the-bone naturalists instinctively find. I gingerly sidestep puddles for fear of slippage. I'm slow. I've been known to kind of crab-walk down a semi-steep hill to avoid a spine-severing spill, while my agile kids giggle as they skip lightly past me.

But still—I love nature, even if we're a funny fit for each other. I love my muddy palms after a good crab-walk. I crave air and silence, and walk and run long and often, usually toward trees. It's nostalgia, perhaps, for a time when I wasn't so urban and brittle in my body and mind. As a rather sullen, Goth-inclined fifteen-year-old, trees saved me. In tenth grade, on a

whim, I enrolled in a one-year outdoor education program, a
public school version of Outward Bound. "Really?" said my dad,
eyebrows raised. "You?" But I was curious and bored, a good
formula to follow for most of life's important decisions.

My class of thirty rushed through our academics in one
semester, and then spent four months on trips to parts of British
Columbia I'd seen only on maps. We slept in snow caves. We
canoed ten days through a channel of rivers without coming
into contact with anyone but each other. We cross-country
skied in avalanche zones. I was ripped from sulkiness, pushed
physically and mentally, jarred repeatedly by surprise and wonder. On a canoe trip, two girls almost died when their boat
careened to the edge of a waterfall. Somehow, they J-stroked
out of the rushing currents, their arms alone moving a boulder
stuck in quicksand. The rest of us watched this feat of super-
human strength, paralyzed in our canoes in the still water up
high, silent, not breathing, barely able to look upon the scene.

For a lot of the kids in the program, that year bred a lifelong connection to nature: many became environmental lawyers
and activists; one is a prominent nature photographer; another
a naturopath. I'd reverted to my pop culture obsessions and
black eyeliner by fall, but I never forgot the new self I'd been that
year, how tough I was. It's not that I was fearless; in fact, I was
never more fearful. Out in the woods, I feared bears and snakes,
rockslides, being buried alive in an ice cave. But I survived, and
learned that fear is not immovable. My body pushed through the
final miles of a three-day-long bike ride. I repeated David Bowie
lyrics a million times in my head to finish the climb to the top

of a mountain, my heel bleeding through the moleskin and into my boot. Over and over that year, I looked up and saw trees, so many trees; the rise of them pulled me up, too, to the tips of the branches, out of myself. I discovered, in those teen years of profound narcissism, that I wasn't the most important force in the universe. There was wonder, and I could access it simply by leaving the concrete for the woods, inhaling the air, by putting one foot in front of the other in the presence of mossy, dirty life.

Over the many years since, I've learned that when I go too long without a dose of the natural world, I'm not quite myself. But I live, as over half the world does now, in a city, and not just in a city, but downtown. I hear streetcars rattling and see the CN Tower from my bedroom window, blinking in a forest of skyscrapers every night. As a family, we don't get out of the city as much as we'd like. On a Saturday or Sunday, when we might be able to slip away, the work grind is a stronger pull than the natural world. Work is at hand; nature takes effort.

Research out of the University of Illinois at Chicago suggests that the percentage of Americans spending time in nature for recreation (camping, fishing, hunting) declined by more than 1 percent a year between the late 1980s and the late aughts. One survey found that Americans spend 87 percent of their time indoors and 6 percent in an enclosed vehicle. In both the United States and Canada, national park usage is dropping, too. In America's national parks, more than 9.2 million overnight camping stays were recorded in 1998. By 2003, the number had dropped to 8.54 million; by 2013, it had fallen again, to 7.91 million. A survey by the Outdoor Foundation asked participants why they weren't visiting parks, and the top answer was "a lack of time due to work and family commitments." The loss of this connection is profound.

In the eighteenth century, Samuel Johnson wrote that "deviation from nature is deviation from happiness," and today's science supports him. Richard Louv, journalist and cofounder of the Children & Nature Network, coined the phrase "nature-deficit disorder" in his 2005 book *Last Child in the Woods*. He wrote that the spread of obesity, depression, and attention disorders among children is a direct result of kids being raised in a cautious culture severed from the natural world. With all those activities on their schedules, and parents who are worried about them walking to the store let alone to the woods, they have no time to really savor and experience the outdoors. Writes Louv, "A kid today can likely tell you about the Amazon rain forest—but not about the last time he or she explored the woods in solitude, or lay in a field listening to the wind and watching the clouds move."

When the book came out, adults kept coming up to him with the same complaint: "Hey, I have this problem, too." Well, why wouldn't we? Overscheduled adults breed overscheduled children. Louv has gone on to write that nature-deficit disorder affects adults, too.

Study after study bears him out. Looking out a window at a natural scene may help post-operative patients recover more quickly. The Japanese government has spent $4 million on "forest-bathing" research since 2004, investigating the therapeutic benefits of exposure to nature. Researchers at Chiba

University in Japan found that participants who took slow walks in the woods showed a 15.8 percent decrease in the stress hormone cortisol and a 1.94 percent decrease in blood pressure. Anxiety—on the rise across North America—can be reduced by proximity to green.

One famous 1991 study at Texas A&M University showed that even brief exposure to nature can reduce stress. Researchers showed subjects a ten-minute-long, gruesome film on workplace accidents. Before and after the film, they checked the viewers' heart rates, blood pressure, and muscle tension, and asked them to rate their own stress levels. Next, one group of subjects watched a ten-minute-long tape of natural images, like rivers and forests. The other group was shown urban scenes of malls and crowded sidewalks. "Participants recovered more quickly and more completely from stress when exposed to . . . the nature settings than to the urban settings," said Roger Ulrich, associate dean of the university's College of Architecture, to the LA Times. "By the end of ten minutes, people who viewed the nature scenes were as relaxed or sometimes even more relaxed than before viewing the accident film."

Of course, "nature = good" is hardly an "Extra! Extra!" revelation. Indigenous people have forever placed the natural world at the center of their beliefs and traditions. The American Romantics held close the conviction that the environment is akin to a prelapsarian garden, a state of grace. In his 1836 essay, "Nature," Ralph Waldo Emerson wrote, "In the woods, we return to reason and faith. There I feel that nothing can befall me in life,—no disgrace, no calamity . . . which nature cannot repair."

On nature, poets and scientists may agree, but we don't really know *why* it has such a direct, measurable effect on our well-being. Those who subscribe to the biophilia hypothesis of evolutionary biologist E. O. Wilson believe we're experiencing an evolutionary holdover: we once required a deep connection to nature for our own survival. Now we suffer in its absence.

Despite the pleas of the Romantics, for most nineteenth-century Americans, spending time in nature didn't exactly top the list of leisure activities. The environment was seen as an impediment to progress, a thing to be conquered, not cele-brated. It wasn't until the latter part of the century, in the wake of the Civil War, that a version of today's pro-environmental message went mainstream. In 1869, William Henry Harrison Murray, a clergyman and Yale graduate, published a book called *Adventures in the Wilderness; or, Camp-Life in the Adirondacks*. The book was well timed: a healing prescription for a country reeling from war and the breakneck speed of industrialization. Murray presented the Adirondacks as the cure; 6 million acres of rela-tively untouched (by white people, anyway) land and waterways north of New York. "I deem the excursion eminently adapted to restore impaired health," wrote Murray. The book was a get-away guide aimed at a new urban population that lived in big, loud, dirty cities, especially those "pent up in narrow offices and narrower studies, weary of the city's din, long[ing] for a breath of mountain air and the free life by field and flood." Murray loved providing quirky how-to information, including what to pack ("Stout pantaloons, vest and coat" in "wool and flannel"), and remarking on food ("The first course consisted of trout and pancakes; the second course, pancakes and trout; the third, fish and flapjacks").

His stories of the miraculous healing powers of nature read today with the fervor of late-night infomercial pitches for exercise schemes. My favorite is the lengthy tale of a wealthy young New Yorker struck with consumption—what we now call tuberculosis—and on death's door. Murray notes that when the young man arrived in the north in early June he was unable to walk, so his guide laid him in the boat on a bed of pine, cedar, and balsam boughs and set forth for a group of islands. "Their pungent and healing odors penetrated his diseased and irritated lungs," writes Murray. "The second day out his cough was less sharp and painful. At the end of the first week he could walk by leaning on the paddle. . . . The third week the cough ceased entirely. From that time he improved with wonderful rapidity." By November he "came out bronzed as an Indian, and as hearty."

Racist miracle stories notwithstanding, the book was an instant best-seller. In the summer of 1869, books in hand, swarms of keen urbanites descended on the Adirondacks, transported by new train lines from Boston and New York. It didn't go well. The few lodges couldn't fit them all, and the presence of women offended the hunters. Also, it was a rainy and miserable summer, and a few of the consumptives who'd hoped for resurrection weren't cured, but died en route. For their failed, muddy efforts, the interlopers were tagged "Murray's Fools" by the press and much mocked.

But in the summer of 1870, the weather improved, and city

folk returned, this time gleaning the benefits of Murray's ethos, as Tony Perrottet wrote in an article in *Smithsonian* that credits Murray with inventing the American vacation. For many, this version of the natural world didn't mean dug-out toilets and trout, but the crafting of elaborate homesteads. Throughout the century, wealthy families like the Vanderbilts and Carnegies built elaborate camps and log cabin compounds that still exist today. As transportation improved, weekend visitors arrived. This is where the word "vacation" comes into common speech, replacing the British word "holiday": the wealthy New York classes would vacate their city homes for the Adirondacks. The summer population went from 3,000 in 1869 to 25,000 in 1900. When the automobile came into play in the 1900s and became the preferred mode of transportation, more and more people could retreat to nature for weekends, and more affordably, into the world of cottage country—a rural hit but with the amenities of the city.

As Witold Rybczynski points out in *Waiting for the Weekend*, the retreat to nature arose alongside the rise of the cities. For farmers, and others who live year-round in rural settings, the rhythms of the weekend have always been largely indistinguishable from the rhythms of the week: livestock need attention seven days a week. The call of the seasons determine what needs to be done for those working the land, and how much free time they have. "The weekend, like the weekend retreat, is an urban habit," writes Rybczynski. "The two developed in tandem as consequences of city life—a time to escape, a place to escape to."

◇◇◇◇

FLASH FORWARD 150 YEARS, and I'm in a crowded coffee shop in Oakland, California, talking to J. Phoenix Smith, a certified "ecotherapist." Over an Americano while dance music blares, Smith tells me that we're not too far from an urban lake called Lake Mary. "It's one of the first national wildlife refuges in the country. Three miles to walk and run around it. I was there on the weekend, and I saw birds I've never seen before!"

I use an exclamation point because Smith is as gleeful about spotting a new bird in the wilderness as others are about spotting a celebrity in the supermarket. She was among the first graduates of the ecotherapy certificate program at John F. Kennedy University in Pleasant Hill, California. Ecotherapy is a burgeoning treatment practice that involves exposing patients to the natural world for physical and psychological healing. But Smith says that, as a kid, she never felt that comfortable in nature; it was something she learned later in life. She grew up in San Antonio, Texas, in a family that stayed close to the air conditioning. On weekends, she says, they mostly shopped.

Smith discovered the outdoors as an adult in crisis. She was living in Washington, D.C., working as a case manager at a women's HIV clinic. Up close to that kind of trauma on a daily basis was stressful; she felt herself burning out, exhausted. A doctor recommended a retreat, which is the kind of advice we all get on occasion, to which we murmur, "Yeah, good idea," and then go back to our lousy feelings. But Smith took her up on it: she went off for a month to study yoga at an ashram in the Bahamas. "All these things opened up in me," she recalls. "I had time to do yoga and be by the ocean. Nature became medicine for me."

Back in her real life, she began to explore the wilderness around D.C., discovering the area's network of public national parks, exploring the Anacostia River and hiking in the Shenandoah.

A few years later, living in San Francisco, she got laid off from her work in public health administration, and she turned immediately to nature to help with the stress of unemployment. "I started reading, and I started walking, and it all clicked. Our destruction of the environment is intimately connected with our own spiritual and mental health," she says.

She was absorbing the writings of Theodore Roszak, a history professor and social critic who coined the term "ecopsychology" in the 1990s to examine the emotional connection between human psychology and the natural world. The environmental crisis is written on our psyches and bodies, and our own mental health—or lack thereof—drives the destruction of the earth. Ecotherapy is the applied practice of ecopsychology, and Smith was living it, reducing the stress of unemployment by returning regularly to her favorite tree and her favorite hike, feeling grounded in these places when the rest of her life was uncertain. Smith, who is African American, started a hiking group for people of color, to push back at the stereotype that black and Latino people don't like the outdoors. Then she became a certified ecotherapist, hanging out her shingle while working a day job in public health. Her biggest client is a San Francisco nonprofit that works with children in foster care who often have behavior and health issues. Smith ran an Intro to Ecotherapy course for the youth workers, taking them on weekend retreats into nature, helping them deal with the high-stress work.

In her sessions, Smith asks clients to consider the ways the environment is already in their lives. Many people, born and raised in cities, will say they have no relationship to nature. Smith refuses to hear this. "I prod and eventually people remember. Everyone has stories: 'Oh—I used to go fishing with my grandfather.' Or, 'My grandmother used to make this special meal growing this special grain in the garden.'" Smith found a photograph of her own grandmother in a garden, and she learned that in the segregated South in the early twentieth century, there were few stores black people could access, so her grandmother grew her own food. This story is a historical link to the plants and vegetables Smith grows today.

In the United States, ecotherapy is still a relatively new field, not yet recognized by any medical association. I mentioned it to a friend who has a farm and she rolled her eyes: "We get to commune with nature every f'n day, not just on weekends." Several articles on ecotherapy snicker about ecotherapists who recommend holding moist soil for mood-enhancement, which, granted, seems like advice delivered through a cloud of bong smoke. (It also seems to be true: University of Bristol researchers found that soil bacteria injections in mice generated serotonin in their brains, a natural antidepressant functioning like Prozac.)

In the U.K., however, ecotherapy has gained a foothold in the medical world as a legitimate mental-health treatment. An organization called Mind funded 130 ecotherapy projects across England between 2009 and 2013. In these studies, twelve thousand people, a wide societal swath with varying mental-health issues, participated in outdoor activities including gardening, food growing, and conservation work. The results were dramatic. Participants reported improved mental and physical health. Unemployed people, now less isolated and happier, became more employable. Participants spoke of a renewed sense of community and well-being. One new gardener in Bournemouth said, "I used to spend a lot of time on my own, I didn't want to leave the house, I slept constantly and felt like I had nothing to get up for, I felt alien. Now I'm part of the team and I feel like I have something to get up for in the morning. I enjoy the fresh air and gardening and I get a real sense of achievement and satisfaction when we finish a garden."

Mental-health issues are a financial burden on any state, costing the U.K. over 21 billion pounds per year in care costs alone, on top of billions more lost to human suffering and unrealized economic output. But ecotherapy is cheap; the Mind program cost very little—7.5 million pounds, lottery funded. An audit found that enrolling just five people with mental-health issues into ecotherapy programs saved more than 35,000 pounds per year in medication, employment insurance, and health care.

The other savings may be more significant. Smith has seen her clients become invested in the natural world. They return to the same settings year after year, saying, "Oh, there's my tree, my rock." This personal connection may have a wider impact, one that sits at the center of ecotherapy: connection to the environment leads to a compulsion to preserve it. She encourages her clients to create a weekend ritual around nature. These can be small steps: a walk every Saturday, a bike ride to a new park on a Sunday morning. "Go explore. Is there a park within ten miles of where you live that you didn't even notice? Start there," she says. Doing so is as urgent as medication. We just have to work harder to fill the prescription. "We had to fight for the forty-hour workweek, we had to fight for the weekend," says Smith. "Now we have to fight for our time in nature. We've got to make it happen."

EILEEN LIVES IN Portland, Oregon. She's a retiree who worked as an art therapist and taught in public schools for forty years. Now in her early seventies, Eileen is one of those people who makes every single nanosecond of her leisure count. During the week, she volunteers. On the weekends, she's in clubs, on a seasonal rotation: a hiking club, snowshoe club, origami club. She sees theater and plays and meets with friends at night. "People in their seventies and eighties, without the obligation of kids, we understand that you have to do something active, and you have to do something intellectual. There has to be a balance, or what are we here for?" she says.

She left New Jersey a few years ago to follow her grown sons to Portland, but also because she wanted a better climate for her active lifestyle. She's always been athletic, competing in bike races and triathlons. But of all her ridiculous long list of activities, it's the retreat to nature that Eileen finds most rejuvenating. She recently took up cross-country skiing, which she claims—though I very much doubt it—to be bad at. But she gives zero cares about the quality of her skiing: she needs the beauty, the air. I talked to her on a Monday, after she'd spent her Sunday skiing, and she told me, "I was thinking yesterday as I'm skiing up in Pocket Creek, there was the snow on the trees, the air was so great. I put my hand out and a bird sat on my head." I stopped her there, and she said it again. "Yes, it's true, a bird sat on my head. It was like a Christmas card where I was. I was restored. I was in nature. That's what I need. We get older and we need to intercept aging. We need to feel fully alive."

ON THE OTHER SIDE of the country, on the same weekend, Torr stands at the top of a cliff on Bear Mountain, looking across at the Manhattan skyline, feeling the awe. He is bearded and barefoot, in the middle of a twenty-mile run with a dozen other people who make up the Brooklyn Trail Runners group. They meet every Saturday at a location outside of New York City and go running where people are really meant to hike, on the kinds of rocky, dirty trails that inspire more tentative types to crab-walk.

Soon after this moment of taking in Manhattan, around hour three of the run, beneath a mossy cliff canopy, one of the runners says, "It's beautiful," and then—smash. She falls, slicing open her knee, down to the bone, "like someone had dug out her knee with a teaspoon," says Torr. Blood is not an infrequent occurrence on these outings. Torr helps her get to a car, back to the city, and while he is certainly concerned, there's acceptance, too. "It's actually kind of a bonding thing, when someone gets injured," he says. And they do get injured: one trail is nicknamed "Six Stitches."

Torr is a designer at a start-up in Chelsea, and when working, it's at the usual kind of breakneck pace that's required. But when it's the weekend, he turns his phone off, and by doing so, he's left alone. "I don't stress about it. It's how I want to live," he says.

How he wants to live is large. He's a vegan. He started a sandal company at one point under the moniker The Sandal Guy. He does "ultra running," training for seventy-mile runs by running barefoot. Let me reiterate: HE RUNS BAREFOOT ON TRAILS.

But shoelessness is not mandatory; Torr set up the club to be accessible to all. He posts a description of the run online, with public transportation routes to the start of the trail. It's free, but it does take a full Saturday. Runners get up at 6:00 a.m. to catch an 8:30 train from Penn Station. Most people won't get back until 5:00 or 6:00. In the summer, there are swims and beach runs.

The trails are all within a half hour or so of Manhattan. At the start, the runners stash a change of clothes in bushes, and they set out in different pace groups, depending on how many people show up. It's a different scene each Saturday. Torr has run with a teenager and a family; a couple of people in their sixties. Sometimes there's a dog named Betty. The loops are six or thirteen miles, depending, and they don't have to involve anything as dramatic as a gouged leg. Often they are running toward brunch, or beer, so there's a social component, too. What Torr notices when he talks to people is their surprise that the natural world is so close at hand, even near Manhattan; they aren't as cutoff as they thought they were.

"People in New York City just don't know all the nature

that's around them within a half-hour train ride. We do a run in Prospect Park, and every time we do that trail run people say, 'I've been to this park a million times, I had no idea these trails were here.'"

Extreme outdoor recreation has boomed in the past few decades, with rising participation in rock climbing, outdoor adventure sports, and X Games. Dangerous ski and snowboard tricks go straight to YouTube. ER rooms have noticed, with an estimated forty thousand injuries per year in the United States among participants in seven extreme sports, including snow-boarding, motocross, and mountain biking.

Sociologist Stephen Lyng calls risky but regulated experien-ces "edgework," borrowing the term from Hunter S. Thompson's *Fear and Loathing in Las Vegas*. Edgework is voluntary risk-taking that leads to a kind of hyperreality; experiences that negotiate the space between "life and death, consciousness and uncon-sciousness, and sanity and insanity" (Thompson called this "dangerous lunacy"). It's a big umbrella that holds beneath it not just avalanche skiing but stock trading, self-starvation, and S&M.

Often, extreme sports involve taking nature—already kind of awesome—and turning it up to eleven; the risk is the reward. The number of people who have climbed Everest has quad-rupled in the last decade. For the overworked masses trapped in thankless jobs, a weekend that includes a hit of extreme adven-ture can be a kind of salvation, a moment of intensity to break the drudgery and feel what it is to be truly alive. For the most for-tunate, these are safe times; it's hard to imagine bungee-jumping businesses doing really well during a war. Much of today's work takes place in front of computers, which is physically safe, and often emotionally draining. The urge for controlled chaos is a primal need to switch up that formula, to jeopardize our bodies in order to soothe our minds.

The need for thrills may be universal, but extreme sports are very particular, and usually the domain of the privileged. BASE jumping and skydiving require a huge outlay of cash. To waterfall-rappel on a Saturday in New Hampshire's White Mountains can cost over $700. Nature can be bought, and conquering it becomes a sign of physical vigor to match one's corporate accomplishments. *The Economist* reports on a new breed of "SuperBoss" engaged in nonstop hyperactivity. On weekdays, CEOs report waking up at 3:30 a.m. for a workout (and to work on the novel, take a meeting, and have morning sex). On weekends, they take their overachievement to the natural world: "Sir Rocco Forte of Rocco Forte Hotels and Michael Johnson of Herbalife are among the bosses who take part in regular 'CEO Challenges' in which they push themselves to their physical limits through such things as triathlons and 100-mile mountain-biking trails."

For these highfliers, leisure becomes an extension of the values of our post-capitalist world: more-better-faster isn't just what drives productivity, but play, too. The bar keeps getting higher, and the experience bigger, no matter how dangerous the lunacy. Even outside our urban settings, we need a goal; we need to win. Nature becomes a weekend job, a badge of success—a thing to be conquered, not experienced.

The Brooklyn Trail Runners are not exclusive, except to the able-bodied and willing. But perhaps what links them to the millionaire triathletes is the quest for "peak experiences." Psychologist Abraham Maslow coined the term to describe those moments when your vision of the world changes—you are in awe, near-mystical rapture; the emotional response is one of "reverence, of humility and surrender." The need to experience a simpler, more atavistic way of being can't usually play itself out during the week, but it can—even for a limited time—on the weekend.

I ask Torr what it feels like to be out there, and he talks about how being on the trails, pushing the body in nature, changes his relationship to time.

"At the end of the run, I'll say to people, 'That was thirteen miles,' and they're like, 'Was it?' When you're pounding the pavement you know it's thirteen miles. But when you're watching every single step on a trail, and you have to be mindful every time you put your foot down—it's a place to live in the now. All your thoughts are gone for those few hours. There's no worries in the world."

I'M NOT INSPIRED to trail run like Torr because I prefer to never ever see the bones that I'm told sit within my body. But mere mortals can access awe, too, and tap into the benefits of the natural world. I wouldn't mind if a bird landed on my head.

On a cold Sunday in February, with Smith's fight-for-nature battle cry in mind, we declare an "OFF DAY" and ditch the kids' hockey commitments. We put the dog in the back of the car and drive out of the city toward a nature sanctuary.

Here is what I want from this Sunday: air, open space, decompression. It's been a stressful time at work, and I need to still the "I suck" ticker tape that's running through my head. In a Stanford-led study on the mental benefits of nature, researchers call this voice "rumination, a maladaptive pattern of self-referential thought that is associated with heightened risk for depression and other mental illnesses." I'm nowhere near the mental illness zone, but I am overwhelmed by a deadline for a show I'm working on, caught up in the minutiae of office politics. My sleep is broken. I feel a little sideways, raw.

The Stanford study sent two groups walking for ninety minutes, one in a grassland area and the other along a four-lane roadway buzzing with traffic. Physiologically, both groups emerged the same. But the group that was exposed to oak trees and shrubs demonstrated a change in the neural activity in the subgenual prefrontal cortex—a brain region that activates during rumination. Rumination decreased; the urban walkers didn't get that benefit.

This is only one of many studies exploring the connection between urban life and mental illness, though no causal link has been proven yet. But if you live in a city, you have a 20 percent higher risk of anxiety disorders and a 40 percent higher risk of mood disorders than do people in rural areas. But most of the world lives in cities now, and the trend is only moving upward. To buffer ourselves from the abrasions of modern life, we need to get back to nature.

Unfortunately, everyone else seems to know this, too.

When we arrive at the sanctuary, the parking lot is full, and I worry that there will be no real break from the throngs. But we get out, and take in the air. We keep walking, up a hill, into an open, snow-covered field. The crowd thins. Mia jumps on a frozen pond, waving. I remember that we visited this preserve once in the fall years ago, and saw the leaves change, gold to red. We do, as J. Phoenix Smith advised, have a connection to the place.

The dog is unhinged, this lunatic rescue that chases the occasional cross-country skier. But we keep walking, and then finally, there's no one for her to bug.

I get a chance talk to my son about his new school, and check in with him about how it's going (it's hard). We are out there for only a couple of hours before my hands go numb. I fall only twice, on icy patches. I don't think I really experience awe, but I feel the breaking of the routine, the split from the ordinary. We are laughing, and together, and we have a Sunday more memorable than all the ones that came before that month, locked in the hockey arena. We are alive.

That night, I check my agitation levels, measuring the Sunday night letdown that precedes the start of a new work-week. It is fainter; a whisper, not a hum.

ART WORKS

I am standing in front of a Picasso with my friend Rebecca, who is an artist, which feels like it should be an advantage in a museum. The painting is a portrait of Daniel-Henry Kahnweiler, a German art dealer who championed Picasso and his fellow Cubists a century ago, when the art world cold-shouldered the outsiders.

I only know this about the painting because of the volunteer guide who is leading our little Saturday morning tour group through several key moments in Modernism. Daniel-Henry himself is kind of hard to see, slipping across the canvas in shimmery pieces, recognizable only as a man of means and influence by the faint outline of his briefcase.

This is all very interesting, but Rebecca and I can't stop giggling, and that's pretty much how our morning at the Art Institute of Chicago goes. I thought that having an artist with me in a museum would alter my experience of the place, and it does, but not exactly how I'd imagined. For an hour, there's a pattern: we stand in front of a piece of beautiful art and then Rebecca makes me laugh (she does a Ferris Bueller routine about Cameron's face looking at Georges Seurat's pointillist *A Sunday Afternoon on the Island of La Grande Jatte*—perhaps the most famous painting of people at leisure on the weekend) or bringing up some stupid moment from high school. Afterward, we have tea in the lounge. It's a great day.

Though this is not one of those, there are times when I've been in museums and found myself surprisingly, profoundly moved by a piece of art. Pretentiously, one might even say— tears and all. I'm not an art expert by any means, though I took some art history classes in university, so I have a rudimentary understanding and a few biases. But I love museums. All my best weekends include them. It doesn't matter what's inside: I love the buildings, not just for their grandiosity but for their quiet corners, and the vulnerability of the people moving past, uncertain and blank, rapturous and whispering. The museum is like the weekend: a break in time, an excuse to step out of the rushing stream and stand still on the bank for a moment. Everyone around you is having a private moment in public— how intimate, to be moved alongside strangers!—and you're all united in the experience of the art, and also in the quiet of the space, the calm. One study found those who attend museums report significant benefits beyond learning: they find them to be places of restoration, and relievers of stress and anxiety. (Note to armchair sports dudes: for unclear reasons, men, in particular, appear to reap the physical advantages of a museum visit.)

We need art, in all or any of its forms, to feel human. I will spare you a debate about aesthetics or the mathematical explanations of beauty. (You know about the golden ratio, right? The perfect ratio for a face? No? Good. It doesn't matter.) Expertise is excellent, but it's the experience of art that makes it so necessary. Even if the art itself is repelling, it stirs and digs down into our most emotional selves, waking us up. Someone in our tour group gets very angry about Marcel Duchamps's *Hat Rack*, which is literally a little wooden hat rack hanging in space. "Is that art?" he keeps asking the guide. He asks this with much agitation, several times. I say to my friend, "Well, that's kind of great to be feeling anything so deeply this early on a Saturday!"

Museums are becoming increasingly social places, especially on weekends. Jacqueline Terrassa, the chair of museum education at the Art Institute of Chicago, tells me that weekend programming is designed to be social, and interactive. Like most museums, this means the Art Institute has classes and drop-in sessions, where people can stay for as little or as long as they want. "Digital culture has changed learning. No longer do you go to a museum just for information. The question now is how to interact, how to be more immersed in things," she says. "How do we create a participatory creative culture? That's where we're at as a society. People crave community, in person, and the museum has to be a living, social space to make it worth their while."

When Rebecca and I go, it's a social pursuit; we're catching up, and it's part of a bigger day of hanging out during my visit to her city. But the experience of art alone, in silence and solitude, is perhaps a deeper kind of weekend experience. If museums are secular cathedrals, then it makes sense that within their walls we can find ourselves near prayer state, or at least in contemplation. There aren't many places in the world where a person can just stand silently with his thoughts and not be regarded as totally creepy.

Rebecca would always take her stepson to the Art Institute on weekends when he was small. She loved watching him get excited about art, seeing things through his eyes. "But I mostly enjoy going to art museums alone," she says in an email. "I get lost in color and line. Clever ways of envisioning the world. Historical pieces leading to new insights to places in the past. Filling in gaps or puzzle pieces of places in time and space that never totally made sense or held my attention before in the same way—or totally waking up to something completely new and different that I have never seen before. I take pictures of a lot of things I see, and want to be reminded of later. For sure it stimulates ideas for me and my own artistic aspirations."

Experiencing art has all kinds of benefits that resemble those resulting from exposure to nature, suggesting that awe is awe is awe. Recent brain-mapping research suggests that exposing a subject to a beautiful piece of art can trigger the release of dopamine, the feel-good chemical, into the orbitofrontal cortex—the pleasure center—of the brain. People who engage with art report "peak experiences" similar to those described by mountain climbers and trail runners—a kind of ecstasy. And it's not just visual art that triggers this joy. In an online survey of 45,000 Brits ranking their top six happiness-inducing activities, sex and exercise top the list, but the other four are all arts-related: theater; singing/performance; exhibitions; craft-related hobbies.

And yet, we are not spending our weekends with art. According to the National Endowment for the Arts in the United States, participation in arts activities has been declining over the past decade. Museum attendance is down, too. Of surveyed parents with kids under six, the main reason given for not engaging with the arts is lack of time. There may be also an intimidation factor: *To set foot in a museum, I have to know all about Daniel-Henry Kahnweiler first.*

A few years ago, I picked up a book called *Art as Therapy*. In it, philosopher Alain de Botton and art historian John Armstrong call for a demystifying of art galleries, and a restructuring of art museums away from arrangement according to date and the offering of factoids. Instead, they propose that art galleries should emphasize "feeling," or a "psychological reading" of the work. Art should be understood as a therapeutic force—"an aid to living and dying," wrote de Botton. Needless to say, many critics hated this narrowing, and when they revamped some rooms at the Rijksmuseum in Amsterdam, one wrote off the exhibit as "shallow" and "obvious."

I don't know if captioning pictures to make them more relevant to our lives—e.g., looking at Claude Monet's *Water Lilies* in a room where all the pictures fit the theme "Hope"—will help bring busy, time-strapped people to museums. But won't they be missing something meaningful if they *don't* come? I emailed Armstrong and he challenged my question: "I'd be asking: 'What would happen if many more people had better relationships with art works and with beauty?' And I think the answer is that we'd ideally deal better with the ordinary problems of existence: we'd be kinder, more patient, more noble minded, more able to face practical challenges, more stoic in the face of inevitable suffering and difficulties."

GUSTAVE FLAUBERT SPENT his Sundays reviewing his week's writing. He would enlist his pal, the poet and playwright Louis Bouilhet, to sit and listen as he read aloud all the writing he'd done the week before. Bouilhet—one patient fellow—didn't mind; he would offer advice and cheer him on, and Flaubert would feel fortified and jazzed for the week to come.

This arrangement seems like a better deal for Flaubert,

though Bouilhet must have got something out of engaging with the great artist's work, too. But when there's so little free time on the weekend, a question arises: What's a better use of my tiny leisure slot—consuming art or creating it?

For therapeutic purposes, creating art has as much value as experiencing it. In one study, students were asked to write down their innermost thoughts on a significant emotional issue for fifteen to thirty minutes, without stopping. This act of self-expression has been shown, in dozens of replicated studies, to positively affect immune function, lower blood pressure, and decrease the frequency of doctor visits. Expelling a story that's lodged deep down, putting emotions on the page—these creative acts give meaning and purpose to the day, to our lives.

That sense of purpose is surely part of the rise in the popularity of "handcrafts" like pottery and knitting. The Maker Faire movement has sprung up all over the world: weekend gatherings of people displaying their DIY inventions in science, technology, crafts, arts. At these weekend events (131 of them were held around the world in 2014), anyone who wants to can show off an invention, as long as it's self-made. It's the coolest county fair ever. In New York in 2015, 95,000 people showed up to observe inventions like the "Barbie's Dream Drone," a life-sized mousetrap, and a giant eyeball mask described as a "visual and sound interface." We have the urge to use our hands, away from devices—to create rather than consume.

On Saturday mornings, Dale takes a pottery class. He signed up because his husband became a marathoner and was gone on weekend mornings. While his husband was off exercising and making all kinds of friends, Dale says he was sleeping in until eleven and then waking up ashamed and guilty at his slothfulness. So he signed up for a class, but discovered on the first day that he would be throwing pots next to children. "Not my idea of a weekend retreat, being surrounded by noisy, untalented children," he jokes. He got his money back and found a spot in the Brooklyn studio where he'd been wait-listed (pottery is hot in Brooklyn these days). For the past three years now, on Saturday mornings, he takes a car service down Atlantic Avenue, when Brooklyn is still sleepy. It is the beginning of the pottery ritual. "Usually when I ride in a car I just look at my phone and zone out, but this ride on Saturday becomes a very active period of studying Brooklyn and Atlantic Avenue. It's really become an exercise in mental awareness. I look out the window of the car and I note things and I appreciate things. Maybe I'm getting ready to be visually aware."

Dale is a trained artist and designer who now works as an editor at a newspaper. His days are long, and he's online every weekend, monitoring the traffic on the website and checking in with his staff. But during these few hours at pottery on Saturday he doesn't think about that; he retreats to a different part of his identity. "It was part of a reawakening of my whole self. I go back to my childhood, to my adolescence, to my college training as a painter and pick up a thread that had been lost," he says.

Once inside the studio, he claims his wheel by the door, where there's a patch of sunlight. Then he goes to the café next door for a coffee with skim milk and a Rice Krispie square. When the potting begins, it's a mellow vibe; there are ten wheels and big hand-building tables.

"When you're not too frazzled and you have mental energy to approach it calmly and systematically, pottery takes you out of the mind loop of worry. You're focusing on something that requires your full attention, and if you're not fully in the moment and concentrating, you're not going to be able to throw. The need to do that saves you from your own distracted mind," he says. "And I feel like I've been purposeful so it gives me permission to goof off later."

He makes beautiful objects: pussy-willow-green bowls, and small gourds; a pitcher with a diagonal slash of glaze. When he's finished, Dale will place his work on a table in the garden behind the studio and take a photo, for Instagram, naturally. But this part of the ritual is not only to collect Likes, it's a part of the process to share the work. "After you've created something there's the contemplation of it, the period of evaluation," he says. His weekend hit of beauty is self-made.

Most of us will never create such transcendent objects, but we can benefit from proximity. And the experience of beauty isn't limited to museums or galleries. There is no better way to explore a place than by looking up high, at the sky or the graffiti. My husband comes from a small town in Nova Scotia. When we visit, I always try to walk through the downtown, which is a bit sad and haunted in the way of small towns where commerce has fled to the suburban mall. But for reasons best known to some gung-ho city official long ago, it's also a town of murals, weird and colorful. One tells a ghost story; another shows a very oddly proportioned crowd of Victorian citizens where the heads don't quite match the bodies. I love these murals. They bring a lot of pleasure. Public art, found art, free music in churches and community centers—it's accessible and available, waiting to transform you, next weekend.

All of us want to come alive to the scope and sublimity of the world. The effects of a weekend that incorporates the beautiful will linger through the week, shadows of the things you saw, the things you made. Beauty stays; it's the best kind of Monday hangover.

CHAPTER 7

MANIFESTO FOR A GOOD WEEKEND

MY WEEKENDS look different these days. I bust out phrases I rarely used before: "Let's skip the sports today" and "Who wants to play cards?" and "I'll see you guys later." My bathroom is dirtier. I try to go twenty-four hours with absolutely no Internet. Seriously. We almost always have a formal Sunday dinner.

As a result, I am perfect and my family is totally happy. Okay—not really. We're still juggling commitments, and sometimes we're separate even when together, locked on our devices in different corners of home. Full confession: I'm writing this on a Sunday.

But I know, for certain, that I won't work next Sunday, when this deadline has passed. And I didn't work Saturday. What's changed, above all, is a new attentiveness to the drift. When the weekend gets bogged down with kid commitments, and work emails start piling up, I swear I can hear time leaking, like a bicycle tire. And when the weekend is getting away, I take small but aggressive steps to take it back. I try to stay committed to Aristotle's ideal, the simple notion that the "good life" includes leisure, and leisure is freedom. The work—while important, and often even gratifying—is not who we are.

There are two cultural shifts ahead in many developed economies: the mass retirement of the Baby Boomers, and the rise of automation. Both of these changes—for better or worse— mean that free time is coming, for some people, at least; will we know what to do with it? Maybe we need to look at the weekend as a practice run, an opportunity to learn how to make the most of time outside work, and redefine ourselves in terms of our passions, our relationships, our values.

Now you say: "But the weekend is approaching, and I still have work to do. This book has not magically made the work go away!" Two nuggets of advice. One, try to be more efficient at work during the week. And if work still lingers on the weekend, then, two, block off a few hours and go do the work, far from any distractions. (Please don't send emails to people you work with unless there is a fire-level crisis. If the email must be composed, leave it in your Draft box until Monday. Don't be a weekend-stealer.) And when those hours are up, it's done. Don't go back to it. Go live your life. You'll finish it faster on Monday anyway.

I know that the good weekend is not always possible. There

are all kinds of social and economic forces in place to ensure overwork: employment uncertainty; lack of child care; inadequate support at home; a free market designed to take and take workers' time. Maybe, as we fight to tackle those kinds of anti-leisure structures, having a good weekend is the ultimate "screw you" to a system designed to keep us members of the cult of overwork, a way to dodge the traps that are set to stop us from truly experiencing the "free" in free time. When a small pocket of time does open up on the weekend, it's an act of necessary rebellion to refuse to fill it with work. Keep close at hand the phrase New Agers love: "Busy is a decision." Make it a mental bumper sticker.

There are key components to a good weekend. It's hard to hit all the notes of leisure every single Friday-to-Sunday, but even nailing just a couple will shift how you feel, inside and out. Then, perhaps, you'll be inspired to seek other kinds of leisure next weekend, or—better yet—during the week. Lo and behold, it turns out that *all* your time is important—all seven days—and worthy of careful, and joyful, cultivation. Eventually, we may no longer be scrambling with futility to balance work and life, but living all the time, fully and well. Seneca knew the deal: "No one will bring back the years; no one will restore you to yourself." The weekend is sanctuary, a laboratory in which to lead the life you want.

Now is your time. How will you use it?

◇◇◇◇

MANIFESTO FOR A GOOD WEEKEND

Connect.

Do this in person: An old friend. A new one. A neighbor. A neglected relative. Extend yourself.

Care.

Offer your time. Volunteer. Become an activist for a cause you believe in. Write an angry letter to someone in government. Go hang out with a group of people who care about something more than you do and let it rub off.

Play.

For every passive activity, do two active ones.

Go green.

Define nature any way you choose. Get close to it. Return to that place every few weekends until it's sacred ground.

Seek beauty.

Expose yourself to art that takes your breath away. Make something with your hands. Stand outside a church on a Sunday morning and listen to the choir. Join the choir.

Do less.

Less shopping. Less cleaning. Less decluttering (this does not mean more cluttering!). Less hovering over the kid.

Don't make plans, make space.

Wander.

Wonder.

Be.

Repeat next weekend.

ACKNOWLEDGMENTS

I want to thank Jennifer Lambert and Julia Pastore for their astute editorial guidance and kindness, and Genoveva Llosa for seeing the book's potential early on. Big thanks to Jackie Kaiser, who first mourned the weekend and helped formulate the pitch. I feel incredibly lucky to have had Christy Fletcher and the amazing people at Fletcher & Co. on my side, finding the book a home. Christy also spent a year answering my anxious queries with humor, intelligence, and—oh so much—patience. The uncannily calm young journalist Leah Jensen was my savior assistant at both the research and the fact-checking stages; thank you, Leah.

Obviously, I am acutely aware of how little time we have, and so I want to thank those who generously gave me theirs.

I'm hugely indebted to the many brilliant people cited in this book who have spent their impressive careers researching work and leisure while I've been a tourist journalist. Please seek out their writing. Witold Rybczynski's *Waiting for the Weekend* is the seminal book on this subject. Benjamin Hunnicutt, Juliet Schor, Judith Shulevitz, Sherry Turkle, George Vaillant, Robert Stebbins, Anna Coote, David Levy, Katherine Losse, Kate Edwards, Scott Schieman, Evan Robinson, Richard Louv, David Roediger and Philip Foner, Shawn Micallef, Courtney Carver, Michele Weiner-Davis, Josh Davis—and many others—all contributed, directly and indirectly, to this project. Two recent books that provided much inspiration, and go deeply where I go lightly, are Bridget Schulte's *Overwhelmed* and Anne-Marie Slaughter's *Unfinished Business*.

Much gratitude to all the innovative business leaders I spoke to who are actively protecting their employees' quality of life and redesigning the way we work, especially Felicitas Betzl, Jason Fried, and Dustin Moskovitz.

To all the working and playing people who let me ask intrusive questions about their weekends, you are too many to name, but I thank you. The stories in this book are real, and the subjects are not composites, though I used first names to (nominally) protect privacy. A few interviewees did not want their names or identifying features used, so in those cases I used pseudonyms.

Family and friends are forced to live with an uninvited level of exposure just by knowing me; for that I grovel, apologize, and offer thanks. My parents, Gary and Cindy, always worked to live, and live well. Their example hovers above this project. My in-laws, Brian and Valerie, offered support and bird talk. Many friends suffered through this birth with me, and I thank everyone who listened and offered wisdom along the way, but especially Maryam, Stephanie, Katie, Sarah L., Lisa, Miranda, and Andi. I highly recommend surrounding yourself with women as smart as these.

And most of all, for enduring the absences, mental and physical and sometimes on the weekend, I thank my family: Julian, Judah, and Mia. You make all the days matter.

NOTES

INTRODUCTION: SUNDAY NIGHT LETDOWN

2   *A 2014 paper from the U.S. National Bureau of Economic Research*: Daniel
S. Hamermesh and Elena Stancanelli, "Long Workweeks and Strange
Hours," *ILR Review*, Cornell University, ILR School, Vol. 68, No. 5
(October 2015): 1007–18.

4   *"Sunday night is the new Monday morning"*: Beth Teitell, "How Sunday
Night Became the New Monday Morning," *Boston Globe*, October 26, 2015,
https://www.bostonglobe.com/lifestyle/style/2015/10/25/how-sunday
-night-became-new-monday-morning/GWRM2sNRKVwVArl9rtTrNM
/story.html.

5   *In a 2013 survey*: Yolanda Wikiel, "This Is Why You Feel So Sad on Sunday
(and How to Fix It)," *Real Simple*, http://www.realsimple.com/health
/mind-mood/emotional-health/why-you-feel-sad-on-sunday.

CHAPTER 1: WHAT IS A WEEKEND?

9   *"Parkinson's law of efficiency"*: "Parkinson's Law," *The Economist*, November 19, 1955, http://www.economist.com/node/14116121.

13 *"more-faster-better philosophy of life"*: David M. Levy, "More, Faster,
Better: Governance in an Age of Overload, Busyness, and Speed," *First
Monday*, Special Issue No. 7 (September 2006), http://firstmonday.org
/issues/special11_9/levy/index.html.

CHAPTER 2: THE RISE AND FALL OF THE WEEKEND

14 *Ancient civilizations loved seven*: Hutton Webster, *Rest Days: A Study in Early Law and Morality* (New York: Macmillan, 1916), 212.

15 *Roman emperor Constantine shifted the calendar*: Witold Rybczynski, *Waiting for the Weekend* (New York: Penguin, 1991), 50.

15 *some scholars maintain*: Zerubavel, 26.

16 *his lot "have barely sufficient time"*: David R. Roediger and Philip S. Foner, *Our Own Time: A History of American Labor and the Working Day* (New York: Greenwood Press/Verso, 1989), 7.

16 *work wasn't virtuous*: Benjamin Kline Hunnicutt, *Free Time: The Forgotten American Dream* (Philadelphia: Temple University Press, 2013).

18 *A group of Philadelphia carpenters*: Roediger and Foner, 7.

19 *the "10 Hour Movement"*: Ibid.

19 *the Ten-Hour Circular*: John R. Commons et al., eds., *A Documentary History of American Industrial Society* (Cleveland: Arthur H. Clark Co., 1910), 95; https://archive.org/stream/documentaryhisto06amer#page/94/mode/2up.

19 *"From 6 to 6"*: Priscilla Murollo, *From the Folks Who Brought You the Weekend* (New York: The New Press, 2001); Roediger and Foner, 31–33.

20 *fired or blacklisted*: Roediger and Foner, 58.

20 *The "mill girls"*: Norman Ware, *The Industrial Worker, 1840–1860* (Boston: Houghton Mifflin, 1924), 134.

20 *historian E. P. Thompson wrote*: E. P. Thompson, "Time, Work-Discipline, and Industrial Capitalism," *Past & Present*, No. 38 (December 1967): 56–97, http://www.sv.uio.no/sai/english/research/projects/anthropos-and-the-material/Intranet/economic-practices/reading-group/texts/thompson-time-work-discipline-and-industrial-capitalism.pdf.

20 *as one factory worker wrote in his memoirs*: James Myles, *Chapters in the Life of a Dundee Factory Boy: An Autobiography* (Dundee: James Myles, 1850), 13.

21 *various biographies describe him as a "dreamer"*: "Robert Owen: The Dreamer," *The Outlook*, December 21, 1907, 869–72. Review of Frank Podmore, *Robert Owen: A Biography* (New York: D. Appleton & Co., 1906).

21 *school for workers*: J. F. C. Harrison, *Robert Owen and the Owenites in Britain and America: The Quest for the New Moral World* (London: Routledge, 1969), 132–35.

22 *Eight hours' labor*: G. D. H. Cole, *Life of Robert Owen*, 3rd ed. (London: Frank Cass & Co., 1966).

22   *From 1881 to 1885*: Roediger and Foner, 131.

22   *and the dreaded boom-and-bust economic cycle*: James Green, *Death in the Haymarket* (New York: Random House, 2006), 167.

22   *On April 15, 1872, in Toronto*: Sally Zerker, *The Rise and Fall of the Toronto Typographical Union* (Toronto: University of Toronto Press, 1982), 90.

23   *labor historian James Green describes the strangeness of the day*: Green, 164.

24   *By 10:00 p.m., as the sky darkened*: Ibid. 185.

24   *Six police officers . . . At least three protestors*: Wilbur R. Miller, *The Social History of Crime and Punishment in America: An Encyclopedia, A–De* (Thousand Oaks, Sage Publications, 2012), 1784; Green, 10.

24   *setting off a cigar-shaped bomb*: "Lingg's Fearful Death," *Chicago Tribune*, November 11, 1887, 1.

25   *Benjamin Franklin*: Benjamin Franklin, *The Autobiography of Benjamin Franklin* (New York: Maynard, Merrill and Co., 1892), 51.

25   *popular pastimes included*: Douglas A. Reid, "The Decline of Saint Monday, 1766–1876," *Past & Present*, No. 71 (May 1976): 82.

25   *On Monday everything is in favour*: Thomas Wright, *Some Habits of the Working Class by a Journeyman Engineer* (London: Tinsley Brothers, 1867), 12.

25   *The idea of the weekend*: Dennis Jacobe and Jeffrey M. Jones, "Consumers Spend More on Weekends, Payday Weeks," *Gallup*, http://www.gallup.com/poll/123839/consumers-spend-more-weekends-payday-weeks.aspx.

26   *In* Waiting for the Weekend: Rybczynski, 122–23.

26   *Saint Monday faded*: Ibid. 141.

27   *An affluent British family*: Pamela Horn, *Ladies of the Manor* (Phoenix Mill, UK: Sutton, 1991), 158–59.

27   *a well-known anti-Semite*: Neil Baldwin, *Henry Ford and the Jews: The Mass Production of Hate* (New York: Perseus, 2001).

27   *Thousands showed up*: Vincent Curcio, *Henry Ford* (New York: Oxford University Press, 2013), 80.

27   *an incentive to spend*: Richard Snow, *I Invented the Modern Age* (New York: Simon and Schuster, 2013), 215–20.

27   *"People who have more leisure"*: Douglas Brinkley, "The 40-Hour Revolution," *Time*, March 31, 2003, http://content.time.com/time/specials/packages/article/0,28804, 1977881_1977883_1977922,00.html.

28   *In* The Sabbath World: Judith Shulevitz, *The Sabbath World: Glimpses of a Different Order of Time* (New York: Random House, 2011), xxviii–xxix.

28 *Kurzarbeit*: Andreas Crimmann, Dr. Frank Wießner, and Professor Lutz Bellmann, *The German Work-Sharing Scheme: An Instrument for the Crisis* (Nuremberg: Institute for Employment Research, 2010), iii.

29 *The long, work-tethered week*: Juliet Schor, *The Overworked American* (New York: Basic Books, 1991), 46–47.

29 *as many as 156 holidays*: Benjamin Kline Hunnicutt, *Free Time: The Forgotten American Dream* (Philadelphia: Temple University Press, 2013), 27.

29 *one-third of his year on leisure*: Schor, 47.

29 *writes Juliet Schor*: Ibid. 44.

30 *Oman switched from*: "Why Is Saudi Arabia Thinking of Moving Its Weekend?" *The Economist*, May 9, 2013, http://www.economist.com /blogs/economist-explains/2013/05/economist-explains-why-saudi -arabia-might-move-weekend.

30 *Saudi Arabia followed suit*: Samuel Potter and Glen Carey, "Saudi Arabia Changes Weekend to Friday, Saturday," *Bloomberg,* http://www.bloomberg .com/news/articles/2013-06-23/saudi-arabia-changes-weekend-to-friday -saturday-spa-reports.

31 *calls for a full, two-day Friday-Saturday weekend*: Ethan Bronner, "Israel Debates Two-Day Weekends, and Its Lifestyle," *The New York Times*, July 6, 2011, http://www.nytimes.com/2011/07/07/world/middleeast /07israel.html.

31 *a bill for six three-day weekends per year*: Tali Heruti-Sover, Janan Bsoul, and Zvi Zrahiya, "Three-Day Weekend Edges Closer to Reality in Israel," *Haaretz,* http://www.haaretz.com/israel-news/business/.premium-1.728240.

32 *"love of money as a possession"*: John Maynard Keynes, *Essays in Persuasion* (New York: W. W. Norton & Co., 1963), 358–73.

33 *living among the artists and intellectuals*: Louis Menand, "Buried Treasure," review of Robert Skidelsky's *John Maynard Keynes: Fighting for Freedom*, in *The New Yorker*, January 28, 2002, http://www.newyorker. com/magazine/2002/01/28/buried-treasure-5.

33 *a panicked article in Life*: Ernest Havemann, "The Task Ahead: How to Take Life Easy," *Life* magazine, February 21, 1964, 85.

34 *"the leisure gap"*: Derek Thompson, "The Myth That Americans Are Busier Than Ever," *The Atlantic*, May 21, 2014.

34 *In 1965, college-educated men had more leisure*: Mark Aguiar and Erik Hurst, "A Summary of Trends in American Time Allocation: 1965–2005," *Social Indicators Research*, Vol. 9, No. 1 (2009), 57–64.

34   *the "substitution effect"*: "Nice Work If You Can Get Out: Why the Rich Now Have Less Leisure Than the Poor," *The Economist*, April 19, 2014, 71.

34   *single mothers*: Susan M. Bianchi, John P. Robinson, Melissa A. Milke, *The Changing Rhythms of American Family Life* (New York: Russell Sage Foundation, 2006), 173.

34   *a worker's average annual hours*: Organization for Economic Co-operation and Development, "Average Annual Hours Actually Worked per Worker," https://stats.oecd.org/Index.aspx?DataSetCode=ANHRS.

34   *a separate poll, conducted by Gallup*: Lydia Saad, "The '40-Hour' Workweek Is Actually Longer—by Seven Hours," *Gallup*, http://www.gallup.com/poll/175286/hour-workweek-actually-longer-seven-hours.aspx.

35   *29 percent of Americans said they perform paid work*: Hamermesh and Stancanelli, 12.

35   *Britain comes in a close second*: Ronald J. Burke and Cary L. Cooper, eds., *The Long Work Hours Culture: Causes, Consequences and Choices* (Bingley, UK: Emerald Group, 2008), xii.

36   *interacting with work 13.5 hours every workday*: Jennifer J. Deal, "Always On, Never Done? Don't Blame the Smartphone," White paper, Center for Creative Leadership, 2015, http://insights.ccl.org/wp-content/uploads/2015/04/AlwaysOn.pdf.

36   *about 150 times per day*: Mary Meeker and Liang Wu, "Internet Trends D11 Conference," Kleiner, Perkins, Caufield, Byers, May 29, 2013, http://www.kpcb.com/blog/2013-internet-trends.

36   *"yuppie kvetching"*: Daniel S. Hamermesh and Jungmin Lee, "Stressed Out on Four Continents: Time Crunch or Yuppie Kvetch?" Discussion Paper No. 1815, Institute for the Study of Labor (Bonn, Germany), October 2005.

37   *Research suggests that 80 percent of working parents feel rushed*: "Raising Kids and Running a Household: How Working Parents Share the Load," Pew Research Center, November 4, 2015, http://www.pewsocialtrends.org/2015/11/04/raising-kids-and-running-a-household-how-working-parents-share-the-load/.

37   *Brigid Schulte, journalist and director of The Better Life Lab*: Brigid Schulte, *Overwhelmed* (Toronto: HarperCollins, 2014), 13.

37   *half of all jobs are deemed "insecure"*: Sara Mojtehedzadeh and Laurie Monsebraaten, "Precarious Work Is Now the New Norm . . ." *The Toronto Star*, May 21, 2015, https://www.thestar.com/news/gta/2015/05/21/precarious-work-is-now-the-new-norm-united-way-report-says.html.

38   *stress of job insecurity*: Rachel Pugh, "Job Insecurity Is Bad for Your Health," *The Guardian*, December 17, 2008, https://www.theguardian.com /society/2008/dec/17/job-insecurity-health.

38   *The Urban Worker Project*: Urban Worker Project, http://www.urbanworker.ca/.

39   *stress hormones*: Daniel J. Levitan, "Why the Modern World Is Bad for Your Brain," *The Guardian*, January 18, 2015, https://www.theguardian .com/science/2015/jan/18/modern-world-bad-for-brain-daniel-j-levitin -organized-mind-information-overload.

40   *brings weight gain and increases anxiety levels*: C. W., "Get a Life—Or Get Fat," *The Economist*, October 14, 2014, http://www.economist.com/blogs /freeexchange/2014/10/working-hours.

40   *risk of stroke*: Tanya Basu, "Working Long Hours Could Increase Your Risk of Stroke and Heart Disease," *Time*, August 18, 2015, http://time.com /4003902/working-long-hours-stroke-heart-disease/.

40   *lack of sleep is linked to obesity*: "Sleep Deprivation and Obesity," Harvard University, T. H. Chan School of Public Health, http://www.hsph.harvard .edu/nutritionsource/sleep/.

40   *President Donald Trump*: Abby Haglage, "Donald Trump's 4-Hour Sleep Habit Could Explain His Personality," *The Daily Beast*, April 2, 2016, http://www.thedailybeast.com/article/2016/04/02/donald-trump-s-4 -hour-sleep-habit-could-explain-his-personality.html.

40   *a podcast called Inquiring Minds*: Indre Viskontas, "9 Reasons You Really Need to Go to Sleep," *Mother Jones*, January 16, 2015, http://www .motherjones.com/environment/2015/01/inquiring-minds-matt-walker.

41   *"death from overwork"*: Sookhan Ho, "Are the Japanese Worked to Death?" *Science from Virginia Tech*, 1995, http://www.research.vt.edu/resmag /sciencecol/AFDC95.html.

41   *One estimate holds*: "Jobs for Life," *The Economist*, December 19, 2007, http://www.economist.com/node/10329261.

41   *compensated by insurance companies*: Ibid.

41   *the new Chinese word guolaosi*: Shai Oster, "In China, 1,600 People Die Every Day from Working Too Hard," *Bloomberg*, July 3, 2014, http://www .bloomberg.com/news/articles/2014-07-03/in-china-white-collar-workers -are-dying-from-overwork.

42   *a lengthy article in **Der Spiegel***: Christoph Scheuermann, "High Stakes: Making Sense of a Banking Intern's Death," *Der Spiegel*, October 11, 2013.

43 *Abdurahman Moallim, twenty-one, a former intern*: Shiv Malik, "Moritz Erhardt Intern Death Spurs Bank of America Merrill Lynch review," *The Guardian*, August 23, 2013, http://www.theguardian.com/business /2013/aug/23/intern-death-bank-of-america-merrill-lynch.

43 *9:00 a.m. to 5:00 a.m.*: Kevin Roose, "Will a Dead Bank of America Intern Change Wall Street's Pledge-Class Culture?" *New York* magazine, "Daily Intelligencer," August 21, 2013, http://nymag.com/daily /intelligencer/2013/08/bofa-intern-death-and-wall-streets-culture .html#.

43 *An autopsy found*: Maev Kennedy, "Bank Intern Moritz Erhardt Died from Epileptic Seizure, Inquest Told," *The Guardian*, November 22, 2013, http://www.theguardian.com/business/2013/nov/22/moritz-erhardt -merrill-lynch-intern-dead-inquest.

44 *it caps interns' hours*: Rupert Neate, "Goldman Sachs Restricts Intern Workday to 17 Hours in Wake of Burnout Death," *The Guardian*, June 17, 2015, http://www.theguardian.com/business/2015/jun/17/goldman -sachs-interns-work-hours?CMP=twt_gu&CMP=twt_gu.

45 *Since the first research on productivity*: Hunnicutt, *Free Time*, 114.

45 *futurist Sara Robinson*: Sara Robinson, "Why We Have to Go Back to a 40 -Hour Work Week to Keep Our Sanity," AlterNet, March 13, 2012, http:// www.alternet.org/story/154518/why_we_have_to_go_back_to_a_40 -hour_work_week_to_keep_our_sanity.

45 *A paper by John Pencavel*: John Pencavel, "The Productivity of Working Hours," Discussion Paper No. 8129, Institute for the Study of Labor (Bonn, Germany), April 2014.

46 *especially Sunday labor*: Ibid.

46 *Erin Reid*: Erin Reid, "Why Some Men Pretend to Work 80-Hour Weeks," *Harvard Business Review*, April 28, 2015.

47 *"greedy institution"*: Lewis Coser, *Greedy Institutions: Patterns of Undivided Commitment* (New York: The Free Press, 1974).

48 *conclusion that short hours win*: C. W. and A. K. J. D., "Get a Life," *The Economist*, September 24, 2013, http://www.economist.com/blogs/freeexchange /2013/09/working-hours.

48 *countries ranked highest*: Anna Bruce-Lockhart, "Which Countries Work the Shortest Hours—yet Still Prosper?" *World Economic Forum*, October 6, 2015, https://www.weforum.org/agenda/2015/10/which-countries -work-the-shortest-hours-yet-still-prosper.

48 *seven of the ten countries with the highest GDP*: "England Fails to Reach Top Ten Most Productive Countries in the World," *Expert Market*, http://payrollservices.expertmarket.co.uk/worlds-most-productive-countries.

49 *far-reaching tragedies*: Leo Hickman, "The Hidden Dangers of Sleep Deprivation," *The Guardian*, February 9, 2011, http://www.theguardian.com/lifeandstyle/2011/feb/09/dangers-sleep-deprivation.

49 *bad medicine, even patient death*: H. R. Colten and B. M. Altevogt, eds., "Sleep Disorders and Sleep Deprivation: An Unmet Public Health Problem," in *Institute of Medicine (US) Committee on Sleep Medicine and Research* (Washington, DC: National Academies Press, 2006), http://www.ncbi.nlm.nih.gov/books/NBK19958/.

49 *the first Mac might have been completed*: S. Robinson.

50 *"creative class"*: Ashley Lutz, "Why the Creative Class Is Taking Over the World," *Business Insider*, July 28, 2012, http://www.businessinsider.com/why-the-creative-class-is-taking-over-the-world-2012-7.

50 *Writing online in Al Jazeera America*: Sarah Leonard, "No Sleep till World Domination: If Bankers Worked 9 to 5, They Might Have to Admit That Finance Is Just a Job," *Al Jazeera America*, March 13, 2014, http://america.aljazeera.com/opinions/2014/3/banker-hours-exhaustionoverwork.html.

50 *Livefyre . . . Evernote*: Christine Lagorio-Chafkin, "World's Coolest Offices: Wide Open Spaces," *Inc.*, October 1, 2014, http://www.inc.com/worlds-coolest-offices-massive-company-headquarters.html.

51 *home-court advantage*: Katherine Losse, *The Boy Kings* (New York: The Free Press, 2012), 3.

51 *an estimated $56 billion*: Katia Savchuk, "Facebook CEO Mark Zuckerberg Gains $3.4 Billion in an Hour after Positive Second-Quarter Earnings," *Forbes*, July 27, 2016, http://www.forbes.com/sites/katiasavchuk/2016/07/27/facebook-ceo-mark-zuckerberg-gains-3-4-billion-in-an-hour-after-positive-second-quarter-earnings/#2c246df727b7.

52 *"When there was nothing else to do"*: Losse, 85.

52 *"enchanted workplaces"*: Robert Howard, *Brave New Workplace* (New York: Viking, 1985).

52 *vulnerable to abuses of power*: J. Boyett and H. Conn, *Workplace 2000* (London: Plume, 1992), 114–15.

53 *"ea_spouse" posted on* Live Journal: ea_spouse, "EA: The Human Story," *LiveJournal*, November 10, 2004, http://ea-spouse.livejournal.com/274.html?page=.

54 *"The stress is taking its toll"*: Ibid.

54   *EA settled*: Nick Wingfield, "Electronic Arts Settles Lawsuit, Will Pay Overtime for Some Jobs," *The Wall Street Journal*, October 6, 2005, http://www.wsj.com/articles/SB112854591447960878.

54   *recent survey by IGDA*: "62% of Developers Indicate Their Job Involves Crunch Time," *International Game Developers Association*, September 18, 2105, https://www.igda.org/news/251411/Press-Release-62-of-Developers-Indicate-Their-Job-Involves-Crunch-Time.htm.

55   *"Facebook is available 24/7"*: Sheryl Sandberg, *Lean In: Women, Work, and the Will to Lead* (New York: Knopf, 2013), 133.

55   *turn over fast*: Anonymous, "Hell Is Working at the Huffington Post," *Gawker*, June 2, 2015, http://tktk.gawker.com/hell-is-working-at-the-huffington-post-1707724052.

55   *Emails fly at all hours*: David Segal, "Arianna Huffington's Improbable, Insatiable Content Machine," *New York Times Magazine*, June 30, 2015, http://www.nytimes.com/2015/07/05/magazine/arianna-huffingtons-improbable-insatiable-content-machine.html.

56   *she herself collapsed*: Valentina Zarya, "Dear Donald Trump, Please Read Arianna Huffington's New Book about Sleep," *Fortune*, April 5, 2016, http://fortune.com/2016/04/05/arianna-huffington-sleep-revolution/.

56   *inhumane conditions in factories*: Spencer Soper, "Inside Amazon's Warehouse," *The Morning Call*, September 8, 2011, http://articles.mcall.com/2011-09-18/news/mc-allentown-amazon-complaints-20110917_1_warehouse-workers-heat-stress-brutal-heat.

56   *employee surveillance*: Simon Head, *Mindless: Why Smarter Machines Are Making Dumber Humans* (New York: Basic Books [Perseus], 2014).

56   *Jodi Kantor and David Streitfeld*: Jodi Kantor and David Streitfeld, "Inside Amazon: Wrestling Big Ideas in a Bruising Workplace," *The New York Times*, August 15, 2015, http://www.nytimes.com/2015/08/16/technology/inside-amazon-wrestling-big-ideas-in-a-bruising-workplace.html.

56   *being berated for turning off his phone*: Hamilton Nolan, "Inside Amazon's Bizarre Corporate Culture," *Gawker*, May 1, 2014, http://gawker.com/inside-amazons-bizarre-corporate-culture-1570412337.

57   *"You can work long, hard or smart"*: Jeffrey P. Bezos, Amazon shareholder letter, http://media.corporate-ir.net/media_files/irol/97/97664/reports/Shareholderletter97.pdf.

57   *according to **Forbes***: "#44 Dustin Moskovitz," *Forbes*, http://www.forbes.com/profile/dustin-moskovitz/.

61 *an interview on* **NPR**: "Shonda Rhimes on Running 3 Hit Shows and the Limits of Network TV," NPR, November 11, 2015, http://www.npr .org/2015/11/11/455594842/shonda-rhimes-on-running-three-hit -shows-and-the-limits-of-network-tv.

61 *op-ed in the Milwaukee* **Journal Sentinel**: Stephanie Bloomingdale, "Walker and GOP Just Took Away the Weekend," *Milwaukee Wisconsin Journal Sentinel*, July 13, 2015, http://www.jsonline.com/news/walker-and-gop -just-took-away-the-weekend-b99536839z1-314775071.html.

62 *Jeb Bush delivered a speech*: David Corn, "Jeb Bush, Americans Already Work Longer Hours: See These Charts," *Mother Jones*, July 9, 2015, http://www.motherjones.com/politics/2015/07/jeb-bush-americans -work-longer-hours-charts.

62 **Time** *magazine quick to point out*: Philip Elliott, "Jeb Bush's 'Longer Hours' Remark Will Haunt Him," *Time*, July 9, 2015, http://time.com /3951396/jeb-bush-longer-hours/.

62 *Germany's Labor Ministry*: Jeevan Vasagar, "Out of Hours Working Banned by German Labour Ministry," *The Telegraph*, August 30, 2013, http:// www.telegraph.co.uk/news/worldnews/europe/germany/10276815 /Out-of-hours-working-banned-by-German-labour-ministry.html.

62 *"right to disconnect"*: Amy B. Wang, "French Employees Can Legally Ignore Work Emails Outside of Office Hours," *The Washington Post*, January 1, 2017.

62 *Bruno Mettling*: Jess Staufenberg, "France May Pass a Law on the 'Right to Disconnect' from Work Emails at Home," *Independent*, February 17, 2016, http://www.independent.co.uk/news/world/europe/france-may-pass-a -law-on-right-to-disconnect-from-work-emails-at-home-a6878571.html.

63 *Dublin Goes Dark*: Laszlo Bock, "Google's Scientific Approach to Work -Life Balance (and Much More)," *Harvard Business Review*, March 27, 2014, https://hbr.org/2014/03/googles-scientific-approach-to-work-life -balance-and-much-more.

63 *Volkswagen announced*: Email interview with Carsten Krebs, director of corporate communications Volkswagen Group of America, July 2015.

63 *Deutsche Telekom, EON, and BMW*: "Banning Email after Work," *DW*, February 20, 2014, http://www.dw.com/en/banning-e-mail-after-work /a-17445387.

63 *Max Schireson*: Max Schireson, "Why I Am Leaving the Best Job I Ever Had," *Max Schireson's Blog*, https://maxschireson.com/2014/08/05/1137/.

63 *Patrick Pichette*: Patrick Pichette, "After nearly seven years as CFO . . ." *Google* +, March 10, 2015, https://plus.google.com/+PatrickPichette /posts/8Khr5LnKtub.

64 *Brent Callinicos*: Ben Geier, "Read This Uber Exec's Heartfelt Resignation Letter," *Fortune*, March 17, 2015, http://fortune.com/2015/03/17/uber -cfo-resignation/.

66 *"total work"*: Josef Pieper, *Leisure: The Basis of Culture* (San Francisco: Ignatius Press, 2009), 78.

67 *"intrinsic motivation"*: Xiaomeng Zhang and Kathryn M. Bartol, "Linking Empowering Leadership and Employee Creativity: The Influence of Psychological Empowerment, Intrinsic Motivation, and Creative Process Engagement," *Academy of Management Journal*, Vol. 53, No. 1 (February 1, 2010): 107–28, http://amj.aom.org/content/53/1/107.abstract.

67 *30 percent of workers have access to some kind of Summer Friday*: Jeff Tyler, "Summer Fridays off Are a Growing Job Perk," *Marketplace*, May 28, 2012, http://www.marketplace.org/2012/05/28/economy/summer -fridays-are-growing-job-perk.

68 *power consumption actually drops*: Choire Sicha, "Letter of Recommen-dation: Summer Fridays," *New York Times Magazine*, July 17, 2015, http:// www.nytimes.com/2015/07/19/magazine/letter-of-recommendation -summer-fridays.html.

68 *43 percent in 2014 versus 38 percent in 2008*: Kenneth Matos and Ellen Galinsky, "2014 National Study of Employers—Society for Human Resource Management," Families and Work Institute, 2014, 22–23.

69 **Fast Company** *reports*: Stephanie Vozza, "How These Companies Have Made Four-Day Workweeks Feasible," *Fast Company*, June 17, 2015, http:// www.fastcompany.com/3047329/the-future-of-work/how-companies -actually-make-four-day-workweeks-feasible.

69 *Amazon announced in 2016 the launch of a pilot project*: David Z. Morris, "Amazon Tests Out 30-Hour Work Week," *Time*, August 29, 2016, http:// time.com/4470544/amazon-tests-30-hour-work-week/.

69 *Lesley Jane Seymour*: Lesley Jane Seymour, "Why We're in Trouble If Only Women Sign Up for Amazon's 30-Hour Work Week," LinkedIn, August 30, 2016, https://www.linkedin.com/pulse/why-were-trouble-only-women-sign -up-amazons-30-hour-work-seymour.

71 *shorter work hours are associated with lower greenhouse gas emissions*: David Rosnick, "Reduced Work Hours as a Means of Slowing Climate

Change," Center for Economic and Policy Research, February 2013.

72 *absenteeism has dropped by half*: "Gothenburg's Six-Hour Work Day Hangs in the Balance," *The Local*, April 21, 2016, http://www.thelocal.se /20160421/gothenburgs-six-hour-work-day-hangs-in-the-balance.

73 *25 percent increase in profits*: Bec Crew, "Sweden Is Shifting to a 6-Hour Work Day," *Science Alert*, September 30, 2015, http://www.sciencealert .com/sweden-is-shifting-to-a-6-hour-workday.

73 *47 percent of American jobs will be automated*: "New Study Shows Nearly Half of US Jobs at Risk of Computerisation," University of Oxford, Department of Engineering Science, http://www.eng.ox.ac.uk/about /news/new-study-shows-nearly-half-of-us-jobs-at-risk-of-computerisation.

73 *four hundred new jobs to offer*: Brian Treanor, *Emplotting Virtue: A Narrative Approach to Environmental Ethics* (Albany: SUNY Press, 2014), 79.

74 *"Hunger in the midst of plenty"*: Roedinger and Foner, 246.

74 *The bill fell*: Ibid. 246–52.

74 *workers staged a mock funeral*: Benjamin Kline Hunnicutt, *Kellogg's Six-Hour Day* (Philadelphia: Temple University Press, 1996), 3.

74 *Writes de Graaf on AlterNet*: John de Graaf, "When America Came 'This Close' to Establishing a 30-Hour Workweek," AlterNet, April 2, 2013, http:// www.alternet.org/labor/when-america-came-close-establishing-30 -hour-workweek.

75 *it was a hit*: Rex L. Facer II and Lori L. Wadsworth, "Four-Day Workweeks: Current Research and Practice," *Connecticut Law Review*, Vol. 42, No. 4 (May 2010): 1044.

79 *"chronophobia"*: Robert Jean Campbell, *Campbell's Psychiatric Dictionary*, 9th ed. (Oxford: Oxford University Press, 2009), 188.

CHAPTER 3: THE NEED TO CONNECT

85 *Our natural reflex is to connect to others*: Matthew D. Lieberman, *Social: Why Our Brains Are Wired to Connect* (New York: Crown, 2013), 42.

86 *"A broken heart can feel like a broken leg"*: Lieberman, 57.

88 *no interaction with neighbors*: Linda Poon, "Why Won't You Be My Neighbor?" *CityLab*, August 19, 2015, http://www.citylab.com/housing /2015/08/why-wont-you-be-my-neighbor/401762/.

88 *the bonds of civic association weaken*: Robert Putnam, *Bowling Alone: The Collapse and Revival of American Community* (New York: Simon and Schuster, 2000).

89   *2010 AARP survey*: G. Oscar Anderson, "Loneliness among Older Adults: A National Survey of Adults 45+," *AARP Research*, September 2010, http://www.aarp.org/research/topics/life/info-2014/loneliness_2010.html.

89   *greater risk for death*: Katharine Gammon, "Why Loneliness Can Be Deadly," *LiveScience*, March 2, 2013, http://www.livescience.com/18800-loneliness-health-problems.html.

89   *UCLA annual national survey*: Kevin Eagan et al., "The American Freshman: National Norms Fall 2014," Cooperative Institutional Research Program at the Higher Education Research Institute at UCLA, 2014, http://www.heri.ucla.edu/monographs/TheAmericanFreshman2014.pdf.

90   *Multitasking different digital media*: Gus Lubin, "Multitasking Is Making You Dumb," *Business Insider*, August 7, 2012, http://www.businessinsider.com/the-perils-of-multitasking-infographic-2012-8.

90   *texting, not talking*: Sherry Turkle, *Reclaiming Conversation: The Power of Talk in a Digital Age* (New York: Penguin Random House, 2015), 3–17.

93   *"online disinhibition effect"*: John Suler, "The Online Disinhibition Effect," *Cyberpsychology & Behavior*, Vol. 7, No. 3 (2004): 321–26.

94   *tracking the trajectories*: George E. Vaillant, *Triumphs of Experience* (Boston: Harvard University Press, 2015).

94   *"the only thing that really matters in life are your relationships"*: Joshua Wolf Shenk, "What Makes Us Happy?" *The Atlantic*, June 2009, http://www.theatlantic.com/magazine/archive/2009/06/what-makes-us-happy/307439/.

95   *"a marked change has come over me"*: Vaillant, 163–70.

95   *body benefits*: D. Von Ah, D. H. Kang, and J. S. Carpenter, "Stress, Optimism, and Social Support: Impact on Immune Responses in Breast Cancer," *Research in Nursing and Health*, Vol. 30, No. 1 (2007): 72–83.

99   *ritual creates "belief" and "belonging"*: Douglas A. Marshall, "Behavior, Belonging, and Belief: A Theory of Ritual Practice," *Sociological Theory*, Vol. 20, No. 3 (November 2002): 360–80.

99   *site of experience*: E. Durkheim, *The Elementary Forms of Religious Life*, trans. J. Swain (New York: The Free Press, 2008).

104 *number of Americans who don't identify*: Pew Research Center, *America's Changing Religious Landscape*, 2015, http://www.pewforum.org/2015/05/12/americas-changing-religious-landscape/.

104 *Trust in religious institutions*: Lydia Saad, "Confidence in Religion at New Low, but Not among Catholics," *Gallup*, June 17, 2015, http://www

.gallup.com/poll/183674/confidence-religion-new-low-not-among
-catholics.aspx.

105 *Hunnicutt said in an interview at OfSpirit.com*: Linda Marks, "The Loss
of Leisure in a Culture of Overwork," OfSpirit.com, http://www.ofspirit
.com/lindamarks12.htm.

106 *"third places"*: Ray Oldenburg, *The Great Good Place* (Philadelphia:
Perseus, 1999).

106 *levels of social connectedness*: "The Social Capital Community Benchmark
Survey," The Saguaro Seminar: Civic Engagement in America, https://
www.hks.harvard.edu/saguaro/communitysurvey/results4.html.

106 *"anomie"*: E. Durkheim, *Suicide: A Study in Sociology*, trans. J. Spaulding
and G. Simpson (New York: The Free Press, 1997).

108 *"tables . . . laid and loaded"*: Aristophanes, *Ecclesiazusae*, in *The Complete
Greek Drama*, Vol. 2, Whitney J. Oates, Eugene O'Neill, Jr., eds. (New
York: Random House, 1938); http://www.perseus.tufts.edu/hopper
/text?doc=Aristoph.%20Eccl.%20848&lang=original.

108 *French salons of the* ancien régime: Bendetta Craveri, *The Age of Conversation*,
trans. Teresa Waugh (New York: New York Review Books, 2005).

108 *"black Harlem first met Greenwich Village bohemia"*: Andrea Barnet, *All
-Night Party: The Women of Bohemian Greenwich Village and Harlem, 1913–
1930* (Chapel Hill, NC: Algonquin Books of Chapel Hill, 2004), 143.

110 *a deep sense of wonder*: David Masci and Michael Lipka, "Americans May
Be Getting Less Religious, but Feelings of Spirituality Are on the Rise,"
Pew Research Center, January 21, 2016, http://www.pewresearch.org
/fact-tank/2016/01/21/americans-spirituality/.

111 *37 percent of Americans*: "U.S. Public Becoming Less Religious," Pew
Research Center, November 3, 2015, http://www.pewforum.org/2015/11
/03/u-s-public-becoming-less-religious/.

111 *less than half that*: G. Jeffrey MacDonald, "'By 2050, 10% of Americans Will
Attend Church,'" *National Catholic Reporter*, February 26, 2009, https://www
.ncronline.org/news/faith-parish/2050-10-americans-will-attend-church.

112 *heated town meetings erupted:* Ray Hanania, "Will Controversy Follow
Recent Sale of Palos Church to Muslims?" *American Daily News*,
November 7, 2016, http://www.illinoisnewsnetwork.com/2016/01/28
/will-controversy-follow-recent-sale-of-palos-church-to-muslims/.

112 *one of the largest Arab communities in the United States*: Louise Cainkar,
"Islamic Revival among Second-Generation Arab-American Muslims:

The American Experience and Globalization Intersect," Bulletin of the Royal Institute for Inter-Faith Studies (Autumn/Winter 2004): 99–120.

112 *first wave*: "Palestinians," *Encyclopedia of Chicago*, http://www.encyclopedia .chicagohistory.org/pages/946.html.

113 *less than 1 percent of the American population is Muslim*: Besheer Mohamed, "A New Estimate of the U.S. Muslim Population," Pew Research Center, January 6, 2016, http://www.pewresearch.org/fact-tank/2016/01/06/a -new-estimate-of-the-u-s-muslim-population/.

113 *Almost 70 percent of Muslim Americans*: "Muslim Americans: No Signs of Growth in Alienation of Support for Extremism," Pew Research Center, August 30, 2011, http://www.people-press.org/2011/08/30/section-2 -religious-beliefs-and-practices/#most-see-religion-as-very-important.

117 *A 2012 study published in* **Psychological Science**: Cassie Mogilner, Zoe Chance, and Michael I. Norton, "Giving Time Gives You Time," *Psychological Science*, Vol. 23, No. 10 (2012): 1233–38.

118 *volunteer work on weekends*: "American Time Use Survey," U.S. Department of Labor, Bureau of Labor Statistics, http://www.bls.gov/tus/charts /volunteer.htm.

118 **Lack of time**: Norah McClintock, *Understanding Canadian Volunteers*, Canadian Centre for Philanthropy, http://www.imaginecanada.ca/sites /default/files/www/en/giving/reports/understanding_volunteers.pdf.

118 *lower depression rates*: Caroline E. Jenkinson et al., "Is Volunteering a Public Health Intervention? A Systematic Review and Meta-analysis of the Health and Survival of Volunteers," BioMed Central, August 23, 2013, http://bmcpublichealth.biomedcentral.com/articles/10.1186/1471 -2458-13-773.

118 *shown to promote empathy*: Lea Winerman, "Helping Others, Helping Ourselves," *Monitor on Psychology*, Vol. 37, No. 11 (December 2006): 38; http://www.apa.org/monitor/dec06/helping.aspx.

119 *brain-imaging study headed by cognitive neuroscientist Jordan Grafman*: Jorge Moll et al., "Human Fronto–mesolimbic Networks Guide Decisions about Charitable Donation." *Proceedings of the National Academy of Sciences*, Vol. 103, No. 42 (2006): 15623–28.

119 *Utah beats all the other states*: Morgan Jacobsen, "Utah Gets Top Spot for Charitable Giving, Volunteering," *Deseret News*, December 8, 2015.

124 *"voluntourism"*: Richard Florida, "There's a Remarkably Strong Link between Community Service and Happiness," *CityLab*, August 12, 2014,

http://www.citylab.com/cityfixer/2014/08/theres-a-remarkably-strong-link-between-community-service-and-happiness/375960/.

125 *people in sexless marriages*: Tara Parker-Pope, "When Sex Leaves the Marriage," *The New York Times*, June 3, 2009, http://well.blogs.nytimes.com/2009/06/03/when-sex-leaves-the-marriage/.

125 *having sex at least once a week*: Amy Muise, Ulrich Schimmack, and Emily A. Impett, "Sexual Frequency Predicts Greater Well-Being, but More Is Not Always Better," *Social Psychological and Personality Science*, November 2015.

126 *A pair of British therapists*: David Delvin, "Work Woes: Sex Difficulties in Busy People," *netdoctor*, January 23, 2013, http://www.netdoctor.co.uk/healthy-living/sexual-health/a10613/work-woes-sex-difficulties-in-busy-people/.

126 *Cynthia, a blogger and journalist*: I spoke to Cynthia by phone, and she wrote about her experience here: Cynthia Lawrence, "Six Steps I Have Taken to Keep My Smartphone Addiction from Ruining My Marriage," *xoJane*, February 18, 2015, http://www.xojane.com/relationships/is-your-smartphone-addiction-ruining-your-relationship.

127 *"iPhone separation anxiety"*: R. B. Clayton, G. Leshner, and A. Almond, "The Extended iSelf: The Impact of iPhone Separation on Cognition, Emotion, and Physiology," *Journal of Computer-Mediated Communication*, Vol. 20, No. 2 (August 2015): 132.

127 *"wretched contentment"*: Paul Levy, *Digital Inferno: Using Technology Consciously in Your Life and Work* (West Hoathly, UK: Clairview Books, 2014), 44.

129 *Mira Kirshenbaum argues*: Mira Kirshenbaum, *The Weekend Marriage: Abundant Love in a Time-Starved World* (New York: Harmony Books, 2005), 3.

130 *couples participated in a new activity*: Arthur Aron et al., "Couples' Shared Participation in Novel and Arousing Activities and Experienced Relationship Quality," *Journal of Personality and Social Psychology*, Vol. 78, No. 2 (February 2000): 273–84.

130 *recreate those initial feelings*: Tara Parker-Pope, "Re-inventing Date Night for Long-Married Couples," *The New York Times*, February 12, 2008, http://www.nytimes.com/2008/02/12/health/12well.html?_r=0.

Chapter 4: Binge, Buy, Brunch, Basketball

135 *most common waking activity*: "Economic News Release. Table 2. Time

Spent in Primary Activities and Percent of the Civilian Population Engaging in Each Activity, Averages per Day on Weekdays and Weekends, 2015 Annual Averages," U.S. Department of Labor, Bureau of Labor Statistics, http://www.bls.gov/news.release/atus.t02.htm.

135 *spend more money on weekends*: Jacobe and Jones.

136 *a 1926 editorial in* **The Nation**: "Restlessness and Recreation," *The Nation*, November 10, 1926. Cited in Robert Goldman, "We Make Weekends: Leisure & the Commodity Form," *Social Text*, Vol. 8 (Winter): 84–103.

137 *It will be said that, while a little leisure is pleasant*: Bertrand Russell, "In Praise of Idleness," *Harper's Magazine*, October 1932.

138 *two main categories of leisure*: Robert A. Stebbins, *Between Work and Leisure: The Common Ground of Two Separate Worlds* (New Jersey: Transaction, 2004). I also interviewed Dr. Stebbins in 2016.

138 *stadiums were built*: Goldman, 86.

139 *called* **Christianity and Amusements**: Richard Henry Edwards, *Christianity and Amusements* (New York: Association Press, 1915), 14.

139 *"Unlike the landsmen's lodges and union halls*: David Nasaw, *Going Out: The Rise and Fall of Public Amusements* (Boston: Harvard University Press, 1999), 2.

140 *The first tailgaters gathered in Virginia in 1861*: The Editors of *Time, 100 American Originals: The Things That Shaped Our Culture* (New York: Time Books, 2016), 60–62.

141 *like nearly 70 million Americans each year*: Tom Ryan, "The Tailgating Opportunity," *RetailWire*, September 5, 2008, http://www.retailwire.com/discussion/the-tailgating-opportunity/.

141 *"vestavals"*: Tonya Williams Bradford and John Sherry Jr., "Domesticating Public Space through Ritual: Tailgating as Vestaval," *Journal of Consumer Research*, Vol. 42 (2015): 130–51.

142 *"People have tailgated in the same place for years*: Beth Carter, "Tailgate Parties Are a 'Powerful Impulse' and a Microcosm of Society," *Wired*, September 21, 2012, https://www.wired.com/2012/09/anthropology-of-tailgating/.

142 *gaming may actually be good for a marriage*: "Online Role-Playing Games Hurt Marital Satisfaction, Says BYU Study," *EurekAlert!*, February 14, 2012, https://www.eurekalert.org/pub_releases/2012-02/byu-org021012.php.

143 *"amusing ourselves to death"*: Neil Postman, *Amusing Ourselves to Death* (New York: Penguin Books, 1985).

143 *every season of* **The Good Wife**: Chelsea Stone, "How Unhealthy Is Binge Watching? Press Pause, and Read On," *Reader's Digest*, http://www .rd.com/slideshows/binge-watching-unhealthy/#ixzz3dvBZKa3H.

144 *feeling depressed when a series ended*: https://www.eurekalert.org/pub _releases/2015-01/ica-fol012615.ph.

145 *Sixty thousand visitors pop by daily*: J. B. MacKinnon, "America's Last Ban on Sunday Shopping," *The New Yorker*, February 7, 2015.

147 *"no woman shall kiss her child on the Sabbath"*: Samuel Peters, *A General History of Connecticut*, 1829. In the Library of Congress online, at p. 69: https://archive.org/details/generalhistoryof00peter.

147 *eighteenth-century meaning of the word "blue"*: "Blue law," *Encyclopedia Britannica*, https://www.britannica.com/topic/blue-law.

147 *"No traveling"*: In *The New York Times*, April 22, 1879. Cited on nj.com: http://www.nj.com/bergen/index.ssf/2012/11/by_the_numbers_a _brief_history_of_blue_laws_in_bergen_county.html.

149 *the highest annual retail sales of any zip code in the nation*: Laura Adams, "Billion-Dollar Bergen: Retail Reigns Supreme throughout the County," *Bergen.com*, February 4, 2011.

149 *Hungary banned Sunday shopping*: Pal Belyo, "Hungary: Effects of Ban on Sunday Trading," *Eurofound*, September 28, 2015, http://www.eurofound .europa.eu/observatories/eurwork/articles/working-conditions-quality -of-life/hungary-effects-of-ban-on-sunday-trading.

151 *one of the most common leisure activities*: Timothy J. Dallen, *Shopping, Tourism, Retailing and Leisure* (UK: Channel View Publications, 2005), 15.

151 *ladies didn't go out*: Quoted in Erika Rappaport, *Shopping for Pleasure* (Princeton, NJ: Princeton University Press, 2000).

153 *middle-class malls are fading*: Hayley Peterson, "America's Shopping Malls Are Dying a Slow, Ugly Death," *Business Insider*, January 31, 2014, http:// www.businessinsider.com/shopping-malls-are-going-extinct-2014-1.

153 *"parental escort policy"*: Kayleen Schaefer, "New Policies Exterminating Teen Mall Rats," *ABC News*, September 23, 2010, http://abcnews.go.com /Business/shopping-malls-increasingly-putting-restrictions-teens /story?id=11701470.

154 *"lifestyle center"*: "It's All at the Mall: Consumers Look to Shopping Centers as Community Centers," Nielsen, June 5, 2014, http://www .nielsen.com/us/en/insights/news/2014/its-all-at-the-mall-consumers -look-to-shopping-centers-as-community-centers.html.

154 *"By affording opportunities for social life"*: Ray Hutchison, ed., *Encyclopedia of Urban Studies* (Thousand Oaks, CA: Sage Publications, 2010), 715.

154 *fear of death*: Chris Gayomali, "Why the Fear of Death Makes Us Go Shopping," *The Week*, September 30, 2013, http://theweek.com/articles/459438/why-fear-death-makes-shopping.

155 *"work and spend cycle"*: Juliet Schor, *The Overworked American* (New York: Basic Books, 1991), 9.

156 *activates the brain chemical dopamine*: Tara Parker-Pope, "This Is Your Brain at the Mall," *Wall Street Journal*, December 6, 2005.

156 *"It is inevitable that life"*: Seneca, *On the Shortness of Life*, trans. C. D. N. Costa (New York: Penguin, 1997).

156 *a study out of the University of Chicago*: Rik Pieters, "Bidirectional Dynamics of Materialism and Loneliness: Not Just a Vicious Cycle," *Journal of Consumer Research*, Vol. 40, No. 4 (December 2013): 615–31.

157 *women of Kabul*: Virginia Postrel, *The Substance of Style* (New York: HarperCollins, 2003), ix–xi.

157 *we want to understand the story of the thing*: Paul Bloom, "The Lure of Luxury," *Boston Review*, November 2, 2015, https://bostonreview.net/forum/paul-bloom-lure-luxury.

159 *an 1895* Hunter's Weekly *article called "Brunch: A Plea"*: Jesse Rhodes, "The Birth of Brunch: Where Did This Meal Come from Anyway?" Smithsonian.com, May 6, 2011, www.smithsonianmag.com/arts-culture/the-birth-of-brunch-where-did-this-meal-come-from-anyway-164187758/.

160 *"Empathy," Micallef writes, "does not exist at brunch"*: Shawn Micallef, *The Trouble with Brunch: Work, Class and the Pursuit of Leisure* (Toronto: Coach House Press, 2014), 7.

160 *New York's* Daily News *declared*: Alexander Nazaryan, "It's Crunch Time to Ban Brunch Time: Step Up to the Plate and Turn This Wasteful Meal Into Toast," *Daily News*, August 24, 2012, http://www.nydailynews.com/life-style/eats/crunch-time-ban-brunch-time-step-plate-turn-wasteful-meal-toast-article-1.1143151.

160 *Julian Casablancas*: David Shaftel, "Brunch Is for Jerks," *The New York Times*, October 10, 2014, http://www.nytimes.com/2014/10/11/opinion/sunday/brunch-is-for-jerks.html?_r=0.

165 *Hobbies vs. Jobbies*: "American Time Use Survey—2015 Results," U.S. Department of Labor, Bureau of Labor Statistics, http://www.bls.gov/news.release/atus.nr0.htm.

167 *one in four Brits describes "watching TV"*: Eleanor Harding, "Hobbies? We'd Rather Watch Television," *Daily Mail*, December 26, 2013.

167 *"take work, turn it into leisure"*: Steven Gelber, *Hobbies: Leisure and the Culture of Work in America* (New York: Columbia University Press, 1999).

169 *"autotelic personality"*: M. Csikszentmihalyi, *Finding Flow: The Psychology of Engagement with Everyday Life* (New York: Basic Books, 1997), 117.

169 *less susceptible to dementia*: Rosebud O. Roberts et al., "Risk and Protective Factors for Cognitive Impairment in Persons Aged 85 Years and Older," *Neurology*, Vol. 84, No. 18 (May 5, 2015): 1854–61.

170 *better equipped to recover*: K. J. Eschleman, J. Madsen, G. Alarcon, and A. Barelka, "Benefiting from Creative Activity: The Positive Relationships between Creative Activity, Recovery Experiences, and Performance-Related Outcomes," *Journal of Occupational and Organizational Psychology*, Vol. 87 (2014): 579–98.

171 *"Every action, movement, and thought"*: Mihaly Csikszentmihalyi, *Flow: The Psychology of Optimal Experience* (New York: Harper & Row, 1990).

171 *"When you have a place in the country"*: James Boswell, *The Journals of James Boswell, 1762–1795*, selected by John Wain (Yale University Press: 1991), 286.

172 *the adult coloring book trend took off*: "Feeling Stressed Out? Adult Coloring Books Can Help," American Council on Science and Health, April 16, 2016, http://acsh.org/news/2016/04/16/feeling-stressed-out -adult-coloring-books-can-help/.

173 *The positive effects of coloring*: Ibid.

177 *Americans do exercise more on the weekend*: "American Time Use Survey— 2013 Results: Leisure and Sports," U.S. Department of Labor, Bureau of Labor Statistics, http://www.bls.gov/tus/current/leisure.htm#a2.

177 *those who used their leisure time for physical activities*: X. Yang et al., "The Benefits of Sustained Leisure-Time Physical Activity on Job Strain," *Occupational Medicine*, Vol. 60 (2010): 369–75.

177 *suggests that "networking is a lifestyle"*: "14 Things Successful People Do on Weekends," *Forbes*, February 22, 2013, http://www.forbes.com/sites /jacquelynsmith/2013/02/22/14-things-successful-people-do-on -weekends/2/#361602fa13d8.

178 *The drive to play is nestled in the brain stem*: Stuart Brown, with Christopher Vaughan, *Play: How It Shapes the Brain, Opens the Imagination and Invigorates the Soul* (New York: Penguin Books, 2009).

178 *"The opposite of play isn't work"*: Brian Sutton-Smith, "The Opposite of Play Is Not Work—It Is Depression," Stanford Neurosciences Institute, May 29, 2015, https://neuroscience.stanford.edu/news/opposite-play-not-work-—-it-depression.

180 *a movement for shorter days*: Haskell Wexler, "Sleepless in Hollywood: A Threat to Health and Safety," *Huffington Post*, September 28, 2012, http://www.huffingtonpost.com/haskell-wexler/film-industry-hours-sleep_b_1385766.html.

181 *men spend about 5 hours per week more than women on leisure*: Bruce Drake, "Another Gender Gap: Men Spend More Time in Leisure Activities," Pew Research Center, June 10, 2013, http://www.pewresearch.org/fact-tank/2013/06/10/another-gender-gap-men-spend-more-time-in-leisure-activities/.

181 *women answered: too tired*: "Gender and Stress," American Psychological Association, http://www.apa.org/news/press/releases/stress/2010/gender-stress.aspx.

184 *One study found that kids*: "Childhood Sports Participation Influences Adult Creativity," *UT News*, University of Texas at Austin, October 23, 2014, http://news.utexas.edu/2014/10/23/childhood-sports-participation-influences-adult-creativity.

186 *"devotee work"*: Stebbins, ix.

CHAPTER 5: DO LESS AND BE MORE AT HOME

190 *One British survey suggests*: Jaymi McCann, "No Time for the Family? You Are Not Alone: Parents and Children Spend Less Than an Hour with Each Other Every Day Because of Modern Demands," *Mail Online*, July 14, 2013, http://www.dailymail.co.uk/news/article-2363193/No-time-family-You-Parents-children-spend-hour-day-modern-demands.html#ixzz4R9o5l33T.

192 *Women now make up 47 percent of the American workforce*: from "Women in the Labor Force in 2010," U.S. Department of Labor, Women's Bureau, https://www.dol.gov/wb/factsheets/qf-laborforce-10.htm; "women with children outside home" in "Employment Characteristics of Families—2015," U.S. Department of Labor, Bureau of Labor Statistics, http://www.bls.gov/news.release/famee.nr0.htm.

192 *American mothers are spending nearly double the time on unpaid work*: Wendy Wang, "On Weekends, Dads Find More Time for Leisure Than

Moms," Pew Research Center, April 18, 2014, http://www.pewresearch
.org/fact-tank/2014/04/18/on-weekends-dads-find-more-time-for
-leisure-than-moms/.

192 *"I don't want to lean in"*: Ariel Levy, "Ali Wong's Radical Raunch," *The New Yorker*, October 3, 2016.

193 *women contributed to household incomes*: Pat Hudson, "Women's Work," *BBC: History*, March 29, 2011, http://www.bbc.co.uk/history/british/victorians/womens_work_01.shtml#two.

193 *On Saturdays and Sundays in the 1950s*: Ellen Castelow, "The 1950s Housewife," Historic UK, http://www.historic-uk.com/CultureUK/The-1950s-Housewife/.

194 *"Pinterest stress"*: Rebecca Dube, "'Pinterest Stress' Afflicts Nearly Half of Moms, Survey Says," *Today*, May 9, 2013, http://www.today.com/parents/pinterest-stress-afflicts-nearly-half-moms-survey-says-1C9850275.

195 *"One day, one room"*: Erin Doland, "Stop Spending Your Weekends Cleaning Your Home," *Unclutterer*, December 10, 2007, https://unclutterer.com/2007/12/10/stop-spending-your-weekends-cleaning-your-home/.

195 *"A general level of mess doesn't bother me"*: Vanessa Barford, "Should We Stop Wasting Time on Housework?" *BBC News*, November 12, 2010, http://www.bbc.com/news/magazine-11734314.

195 *Chores are key to developing self-mastery*: Kimberley Dishongh, "Study Finds Having Kids Do Chores Is a Good Thing," *The Washington Times*, July 12, 2015, http://www.washingtontimes.com/news/2015/jul/12/study-finds-having-kids-do-chores-is-a-good-thing/.

198 *44 million Americans provide unpaid care*: Mary Jo Gibson and Ari N. Houser, "Valuing the Invaluable: The Economic Value of Family Caregiving," Public Policy Institute, 2008, http://www.aarp.org/relationships/caregiving/info-2007/ib82_caregiving.html; update, 2015: https://www.caregiver.org/caregiving.

199 *"The weak teach the strong"*: Pamela Cushing, "To Be Fully Human," *Jean Vanier: Transforming Hearts*, http://www.jean-vanier.org/en/his_message/jean_vanier_on_becoming_human/to_be_fully_human. For further reading: Jean Vanier, *Becoming Human* (Mahwah, NI: Paulist Press, 2008).

200 *"We dusted off old dreams"*: Kate Saffle, http://www.cohesivehome.com/. Reprinted with permission of the author.

206 *"the dinner table as a battleground"*: Jane Jackman, "How Food Snobs Guard

the Right to Scoff . . ." *The Independent*, July 28, 1994, http://www.independent
.co.uk/voices/how-food-snobs-guard-the-right-to-scoff-balsamic-vinegar
-and-dinner-parties-keep-the-middle-classes-1416916.html.

206 *average American eats one out of five meals in her car*: Cody C. Delistraty,
"The Importance of Eating Together," *The Atlantic*, July 18, 2014, http://
www.theatlantic.com/health/archive/2014/07/the-importance-of-eating
-together/374256/.

207 *kids who eat with their parents five or more days*: "The Importance of
Family Dinners VIII," National Center on Addiction and Substance
Abuse, September 2012, http://www.centeronaddiction.org/addiction
-research/reports/importance-of-family-dinners-2012.

207 *The number of Americans hosting and attending social events*: White
Hutchinson Leisure and Learning Group, "The Evolution of Socialization,"
White Paper, December 2015, https://www.whitehutchinson.com/leisure
/articles/downloads/the-evolution-of-socialization.pdf.

208 *exorbitant rent and real estate prices*: Teddy Wayne, "The Death of the Party,"
The New York Times, September 16, 2015.

209 *scheduling leisure activities*: Erika Ebsworth-Goold, "How Scheduling
Takes the Fun out of Free Time," *The Source*, Washington University in
St. Louis, March 8, 2016, https://source.wustl.edu/2016/03/scheduling
-takes-fun-free-time/.

210 *"We invest ever more fiercely"*: Oliver Burkeman, *The Antidote: Happiness for
People Who Can't Stand Positive Thinking* (New York: Penguin Books, 2012).

210 *over half of suburban American boys*: Bruce Kelley and Carl Carchia, "Hey,
Data Data—Swing!" *ESPN*, July 11, 2013, http://www.espn.com/espn/story
/_/id/9469252/hidden-demographics-youth-sports-espn-magazine.

212 *"When I was growing up"*: Bruce Feiler, "Overscheduled Children: How
Big a Problem?" *The New York Times*, October 11, 2013.

213 *The last practice*: Katrina Onstad, "Are We the Worst Generation of
Parents Ever?" *Today's Parent* magazine, February 2016.

213 *a poll from NPR*: Scott Hensley and Alyson Hurt, *Shots: Health News from
NPR*, June 15, 2015, http://www.npr.org/sections/health-shots/2015/06
/15/413379700/a-look-at-sports-and-health-in-america; http://media.npr
.org/documents/2015/june/sportsandhealthpoll.pdf.

214 *1 in 2,451 boys playing high school basketball*: Anders Kelto, "How Likely
Is It, Really, That Your Athletic Kid Will Turn Pro?" *Shots: Health News
from NPR*, September 4, 2015, http://www.npr.org/sections/health-shots

/2015/09/04/432795481/how-likely-is-it-really-that-your-athletic-kid
-will-turn-pro.

214 **bored people are likely to become "prosocial"**: Wijnand A. P. van Tilburg, "Boredom and I ts Psychological Consequences: A Meaning-Regulation Approach" (PhD diss., University of Limerick, 2011), https://ulir.ul.ie /bitstream/handle/10344/1938/2011_VanTilgurg,%20Wijnand.pdf.

216 **"Why My Kids Don't Play Organised Sport"**: Margaret Rafferty, "Why My Kids Don't Play Organised Sport," *kidspot*, http://www.kidspot.com.au /school/primary/extracurricular/why-my-kids-dont-play-organised-sport.

218 **"There was one time in high school"**: "Tom Hanks Says Self-Doubt Is 'A High-Wire Act That We All Walk,'" *Fresh Air*, April 26, 2016, http://www .npr.org/2016/04/26/475573489/tom-hanks-says-self-doubt-is-a-high -wire-act-that-we-all-walk.

219 **dual-earner families with kids**: See Scott Schieman's website: http:// individual.utoronto.ca/sschieman/Professional_Home_Page/Home.html.

220 **"leisure deficits"**: Suzanne M. Bianchi, John P. Robinson, and Melissa A. Milkie, *Changing Rhythms of American Family Life* (New York: Russell Sage Foundation, 2006), 15–16.

220 **More hours didn't actually affect children's academic success**: Melissa A. Milkie, Kei Nomaguchi, and Kathleen E. Denny, "Does the Amount of Time Mothers Spend with Children and Adolescents Matter?" *Journal of Marriage and Family*, Vol. 77: 355–72.

221 **At the AA level**: Rachel Giese, "Puckheads: Inside the Crazed Arenas of the GHTL," *Toronto Life*, February 2015.

CHAPTER 6: THE POWER OF BEAUTY

225 **"We find that we slip into the Beautiful"**: John O'Donohue, "Awakening to Beauty," *Utne Reader*, April 2005.

226 **forty-five minutes of arts and crafts**: Girija Kaimal, Kendra Ray, and Juan Muniz, "Reduction of Cortisol Levels and Participants' Responses Following Art Making," *Art Therapy*, Vol. 33, No. 2 (2016): 74; http:// www.tandfonline.com/doi/full/10.1080/07421656.2016.1166832.

226 **"awe" is the underexamined emotion**: Dacher Keltner and Jonathan Haidt, "Approaching Awe, a Moral, Spiritual and Aesthetic Emotion," *Cognition and Emotion*, Vol. 17, No. 2 (2003): 207–314.

227 **"Experiences of awe bring people into the present moment"**: Melanie Rudd, Jennifer Aaker, and Kathleen Vohs, "Awe Expands People's Perception of

Time, Alters Decision Making, and Enhances Well-Being," *Psychological Science*, Vol. 23, No. 10 (2012), http://faculty-gsb.stanford.edu/aaker/pages /documents/timeandawe2012_workingpaper.pdf.

227 *"It's nostalgia"*: My essay on Quest appeared in a different form in *Elle* magazine, August 2007, titled "My Year of Living Dangerously."

229 *the percentage of Americans spending time in nature*: John Nielsen, "Americans Spending Less Time in Nature," *NPR*, February 6, 2008, http://www.npr.org/templates/story/story.php?storyId=18698731; N. E. Klepeis et al., "The National Human Activity Pattern Survey (NHAPS): A Resource for Assessing Exposure to Environmental Pollutants," *Journal of Exposure Analysis and Environmental Epidemiology*, Vol. 11, No. 3 (2001): 231–52, http://www.nature.com/jes/journal/v11/n3/full /7500165a.html.

229 *national park usage is dropping*: Associated Press, "US National Park Statistics Show Long-Term Decline in Number of Overnight Camping Stays," *Canada.com*, May 15, 2014, http://o.canada.com/travel/u-s-national-park -statistics-show-long-term-decline-in-number-of-overnight-camping-stays.

230 *"A kid today can likely tell you about the Amazon rain forest"*: Richard Louv, *Last Child in the Woods: Saving Our Children from Nature Deficit Disorder* (Chapel Hill, NC: Algonquin Books, 2008), 1.

230 *natural scene may help post-operative patients recover*: R. S. Ulrich, "View through a Window May Influence Recovery from Surgery," *Science*, Vol. 224, No. 4647 (April 27, 1984): 420–21.

230 *"forest-bathing"*: Ephrat Livni, "The Japanese Practice of 'Forest Bathing' Is Scientifically Proven to Improve Your Health," *Quartz*, October 12, 2016, http://qz.com/804022/health-benefits-japanese-forest-bathing/.

231 *slow walks in the woods*: Bum Jin Park et al., "The Physiological Effects of *Shinrin-Yoku* (Taking in the Forest Atmosphere or Forest Bathing): Evidence from Field Experiments in 24 Forests across Japan," *Environmental Health and Preventive Medicine*, Vol. 15, No. 1 (2010): 18–26.

231 *brief exposure to nature*: R. S. Ulrich et al., "Stress Recovery During Exposure to Natural and Urban Environments," *Journal of Environmental Psychology*, Vol. 11 (1991): 201–230.

231 *"Participants recovered more quickly"*: Kathleen Doheny, "Nature Has Charms That Can Reduce Stress," *Los Angeles Times*, July 25, 1989, http://articles.latimes.com/1989-07-25/news/vw-261_1_nature-scene; Roger S. Ulrich, Robert F. Simons, and Mark A. Miles, "Effects of

Environmental Simulations and Television on Blood Donor Stress," *Journal of Architectural and Planning Research*, Vol. 20, No. 1 (2003): 38–47, www.jstor.org/stable/43030641.

232 **the biophilia hypothesis**: E. O. Wilson, *Biophilia* (Boston: Harvard University Press, 1984).

232 **"I deem the excursion"**: William H. H. Murray, *Adventures in the Wilderness, or Camplife in the Adirondacks* (Boston: De Wolfe, Fiske & Co. 1869), 11; http://quod.lib.umich.edu/m/moa/afk3913.0001.001/3?q1=trout &view=image&size=100.

233 **In the summer of 1869**: Phillip G. Terrie, *Forever Wild: A Cultural History of the Adirondacks* (Syracuse, NY: Syracuse University Press, 1994), 68–74.

234 **with inventing the American vacation**: Tony Perrottet, "Where Was the Birthplace of the American Vacation?" *Smithsonian*, April 2013.

234 **The weekend, like the weekend retreat**: Rybczynski, 185.

236 **"ecopsychology"**: Theodore Roszak, *The Voice of the Earth* (New York: Simon and Schuster, 1992).

237 **soil bacteria injections in mice**: Christopher Lowry et al., "Identification of an Immune-Responsive Mesolimbocortical Serotonergic System: Potential Role in Regulation of Emotional Behavior," *Neuroscience* (online), March 28, 2007.

238 **The results were dramatic**: Ecominds, "Feel Better Outside, Feel Better Inside: Ecotherapy for Mental Wellbeing, Resilience and Recovery," Mind, 2013, https://www.mind.org.uk/media/336359/Feel-better-outside-feel -better-inside-report.pdf.

242 **forty thousand injuries per year**: Vinay K. Sharma et al., "Incidence of Head and Neck Injuries in Extreme Sports," paper delivered to the American Academy of Orthopedic Surgeons, May 14, 2014, http://www.abstractsonline .com/Plan/ViewAbstract.aspx?mID=3358&sKey=f7e15f94-acd4-4221 -a3e6-ec6bb0a044a0&cKey=eaac6013-9075-4d42-9abe-d5e83ce5292e&mKey= 4393d428-d755-4a34-8a63-26b1b7a349a1.

242 **"life and death"**: Stephen Lyng, "Edgework: A Social Psychological Analysis of Voluntary Risk Taking," *American Journal of Sociology*, Vol. 95, No. 4 (1990): 851–86, www.jstor.org/stable/2780644.

243 **new breed of "SuperBoss"**: Adrian Wooldridge (Schumpeter), "Here Comes Superboss," *The Economist*, December 16, 2015, http://www.economist .com/news/business/21684107-cult-extreme-physical-endurance-taking -root-among-executives-here-comes-superboss.

244 *"peak experiences"*: Abraham H. Maslow, *Toward a Psychology of Being* (New York: Simon and Schuster, 2012).

245 *"rumination a maladaptive pattern"*: Gregory N. Bratman et al., "Nature Experience Reduces Rumination and Subgenual Prefrontal Cortex Activation," *Proceedings of the National Academy of Science*, Vol. 12, No. 28 (July 14, 2015), http://www.pnas.org/content/112/28/8567.full.pdf.

245 *if you live in a city*: Rob Jordan, "Stanford Researchers Find Mental Health Prescription: Nature," *Stanford News*, June 30, 2015, http://news.stanford.edu/2015/06/30/hiking-mental-health-063015/.

248 *relievers of stress and anxiety*: Alice Park, "For Men, Good Health May Be Found at the Museum," *Time* May 24, 2011, http://healthland.time.com/2011/05/24/for-men-good-health-may-be-found-at-the-museum/.

250 *Recent brain-mapping research*: Richard Alleyne, "Viewing Art Gives the Same Pleasure as Being in Love," *The Telegraph*, May 8, 2011, http://www.telegraph.co.uk/culture/art/8501024/Viewing-art-gives-same-pleasure-as-being-in-love.html.

250 *a kind of ecstasy*: Jean Quarrick, *Our Sweetest Hours: Recreation and the Mental State of Absorption* (New York: McFarland & Company, 1989), 149.

250 *top six happiness-inducing activities*: Clayton Lord, "Art and Happiness: New Research Indicates 4 out of 6 Happiest Activities Are Arts-related (!)," *New Beans* (artsjournal blog), December 2, 2011, http://www.artsjournal.com/newbeans/2011/12/art-and-happiness-new-research-indicates-4-out-of-6-happiest-activities-are-arts-related.html.

250 *Museum attendance is down*: "Surprising Findings in Three New NEA Reports on the Arts," *National Endowment for the Arts*, January 12, 2015, https://www.arts.gov/news/2015/surprising-findings-three-new-nea-reports-arts#sthash.bTAbv525.dpf.

251 *"an aid to living and dying"*: Alain de Botton and John Armstrong, *Art as Therapy* (New York: Phaidon, 2013).

251 *one wrote off the exhibit*: David Balzer, "Only Connect: What's Wrong with 'Art as Therapy,'" *Canadian Art*, May 27, 2014, http://canadianart.ca/reviews/art-as-therapy/.

251 *Gustave Flaubert spent his Sundays*: Mason Currey, *Daily Rituals: How Artists Work* (New York: Knopf, 2013), 29–32.

252 *This act of self-expression*: Heather L. Stuckey and Jeremy Nobel, "The Connection Between Art, Healing, and Public Health: A Review of Current Literature," *American Journal of Public Health*, Vol. 100, No. 2 (2010): 254–63.